RETURN
WITH
HONOR

FAVORITE TALKS

FROM

ESPECIALLY FOR YOUTH

RETURN WITH HONOR

EFY·1995

FAVORITE TALKS

FROM

ESPECIALLY FOR YOUTH

BOOKCRAFT

SALT LAKE CITY, UTAH

Chapter 9, "Bats, Bites, and the Vaccine" by Victor Harris, is taken from the talk tape "Hamburger, Fries, Pie and a Drink" by Victor Harris, produced and published by Covenant Communications, Inc., and is used by permission.

Chapter 14, "Santa Claus Is Coming to Town: Some Myths About Faith" by Art E. Berg, is taken from the forthcoming book *Finding Peace in Troubled Waters* by Art E. Berg, to be published by Deseret Book Co., and is used by permission.

Chapter 15, "You Tell on Yourself: What You Are Inside Will Show Up Outside" by Michael Weir Allred, is taken from the talk tape of the same title, produced and published by Covenant Communications, Inc., and is used by permission.

Library of Congress Catalog Card Number: 95-79746
ISBN 0-88494-991-5

First Printing, 1995

Printed in the United States of America

Special appreciation is expressed to the contributors to this work for their willingness to share their thoughts and testimonies with youth. Each author accepts complete personal responsibility for the material contained within his or her chapter. There is no endorsement for this work (real or implied) by The Church of Jesus Christ of Latter-day Saints, the Church Educational System, or Brigham Young University.

CONTENTS

1

"MEN ARE, THAT THEY MIGHT HAVE JOY" (P.S. TEENAGERS TOO)

Sue Egan

Do you remember that "Don't Worry, Be Happy" smiley face emblem that was so popular a few years ago? It could be found everywhere on bumper stickers, signs, posters, and T-shirts. Have you ever wondered why such a simple emblem was so well liked? Perhaps it was because it gave everyone a good feeling; and everybody likes feeling happy.

Many claim they know what brings happiness. Good looks, lots of money, and popularity are a few of the things that some promise will bring joy. But the Prophet Joseph Smith tells us of the true path. He said: "Happiness is the object and design of our existence; and will be the end thereof, if we pursue the path that leads to it; and this path is virtue, uprightness, faithfulness, holiness, and keeping all the commandments of God" (*Teachings of the Prophet Joseph Smith*, Joseph Fielding Smith, comp. [Salt Lake City: Deseret Book Co., 1938], pp. 255–56).

Happiness is found in keeping the Lord's commandments. I've seen that principle manifested in my life and in the lives of many others also. I have worked with hundreds of youth during the last few years and can honestly say that those teenagers who keep the commandments are the most happy.

I recall the week I spent with some young people in Ontario, Canada. I was invited to speak at a youth conference that involved their entire region. About six hundred youth and their leaders attended, and from the opening devotional it was obvious that the week was going to be unusual. Everyone was so excited to be there. Many of them seldom or never saw another Latter-day Saint in their school or even in their community, whereas now they were part of an army of Mormons that flooded a university campus. The youth were eager to get to know each other and to learn more about the gospel. Their devotion to the Lord was apparent.

As we gathered together for the keynote address and the preliminary announcements, we were instructed that throughout the week all the young women would be "escorted" as they crossed the campus. This meant that whenever any girl attending the conference was walking from one building to another, a young man would link arms with her and accompany her to the door of the next class. This was not a romantic gesture but merely an act of respect and friendship. Young men were instructed that they weren't to wait for their "dream date" to walk by; the first unaccompanied conference-attending female they saw was the one they were to walk to class. The rule worked the same for the young women. They weren't to "pick and choose" their escorts—first come, first served. Everyone was equal.

The idea caught on quickly. By midweek, escorting often took the form of large groups of youth linked together. The sidewalks resembled dozens of chorus lines from *The Wizard of Oz*. Social boundaries that often separate people from each other started crumbling. Cliques began to fade. Tall girls walked with short boys, and beauty queens linked arms with guys who had never been close to a member of the opposite sex. Outgoing young men were walking and talking with shy girls. Divisions that occur in most social settings simply weren't there. The youth began accepting one another and caring about each other as equals.

The fruits of their charity grew throughout the week. One night a talent show was held. Some of the youth that were scheduled to perform attended a high school of the performing arts, and they were incredibly talented. Other participants were average. There were also some whose offerings were quite humble. It was this last group that caused concern. How would the audience respond to them?

The first number was a song by a gifted performer. As her piece ended, the audience literally roared with applause. The next participant was a young man. His song was soft and simple. He was shy and didn't make eye contact with anyone in the audience. As he began singing I held my breath, waiting to see how the group would react. They were incredible. Respectfully, they gave the performer their full attention. At the end of the song, the applause was just as loud for him as it was for the previous performer. These youth were coming together in a miraculous way. Their hearts were continuing to be "knit together in unity and in love one towards another" (Mosiah 18:21).

On the last day of the conference we gathered together for a closing devotional. Tears were shed as speakers acknowledged their love for Heavenly Father and for all of his children. In the audience hearts bore silent witness of the "change of heart" (see Alma 5:12–14) that had occurred to them that week. All were bound together by a love for God and for one another that many of them had never before experienced. A feeling of reverence filled the congregation, and the Spirit of the Lord rested upon each of us.

As the meeting was about to come to a close, two young women got up to sing the closing song, "Teach Me to Walk in the Light." The first young woman came up to the microphone and in beautiful tones began to sing, "Teach me to walk in the light of his love. Teach me . . ." Her voice choked with emotion. Unable to continue, she motioned for the other young woman to take over. "Teach me to pray to my Father above," the other continued in sweet, clear tones. "Teach me to . . ." Then she too was overcome with emotion. The piano continued softly, the accompanist playing alone. Neither young woman could regain control of her emotions.

And then it happened. Almost like a wave of spirit, the entire audience rose to their feet, joined hands, and continued, ". . . Teach me, teach me, to walk in the light . . ." As an audience, we sang the next two verses together. Although there were over six hundred united voices, the volume of the song was barely above that of a whisper. With tears streaming down our cheeks we reverently sang praises to our Heavenly Father. We knew he loved us. We knew we loved him. We knew we loved each other. We felt a tangible, exquisite, unspeakable joy! "And it came to pass that there was no contention in the land, because of the love of God which did dwell in the hearts of the people. . . . And surely there could not be a happier people among all the people who had been created by the hand of God. . . . They were in one, the children of Christ." (4 Nephi 1:15–17.)

Why had we experienced such great happiness that week? It was simple. Individually and collectively we focused on keeping the first and second commandments of the gospel. The Savior said: "Thou shalt love the Lord thy God with all thy heart, and with all thy soul, and with all thy mind. This is the first and great commandment. And the second is like unto it, Thou shalt love thy neighbor as thyself." (Matthew 22:37–39.)

First Nephi 11:22–23 describes the love of God as "the most desirable above all things. . . . and the most joyous to the soul." I love that! Every time I read this passage of scripture a smile comes to my face. I want to say: "That's right! Nothing feels more wonderful than loving Heavenly Father, keeping his commandments, and partaking of his love for us! I know that Heavenly Father's love is 'the most joyous to the soul' because I have experienced it."

However, those who love Heavenly Father and keep his commandments are not immune to trials. Bad things happen to the obedient as well as to the disobedient. But the obedient handle trials differently. Take Sarah, for example. I met Sarah a couple of years ago. Sarah has always done her best to attend her church meetings. She is often the first to volunteer for a service opportunity in her Young Women class. Sarah strives to live the "Standards of Personal Worthiness" outlined in her Personal Progress book. Yet last year Sarah's mother committed suicide. Her older brother has left the Church. Her little sister has serious medical problems, and Sarah is often required to care for her. Despite all these challenges, Sarah continues to make righteous choices.

She knows that things are difficult now, and sometimes she feels overwhelmed. Through the help of her loving bishop, Sarah has found a professional counselor she occasionally visits with. And she continues to talk to her Heavenly Father each day through sincere, heartfelt prayer. She shares her feelings with him. And because she is doing her best to keep the commandments, she has the gift of the Holy Ghost to comfort her. She asks Heavenly Father to bless her, and even though the trials continue she knows that her Father in Heaven is making her strong enough to handle her challenges. Sarah is beginning to understand the Lord's words to the Prophet Joseph Smith: "All these things shall give thee experience, and shall be for thy good" (D&C 122:7).

As Sarah experiences trials in righteousness, she still finds happiness. She understands the words of our prophet, President Howard W. Hunter: "Our detours and disappointments are the straight and narrow path to Him" ("The Opening and Closing of Doors," *Ensign,* November 1987, p. 60). And that makes Sarah feel happy. Not the giddy-silly-lightmindedness that some equate with happiness, but true joy. Sarah counts her blessings and turns her trials over to the Lord. Sarah is one of the most thankful people I know, and she's also one of the happiest.

As Sarah has discovered, righteousness, happiness, and gratitude go hand in hand. I was older than Sarah when I learned that lesson, but it was a lesson that I'll never forget. We are commanded, "Thou shalt thank the Lord thy God in all things" (D&C 59:7). I can bear witness that as we keep that commandment our happiness increases.

Several years ago I felt that, despite all my efforts, I simply wasn't feeling happy. I was trying my best to live righteously, but it didn't seem to be paying off. As I would go to bed each evening, I would plead with my Heavenly Father to lift my feelings of discouragement. But upon my awakening each morning, many burdens continued to weigh upon me. I thought perhaps I wouldn't ever feel joyful again.

One evening as I began my familiar "please help-me-feel-happy" prayer, a strong impression prompted me to quit asking for things and instead to offer thanks. The Spirit distinctly directed me to begin to thank Heavenly Father for each one of my blessings. I followed the prompting and slowly began to name my blessings, one at a time.

I was very specific. I began to express thanks for the people I loved, mentioning each by name. Every one of them! I told the Lord why they were a blessing to me. I went back as far as my memory would allow and expressed thanks for things that happened yesterday, last month, last year. I recalled memories of college, high school, junior high, and even events that happened in elementary school. I told Father in Heaven how thankful I was that Mrs. Naylor was my third grade teacher. I was reminded of those wonderful feelings I had as she taught me to love books like *Charlotte's Web* and *The Byrds' Christmas Carol.* I thanked him for the Primary music leader who taught my Firelight class the song, "The Chapel Doors." My mind raced through years of pleasant memories. I began thanking Heavenly Father for everything that was going right with each one of my children. Gratitude for countless blessings poured out of my soul. As the Spirit directed me in that prayer of thanksgiving, the list of blessings grew longer and longer. Once-forgotten memories filled my soul with light and love.

About two in the morning I awoke. I was still kneeling by the side of my bed. I had fallen asleep while offering a prayer of gratitude. Recollections of blessings continued to flow into my mind. Peacefully I climbed into bed.

When I arose that morning, things looked different to me. The cloud was lifted. I recognized the hand of the Lord in my life. Blessings that I had so often taken for granted flooded my heart. Events fell into perspective. My vision ceased to focus on the few things that were going wrong and transferred to the myriad things that were going right. A feeling of joy washed over me, and I began seeing "things as they really are" (see Jacob 4:10–13). I recognized that those small obstacles that had earlier overwhelmed me had purpose in my life. They made me realize my weakness and my dependence on Heavenly Father; he would give me the added strength to cope with those trials. They could actually be consecrated for my gain (see 2 Nephi 2:2). I realized the abundance of blessings that had always been there; blessings that outweighed the burdens! The Spirit whispered that the plan of salvation is "the plan of happiness" (Alma 42:16). My testimony was reinforced that long ago I truly had "shouted for joy" as I chose to follow Heavenly Father's plan (see Job 38:7). Gratitude had literally healed my soul, and I felt happy once again.

We must come to understand the power of President Ezra Taft Benson's statement: "This great principle of gratitude, made a daily part of our lives and our prayers, can lift and bless us" (*The Teachings of Ezra Taft Benson* [Salt Lake City: Bookcraft, 1988], p. 364). That's true. Try it yourself. Offer a sincere prayer of gratitude to your Heavenly Father and see what happens. "Enter into his gates with thanksgiving . . . be thankful unto him, and bless his name" (Psalm 100:4). When we are thankful our happiness increases.

Happiness *is* the object and design of our existence. We are promised that, "the righteous, the saints of the Holy One of Israel, they who have believed in the Holy One of Israel, they who have endured the crosses of the world . . . they shall inherit the kingdom of God, which was prepared for them from the foundation of the world, and their joy shall be full forever" (2 Nephi 9:18). I humbly add my witness to the testimony of our late prophet, President Ezra Taft Benson: "The Church itself is God's great instrument to build and to save and to exalt men everywhere, through the application of the simple principles of the gospel. It is a way of life that will make men happy, and 'men are, that they might have joy' (2 Nephi 2:25)." (*The Teachings of Ezra Taft Benson*, p. 167.)

Sue Egan has attended both BYU and the University of Utah. She has been a professional vocalist and a teacher and is presently a home-maker. An avid student of the scriptures, Sue also loves watching "Dragnet" reruns on TV and "cruising" with her husband in his red sports car. Sister Egan is a popular presenter at EFY and serves in the Church as a stake Young Women president. She and her husband, Richard, have six children.

2

THE GREAT DUNGENESS CRABBING ADVENTURE
OR
AS THE TIDE TURNS

Suzanne Ballard

Remember that old TV commercial—"We've got crab-legs, we've got crab-legs . . . ?" Bet you're humming the tune right now! In our family we don't just sing the tune, we actually go out to the Pacific Ocean and get those "crab-legs!" Each year we make the two-hour trip from our home near Portland, Oregon, to Netarts Bay on the Pacific coastline to go Dungeness crab fishing. It's usually in the late fall or early winter, so the weather is rainy, cold, and miserable, but we take the whole family in search of those delicious Dungeness crabs.

Sometimes they have Dungeness crabs in your local supermarket, so if you've never seen one try looking there. They're about five to eight inches across the back of the shell and have two huge claws with which they tear apart the dead fish and other garbage they find on the sea floor. They are the vultures of the ocean bottom! But, boy, are they good eatin'!

Crabs don't walk frontways—they walk sideways! These crabs can smell something rotten on the floor of the bay and will come running to get it. They're really fast!

A few years ago a new family moved into our ward. They were definitely "land-lubbers" but really wanted to go crabbing with us. To protect their reputation and identity, I'll call them Dan and Fran Smucker (because they really got us into a jam!) They had three sons who went with us. I'll call them Son A, Son B, and Son C. Pretty original, huh!

Well, anyway, we all went together and rented two boats to go out into the bay in search of those delicious crabs. Since the Smuckers hadn't ever been crabbing, we decided that I would go with my youngest daughter, Megan, in Dan and Fran's boat, and my husband, Russ, would take our other three children and Smucker Son A in his boat. Now, these are *not* big boats—they're the kind you see fishermen put on top of their campers. They're about ten feet long and three benches and are only about fourteen inches deep. The water of the bay is really shallow too—only about 15 feet deep at low tide. The small motor attached at the back propelled each boat, and Dan and Russ took over the duty of steering.

Because our family had been crabbing so many times before, we knew the best part of the bay to go to for the largest crabs. Russ immediately headed over that way. Megan and Smucker Son C didn't want to go that far away, so they talked Dan into staying close to the shoreline. We had fun tying fish scraps onto the bottom of our crab cages, throwing our three cages over the side, and watching them sink to the bottom with a buoy floating on the surface to let us know where they were. We could leave the cages down for no more than ten-to-fifteen minutes. If we left a cage down longer, the crabs would come quickly into it and would eat *all* the dead fish, leaving us no more bait.

After ten minutes or so one of us would pull up the crab cage as fast as we could (which would pull up the sides of the cage, trapping the crabs inside.) Each time we would have a dozen or so crabs. Megan and the two Smucker boys delighted in grabbing the crabs that were too small to keep and throwing them back into the bay. Fran and I caught the biggest ones, measuring them and putting the keepers into a bucket.

After an hour or so we'd only collected about three or four crabs. When Russ came to tell us they'd gotten over a dozen large crabs on his side of the bay, Megan and Son C decided they'd rather go back to the campsite. After depositing the two youngest children on the shore, we began to follow Russ.

President David O. McKay once said: "Every action is preceded by thought. If we want to control our actions, we must control our thinking." Dan began thinking—and it got us in trouble.

Dan noticed that the area of the bay where it joins the ocean (called the bar or the breakers because of the big waves there) had no crabbing boats. He kept saying that he was sure the biggest crabs were just in front of the bar near the breakers. Unfortunately, I didn't argue with him. I was along for the ride and was enjoying my conversations with Fran. But even the seals riding in the breaker waves seemed to be calling to Dan to come and try crabbing near the bar.

And then Dan turned the boat towards the ocean. The waves were huge! Dan kept saying that he only wanted to put the three crab cages in the water in the small waves just in front of the bar and that he wouldn't get too close to the breakers. And the seals kept calling us.

Russ finally noticed we were heading out towards the ocean and, turning his boat around, began coming after us, yelling the whole way. The sounds of the ocean and the motor kept us from hearing his warnings.

What we didn't know was that the tide had turned and was pulling the bay water out into the ocean. Dan put the first crab cage into the water while Son B steered the boat—all was well. When he put down the second crab cage, we noticed that we were into rougher waters. Fran asked that they steer the boat away from the breakers to put down the third crab cage.

Just then we realized that the tide had pulled us right into the bar. The enormous waves were crashing down around us! Fran and I started screaming for Dan to steer us out of the waves. The boat was being tossed around. We were hanging on with white knuckles! The seals were laughing at us.

Dan asked Smucker Son B to turn the boat around *between* waves. Just when he thought it was the right time, he turned the boat around. I will never forget what happened next as long as I live. A huge wave came crashing down on our boat, soaking us all with the icy sea water!

Sputtering and wet to the bone, Dan grabbed the motor control from his son and determinedly began steering the boat to safety. Smucker Son B was yelling "We're gonna drown! We're gonna drown! We're gonna drown!" Fran, the sensible one, had grabbed one of the buckets and was bailing out the boat—which now contained about four to six inches of water!

It's amazing to me what people do when they are threatened with a disaster. Some people steer towards safety, some bail out the boat, some scream and yell—and then there was me! I was rescuing crabs from the bottom of the boat! (I could concentrate only on something as trivial and stupid as saving crabs, which can swim just fine!)

Just as we came out of the bar, Russ joined us. I immediately jumped ship and joined his. Smucker Son A decided to help his mom and dad and joined their boat. After Russ had scolded us, he admonished us to follow him to the shore. But Dan worried aloud about the crab cages! Again, thought precedes action. Russ told him to leave them. The next thing we knew, Dan was heading back out towards the bar to rescue the crab cages!

They got two of the cages, but in trying to retrieve the other one they were again sucked out into the bar, were inundated, and barely escaped.

About that time the boat owner came out to rescue them. He was sure mad! Someone on the shore had seen us going out into the bar and had called the Coast Guard, who had called him to rescue us. We found out later that people have died when their boats were overturned in the breakers. We were grateful to be alive.

Later Dan had to pay for the lost crab cages—about a hundred dollars. The owner said *no one* would be foolish enough to go out into the bar to retrieve it. He really chastised us all for our errors in judgment. We were all chilled to the bone, and our great crabbing adventure was over.

Now, you know there has to be a moral to the story, right? Well, here it is: Stay in the safety of Gospel Bay and away from the world's bars—and I don't just mean taverns!

Think about this story and how it relates to you in your life. The bay is the safety of the gospel. Look at how much fun we could have had just staying in the bay! The Dungeness crabs are like the delicious rewards that Heavenly Father provides to those who stay in the safe waters.

The bar represents the temptations of the world. That's danger! That's sorrow! The laughing seals calling to us could represent your "friends" who are experiencing the temptations of the world and don't *seem* to be drowning but are laughing at you for choosing the safe course!

From the scriptures we can learn an important key on how to handle this problem. Remember that the people in the large and spacious building in Lehi's dream "did point the finger of scorn at me and those that were partaking of the fruit also; *but we heeded them not*" (1 Nephi

8:33, emphasis added). That's the key—not paying attention to the seals in the water as we hold fast to the iron rod of the gospel.

Usually there is safety in numbers—unless the driver (leader) is going the wrong way! Just who are your friends? Choose wisely the boat you get into! Are you choosing to board only boats with friends who have your same standards? James 4:4 says that "whosoever therefore will be a friend of the world is the enemy of God." The same writer says in verse 7: "Submit yourselves therefore to God. Resist the devil, and he will flee from you." Another key, then—avoid choosing "friends" who want to do worldly things rather than follow God. Remember, if you follow Heavenly Father, Satan will have no power over you.

Russ's warning cries weren't heard by us in the other boat—they were drowned out by the roar of the waves. Are you learning how to listen to the still, small voice *now*, before you board the wrong boat, or are you letting the noise of the world drown out the sweet sounds of the Holy Spirit? In the Doctrine & Covenants (45:57) we learn that the "wise . . . have taken the Holy Spirit for their guide, and have not been deceived." Here's another key—be wise and learn to recognize the Holy Ghost to avoid being deceived by Satan.

What does that invisible tide represent? If you said Satan, I'm pleased. You're getting good at these analogies. Right on! Satan is an invisible, evil force pulling us out to danger—much of the time without our awareness. You might think it's fun to skirt danger—but if the tide is going out you might instead get sucked into big trouble, as we were in Netarts Bay. Don't skirt danger—stay away from the edge— and you won't be pulled out into dangerous seas. Stay in the safety of the bay. Proverbs 29:25 says it best: "Whoso putteth his trust in the Lord shall be safe." Then the key is to trust the Lord and what he says, right?

We in Dan's boat realized almost too late that we were in trouble— over our heads. Too often this happens in life also. Many youth in the Church have told me about situations—a party, a single date with a person of questionable standards, a gang activity—where they realized they were in over their heads. They've told me about how difficult it is to repent and change their lives after they've been inundated in the icy waters of sin. Dan's "repentance" wasn't easy either—a hundred dollars, ice-cold clothes, and a chastisement; but at least we didn't lose a life. Too many youth have experienced much worse than he did—lives lost, pregnancies, venereal disease, a guilty conscience, loss of self-esteem. Be careful by staying well away from sin!

The scriptures tell us that "joy shall be in heaven over one sinner that repenteth" (Luke 15:7). Repentance is hard but is so worth it! When we've made a mistake, committed a sin, transgressed, then repentance, because of Christ's atonement, can wash us clean again. That is a wonderful key. But remember that repentance for grievous sin is difficult and painful. It is better not to have sinned in the first place.

My concentrating on rescuing crabs in the face of imminent danger could be likened to many of us concentrating on the unimportant in life—material possessions, TV, pride, and anything that is worldly. Jesus said: "Lay not up for yourselves treasures upon earth, where moth and rust doth corrupt, and where thieves break through and steal: but lay up for yourselves treasures in heaven . . . for where your treasure is, there will your heart be also" (Matthew 6:19–21). Dan and Fran did the right thing at that point—they concentrated on the things of worth (getting us out of the mess we were in). Unfortunately many young people who commit a sexual sin, for instance, will continue in that sin and try to cover it up rather than take the first steps in the repentance process to become cleansed.

The Coast Guard being called to rescue us we can liken to our bishop. He is here to help guide us to the safe waters of the gospel. He has the power and authority to show us the pathway back to Heavenly Father.

What are the temptations in the breakers? I'm sure you see them every day at your school and in the media.

Breaking the Word of Wisdom. Sometimes the temptations of coffee or tea or cigarettes or alcohol seem so insignificant when compared to the "bigger" sins, don't they? After all, what's the harm of just *one* drink or *one* cigarette? That's skirting danger. Remember that mind- and body-altering substances dull your ability to hear and heed the Holy Ghost and many times lead to a lifetime addiction. Could the tide then pull you out so far that you can't be rescued? Be wise.

Drugs. I know the awfulness of this temptation. I have seen the heartache that drug use causes in a family. You will never see a drug user who is a success in life—it always catches up with him sooner or later.

A friend of mine I'll call "Bill" tells the story of growing up in

Washington, D.C. His best friend dropped out of high school to sell drugs and used to laugh at Bill for going to college. While Bill ate pork and beans and struggled to make ends meet as a poor college student, his drug-pushing friend was wearing expensive suits, driving a fancy car, and trying to tempt Bill into the drug business.

Bill resisted the temptation. Now he is a successful businessman and recording artist with a six-figure annual income. His so-called "friend" is in the federal prison in Illinois, serving a fifty-year sentence on drug convictions. He has to ask Bill and others to take birthday presents for him to his young child or visit his mother in the rest home. Don't be fooled by the seals calling out to you. Think about the long-term consequences of your actions.

Pornography. Did you know that Ted Bundy, the mass murderer of young women, began his slide by reading a single pornographic magazine? Are you so sure the tide won't pull you into the bar that you want to risk it? Pornography is like an octopus with tentacles that methodically pull its victim into the icy waters of hell. Stay away from it! Avoid it as you would a killer disease. President Gordon B. Hinckley has given this advice: "There is no surer way [to fall under Satan's power] than to become engulfed in the tide of pornography that is sweeping over us. If we succumb to it, it destroys us, body and mind and soul." ("Don't Drop the Ball," *Ensign,* November 1994, p. 48.)

Premarital sex. I have heard from LDS youth who thought that succumbing to this temptation would be OK because "after all, we're in love!" They have all expressed regrets and suffered severe repercussions from that decision. Don't be fooled by those around you in a boat that is heading in the wrong direction—*everyone* is *not* doing it! It's cheap and trashy when engaged in prior to marriage—even with someone you plan to marry. It's wonderful, sensational, fantastic, and *safe* when experienced within the framework of a temple marriage. Please believe me! The bishop can help rescue you if you've gotten this far into the breakers. He can be the Coast Guard to guide you back to safe waters.

Every day we are faced with temptations. A clear understanding of God's plan for our *happiness* will help us avoid them. Satan only wants us to be *unhappy.* "He seeketh that all men might be miserable like unto himself" (2 Nephi 2:27). Remember, "Wickedness never was happiness" (Alma 41:10).

Remember who you are! We are spirit children of a royal Father in Heaven having a mortal experience. Remember your heritage. Please don't debase yourself by playing in the bar and thereby perhaps not being able to make it back to his presence.

I once saw a cartoon of a man fishing in a cow pasture. The caption said: "If you want to catch fish, you must *go* where the fish *are!*" The same is true of our lives. If we want to be physically fit, we don't "fish" for it with a Twinkie in one hand and a TV remote in the other. If we want to be more spiritual, we shouldn't "fish" for it by watching R-rated movies. If we want to be able to recognize the invisible tide and stay out of the bar, we'll need to "fish" for the Spirit and pattern our lives after the example of the Savior.

Be the best you can be! You don't get another chance at this earth life! You are special! You are the son or daughter of royal, heavenly parents! You are the only person on this whole earth exactly like you— ever! Life is too precious to be blown away on drugs, immorality, materialism, and so forth. Dare to be a righteous Latter-day Saint. Stay in the safety of Gospel Bay. Be a beacon of light to your friends. I know you can do it.

I know that Heavenly Father will bless you, Jesus Christ will lead you by the hand, and the Holy Ghost will comfort you, *if* you but ask for their help. They are real. They are there. They really are.

Note: Dan tells me that he and his family went back to Netarts Bay two years later to try Dungeness crabbing again. He worried that the boat owner would remember him and refuse to rent him a boat. But just as our bishop and the Lord forget our sins when we properly repent, so had the boat owner. Dan was so relieved! They stayed away from the bar, got numerous crabs, and thoroughly enjoyed themselves in the safety of Gospel Bay.

Suzanne Ballard teaches early-morning seminary in Vancouver, Washington, where she lives with her husband, Russell. They are the parents of four children. A certified childbirth educator, Sister Ballard was named National Young Mother of the Year in 1985. She has served in leadership positions in Young Women and Relief Society and enjoys traveling, being with her family, public speaking, and "anything to do with the youth!"

3

DID IT REALLY HAPPEN?

Mark Bybee

As nearly as I can recall, the first miracle I ever personally witnessed took place when I was about eleven years old. It happened in front of our home in Columbus, Ohio. As the car stopped across the street from our home, Jack, my younger brother, jumped out of the back door on the curb side, and I heard my mom yell, "Jack, wait on the curb." But Jack ignored Mom, and as I looked over my right shoulder from the back seat I saw him dart between the rear of the car we were in and the parked car behind us. I remember getting my head turned around just in time to see a big car run smack over the top of Jack. His head smashed out the headlight, and then the car ran right over him.

I'll never forget the feeling of incredible fright which ran through me as I saw his little body flying through the air. I wanted to scream and turn back the clock as I saw the five-year-old body come to a rest in a clump on the side of the road. I screamed out, "No!" as I flung the door open and ran to his side. Everything inside of me told me not to touch him, because if I moved him I might cause paralysis. Jack didn't move, and he was bleeding from his head. I turned back toward the car just in time to get between Jack and my mom as she ran screaming, "My baby, my baby." I held her by her arms and pushed against her as I tried to get her not to touch Jack. She finally calmed down and told me to run and get Dad.

Dad was at the kitchen counter, having paid no attention to the screeching tire sounds since they were so common. I yelled to him that Jack had been hit, and he flew out the front door and went straight to his side to check his vital signs. As Dad knelt down he asked me to take Mom inside and pray for Jack.

I'll remember forever the scene of my brothers and sisters kneeling around the sofa praying out loud for Jack. I couldn't stay there, so I ran back out and stood by my dad. I watched as Dad felt for a pulse and listened at Jack's chest. When he looked up at me with a look of futility and deep sadness as he said, "Go comfort your mother," I knew Jack was dead and I didn't want it to be so. As I walked slowly from Jack and Dad, I looked back to see Dad praying with his head down. As nearly as I can recall, Dad was praying that Jack could live and that he could raise his son to manhood. Then by his priesthood authority he commanded Jack to live. I looked down again at Jack, and his little body just lay motionless on the ground.

I went back inside and knelt next to my mom. I didn't have the heart to say anything. The next thing I remember is hearing the sounds of the sirens in the distance. We all jumped up and ran outside as the ambulance pulled up next to Jack and the drivers jumped out and ran to Jack's side. I well recall the scene of Jack sitting up coughing and crying as he held his head and complained of a headache. The attendants put Jack into the ambulance and then sped off to the hospital. Dad said that Jack was seriously injured, with possible broken bones and other injuries. You can imagine our surprise when Jack returned with a concussion and no broken bones.

To anyone else this story seems far-fetched, and as I shared the story with other friends during my adolescent years many laughed and said I had made it up. I would get upset and say, "You don't understand! I was there! I saw it happen! I can't change what happened!"

Since that time of my life I have often thought about Joseph Smith and how difficult it must have been for him to deal with the ridicule that came from people because of his first vision. The challenge in Joseph was that he was there and he saw what he saw and he could not deny what he had seen.

At the time of Joseph Smith's first vision the world had many ideas that were confusing to him. There was an emphasis on the Bible and its completeness. Some religions taught that the Godhead was one personage—and that one was a spirit. Most religions taught that revelation and miracles had long since ceased to exist, and that God's visits to earth and to man no longer occurred because the Bible was the only thing we needed. Some religions were even teaching that Satan was not real, but that he was only placed in the Bible to scare people into submission to the teachings and commandments that it taught. Even today such beliefs flow through the basic ideas of many faiths.

The fourteen-year-old Joseph Smith spent a great deal of time studying the Bible as well as attending the different churches in his area. Although Joseph had been a strong, active child and loved to go off and play, he was nonetheless a very sober person and extremely honest. His friends and family indicated that he was known for his honesty and would not even stretch the truth.

I have often wondered now if my parents would have believed me more if I had told the truth all the time instead of just part of the time. I can imagine coming home at fourteen and telling my mom and dad that I had seen a vision of the Father and the Son. At first my father would have laughed and thought it was a joke, and then he would have been angry and grounded me for a month for lying. It's not because he would not want to believe me but only because I had stretched the truth or lied so many times in my youth. Isn't it curious that Joseph's parents didn't even question him because he had no disposition to lie and had always told the truth? What a great reputation to have and to work for!

What was Joseph really looking for that early spring morning when he walked into the woods? According to his story, he had become confused because the several churches in the area were teaching different doctrines and generating much contention. In addition to the different churches there were revival meetings in the countryside, and his family often attended them. The revivalists too were teaching different doctrines concerning the same principles. It added to his confusion that Joseph's family members had separated themselves in their affiliation with the different churches. Joseph wanted to join the right or true church, and the Bible had convinced him that there must be one. But in all the confusion he could not determine which of the churches *was* the one.

One day in his reading Joseph came across a scripture in the epistle of James which told him that if he asked God for knowledge on an important matter he could get an answer, and God wouldn't be angry at him or chastise him for asking. Joseph had prayed before, but never out loud. I am sure he took a lot of time getting the courage to go into that grove of trees and pray out loud to the Lord. I'm also sure that he didn't expect what he got. In fact, I am sure that he wasn't thinking anything like, "Well, this morning I'm going to have a visit from the Father and the Son and be called to be a prophet." On the contrary, he was just expecting a quick answer from the Spirit as to which of the churches in town was correct, which one he should join. Maybe just a good feeling about one or the other church so he could solve his problem.

What really happened in that grove of trees that morning? As Joseph knelt down to pray he was first seized upon by a powerful evil force. His tongue was bound, and he found himself slowly becoming overpowered. At a point where he was about to sink in despair and give himself over to destruction, he used all of his power to call upon God to deliver him. Just at that moment a bright light appeared above him and came to rest upon him. When the light came, the evil power left him.

Looking into the light he saw two beings standing above him in the air. One of them spoke to Joseph, identifying the other being as the Son of God and telling Joseph to listen to Him. The Son then told Joseph not to join any church, and Joseph understood that he was to continue as he was until further directed. When the vision was complete, Joseph found himself lying on his back looking into the air.

As Joseph left the trees that day he realized that he had seen the Father and the Son; but more important, he knew that God knew that Joseph had seen a vision and Joseph could not deny it.

What can we learn from that great vision of Joseph Smith's? One of the first things is that Satan is real and that he doesn't ever want anyone to succeed, especially a future prophet. I'm sure that Joseph Smith didn't know what he was in store for, just as we don't know what is in store for us. Satan knows us and he also knows our weaknesses and he will always be in our faces seeking to turn us away from our destination. We also learn that Satan leaves when the Father and the Son appear. Isn't it great to know that we can call upon our Father in Heaven in the name of Jesus Christ and free ourselves from the influence of Satan! Section 129 of the Doctrine and Covenants helps us to understand how to handle situations with spirits that we don't want around.

Some of the simple but glorious things that Joseph learned as soon as the Father and Son appeared concerned the nature of the Godhead. Upon looking into the light, Joseph discovered the true doctrine that each member of the Godhead is a separate and distinct personage. The most fundamental thing he learned is that God truly lives and Jesus is his Son. Something that I realized that probably isn't extremely significant, but I thought it was, is that the Father and the Son were not touching the ground. They were standing above Joseph in the air. Perhaps that means that resurrected beings are not subject to the law of gravity.

In the course of the vision Joseph learned that there was no true church on the earth, and he was not to join any church. He also learned that at some future time the fulness of the gospel would be made known to him.

One of the most powerful lessons learned in the First Vision took place when the Father first opened his mouth. Up until a few years ago I thought that the first words from the Father to Joseph were, "This is my Beloved Son, hear him." I discovered by close examination that the first word from the Father was "Joseph." When I discovered this it hit me so hard that I just sat there and broke down in tears. How great it is to know that God knows his children by name, and even with billions of children through the ages, he still knew this fourteen-year-old boy by name! The reason I broke down was that I realized he knew me by name, and it made me feel so cared for and loved and significant. I know now that Father would never look at me and wonder who I was, or hesitate and try to remember who I am or where he saw me last. What a fantastic vision and what great doctrines to learn! The vision teaches such important doctrines—to the youth and to everyone else who will listen.

When I was eleven years old my father took the family to the Sacred Grove for the first time. We walked down the dirt path from the farmhouse to the edge of the grove and then deep into the woods. As we sat on a log, Dad explained the First Vision and the wonderful doctrines to be learned. At the conclusion of his lessons he walked over to a large tree, and touching it he said that the tree just might be old enough to have been there when the First Vision took place. True or not, the idea captured my thinking, and as the family began to move away from the grove I moved over to the tree; and touching it, I spoke these words: "Oh, I wish you could talk so you could tell me what the Father and the Son look like." My childlike faith had convinced me that the vision was real and true.

Over the next seven years Dad periodically took us back to that same spot, and taught us that same lesson. For the first few years I went through the same speech as I touched the same tree. Many trials and great peer pressure came into my life during the next few years, which affected my little speech at the tree. Between the ages of sixteen and nineteen I would touch the tree and say, "I wish you could talk so that you could tell me if it really happened, and then I'd know if there was even a God at all." My childlike faith was gone and my self-worth was nonexistent.

Just before I turned twenty years old, one of my best friends joined the Church, and in the process I became committed to read the Book of Mormon. I read to find out if it was true, and to find out if the First Vision had really happened. I wanted to know for myself.

One evening I knelt next to my bed and, remembering the story of Enos, I told the Lord that I was prepared to stay on my knees all night if I had to in order to get an answer to my prayers. A number of times during the night I fell asleep, and then as I awoke I would remind the Lord that I was still there on my knees and that I really wanted to know if Joseph was a prophet and if the Book of Mormon was true. I remember how sore my knees were the last time I woke up, and I had a kink in my neck. I addressed the Lord concerning my desires once again; and as I finished my prayer I opened my eyes to see the rays of the sun entering my room. I can't really describe the feeling or what happened, but I know my chest was so full and I knew deep inside that Joseph was a prophet, and the Book of Mormon was true. That morning the Spirit bore this witness to my spirit.

A few months later my friend came to me at 2:00 A.M. and proposed that we go to the Hill Cumorah Pageant in New York. I reminded him that he had no car, and that mine would never make it that far. "We'll take my motorcycle, then," he said. So we rode 650 miles from Columbus, Ohio, to Palmyra, New York, in 16 1/2 hours. The ride was very interesting, to say the least. We arrived the next evening about the time everyone was starting to save seats for the pageant. We found my dad, and feeling the saddle sores from riding, we asked to borrow his van to go to the Sacred Grove, which is a few miles from the Hill Cumorah. As we reached the Smith farm, the usual hordes of visitors were gone, and the sun was setting. We walked into the grove, where we knelt together thanking the Lord for our testimonies and our upcoming opportunity to serve on missions. My friend moved to a distant part of the grove in order to have some private moments. I took that opportunity to go over to my tree, and out of habit I began to repeat my usual speech. I stopped and became very emotional as I said to the tree, "Even if you could talk, you couldn't tell me anything that I don't already know, because the Spirit already told me this church is true."

Joseph Smith is a prophet! The Book of Mormon is true! This testimony I bear in the name of Jesus Christ.

Mark Bybee taught seminary and institute for seventeen years. He holds a master's degree in recreational management, and enjoys racquetball, the martial arts, outdoor recreation generally, and high-risk sports such as kayaking and white water rafting. He advises young people to "look forward," to "look to the Savior for help," to "not be discouraged," and to "not let anyone take away their dreams." Mark and his wife, Lisa, have eight children.

4

PRAYER: YOUR PASSPORT TO SPIRITUAL POWER

Vivian R. Cline

Have you ever had a long-distance friend? You were separated by a great distance and your only means of communication was by phone or letter. Remember how happy it made you feel when you saw their letter in the mailbox or heard their voice on the other end of the phone. It was the next best thing to being there with them. You renewed your friendship and shared what was happening in your life. Though the miles were great, you were still very close.

What if you stopped communicating? Would you remain close? As the years went by would you find that the two of you had grown closer? Probably not.

So it is with our Heavenly Father through his Son, Jesus Christ. Though the distance between us may be great for now, we can still be close through the special means of communication he has given us—prayer.

Though the subject of prayer may seem one that is common or familiar, it is amazing how easily it is forgotten or passed off as not very important.

It's easy to understand how this can happen. It's because we are so busy and so smart! Praying takes time, and we are all so pushed for time. Our schedules demand that we get up early and stay up late in order to accomplish everything. We sleep until the last possible minute in the morning and then crash from exhaustion in the evening. Besides, we are smart. We know that Heavenly Father loves us and that we love him. We also know that he knows all that we stand in need of before we even ask. We tend to rationalize that if we obey the commandments and are good, the blessings will continue. *Not so!*

It is my intent in this chapter to turn to the scriptures and find the answers to 1) Why we should pray, 2) When we should pray, 3) How we should pray, and 4) How to recognize when we receive answers.

Why we should pray. We have already established the fact that communication with our Heavenly Father helps us to stay close to him, but there are other reasons as well.

We are told in Matthew 7:7 and 8, "Ask, and it shall be given you; seek, and ye shall find; knock, and it shall be opened unto you: for every one that asketh receiveth; and he that seeketh findeth; and to him that knocketh it shall be opened."

Our Father in Heaven loves us and so has given us the gift of agency. If he gave us everything we need without our asking, that agency would be taken from us. We are reminded, however, in D&C 8:10, "Do not ask for that which you ought not."

We remember the story of Joseph Smith and Martin Harris. Martin wanted to show the Book of Mormon manuscript to his family, but when Joseph asked the Lord he said no. Joseph continued to petition the Lord for his request even though he knew he "ought not." Because Joseph was righteous and continued to ask even though the Lord knew what would happen, he let Joseph have his request. As we know, the manuscript was lost by Martin and was never recovered. Sometimes Father will grant us our desires even though it may not be for the best at that time.

I recall a personal instance in my own life when this happened.

When I was about thirty-four years old I began to complain to the Lord about not having a leadership position in the Church. I had been active in the Church all my life and had served in various positions such as teacher, chorister, pianist, and so on, but had never had what I considered a really responsible job in leadership. All my friends had served in different presidencies, and I felt left out. I began to ask the Lord if he didn't feel that I had leadership qualities, and if I did, why he wouldn't let me use them. As we were talking one day about the subject, my husband reminded me that Father was using my leadership skills as I served the youth of the Church through my speaking. Somehow that didn't satisfy me, and I continued my petitioning.

Lo and behold, one day I got a call from my bishop, and guess what call he extended? I was to be the new Young Women president in our ward.

I was totally elated. Finally, here was my chance to use my leadership skills. Never mind the fact that I had never served in the Young Women program and didn't have a clue how things ran. Never mind the fact that I had a young family of five children who required much attention. Or the fact that at that time in my life my husband and I had to have a second income, and so I taught finishing classes in my home every week. And last of all, never mind the fact that I spoke to the youth of the Church at least once a week and flew out of town almost once a month to do youth conferences.

As you can well imagine, with the schedule just mentioned and the pressure and responsibility of being the Young Women president, the word *stress* took on new meaning for me. Though I may have had the ability to do the job, the time wasn't right. However, I asked what I "ought not" and the Lord said, "OK, you asked for it (over and over and over), you got it." It was a hard lesson for me to learn, but I now know to always add "but thy will be done" at the end of my requests.

We are also told, in Matthew 26:41, to pray "that ye enter not into temptation." Our prayers draw us closer to the Lord and give us added strength to resist the temptations of Satan.

We are counseled in Alma 13:28 to "watch and pray continually, that ye may not be tempted above that which ye can bear." How comforting to know that our prayers will prevent the adversary from tempting us more than we can handle!

Last of all we are told by Alma again (37:37), "counsel with the Lord in all thy doings, and he will direct thee for good." When we ask the Lord what we should do in all our affairs it's like asking for his advice. Any loving parent will gladly give advice when it is asked for.

All this is fine and good, you might be saying to yourself right now, but what if I just don't feel like praying?

That is the very time you should pray!

Nephi warns us, "the evil spirit teacheth not a man to pray, but teacheth him that he must not pray" (2 Nephi 32:8). The very minute you don't want to pray is the minute you should kneel and ask the Lord to bless you with his Spirit that you may not be tempted by the promptings of Satan.

Satan is very cunning and knows that one of the greatest weapons we have against him is prayer. He will do everything in his power to try to stop you from praying. He will tell you that you don't need to pray, that you are too tired to pray, or that you are too busy to pray. Anything to get you away from prayer so your resistance will be weakened.

When we should pray. Our first prayer of the day should be in the morning, preferably when we first get up. Tired as you may be when you drag out of bed, if you hit your knees to the floor and pray you will find that your entire day will go smoother.

Amulek tells us to pray "both morning, mid-day, and evening" (Alma 34:21). If you are at school and you need a little extra help on an exam, or you need some extra patience with a friend or teacher, or maybe you got an exam back that you did well in, a short silent prayer is very appropriate.

Naturally you will want to end your day with prayer. This is a great time to really pour your heart out to Father and discuss your day and any problems you may have.

We have been asked to give thanks over each meal we have. For most of us that is three times a day. And our prophet has asked us to have family prayer both morning and night. The Savior himself commanded us to have family prayer as well as personal prayer (see 3 Nephi 18:21).

Wow! Do you know how many prayers that is in one day? At least two personal, two family, and three meals. That's a total of seven prayers. Can you imagine how close to the Spirit you can be if you pray seven times a day? Satan won't even stand a chance with all that spiritual power!

Though *how we should pray* may seem elementary to some, I find as I listen to others pray that many are unaware of a few simple guidelines.

In Matthew 6:9 we find the perfect opening format. We open with "Our Father which art in Heaven" or a salutation which includes Heavenly Father. Next we give him thanks. This may include specifics or things in general, or both. We then ask him for the things we are in need of. We are usually very specific in this area. Before we close we ask him to "forgive us" of our sins or wrongdoings and then pray for those who have wronged us. You may not want to pray for those who have hurt you, but we are told quite clearly that "if ye forgive men their trespasses, your Heavenly Father will also forgive you" (verse 14).

As you "pray for them which despitefully use you, and persecute you" (Matthew 5:44) you will find your feelings of ill will begin to melt away. In praying for them you will find yourself being healed. When it is appropriate we should pray vocally. There will be times, however, when silent prayer is proper. Doctrine and Covenants 19:28 makes this clear. "And again, I command thee that thou shalt pray vocally as well as in thy heart; yea, before the world as well as in secret, in public as well as in private."

We of course never want to make a spectacle of ourselves as the Zoramites did on their Rameumptom (see Alma 31:12–22), but we should also never be ashamed to discreetly bow our head in public and offer a quick prayer. There is nothing wrong or embarrassing about letting people know that we are Christians. They may not tell you, but secretly they will admire you for your courage to do what you think is right.

Now for the *answers* to our prayers. How do we know when we have received an answer?

There are several ways in which our Heavenly Father gives us answers. One well-known way is given to us in D&C 9:8–9. After you "study it out in your mind; then you must ask me if it be right, and if it is right I will cause that your bosom shall burn within you; therefore, you shall feel that it is right. But if it be not right you shall have no such feelings, but you shall have a stupor of thought that shall cause you to forget the thing which is wrong."

Is that easy or what? If we feel excited about our decision we will know that it is right. But if we don't feel excited and we still question our decision and tend to put it off or not think about it, then the decision is probably wrong.

I have personally been blessed with an added way of knowing whether a decision is wrong. When I make a bad decision I get the most horrible pit in my stomach. It stays there until I have changed my mind. I may end up with ulcers someday, but so far this has been a sure-fire method of knowing right from wrong!

Another method which Father uses to answer our prayers is through others. Let me share a personal example with you.

In the early part of my marriage my husband and I found ourselves with five small children, a large mortgage payment, and plenty of debt and expenses. Money was never so tight, and more than once I considered going to work outside the home.

One day I received a phone call from a woman who was a professional "head hunter." Now, before you think she was after my head, let me tell you what that means. In the business world, large businesses who need employees in a particular area of expertise often go to an employment agency that specializes in finding those employees. The agency doesn't run ads but actively seeks out people who are usually employed elsewhere and convinces them that a move to this new company would be more profitable for them. In return they are paid a handsome fee for their service.

The woman said that she knew of me and that she had a selling position with a very large jewelry company that would be perfect for me. The job paid a lot of money and started right away. She asked me to come in for an interview and discuss the possibilities with her.

I was so excited! You see, my husband and I had been praying earnestly for some time that the Lord would bless us with the ability to get out from under our financial strain. This had to be an answer to prayers. I could go to work and make tons of money, and not only could we pay off our debts but we would also have extra with which to take our children to Disneyland and on other vacations.

The next day I went in for the interview. Not only did the interview go well with the head hunter but also she wanted me to meet the owner of her firm and interview with him. Again the interview went super. They both confirmed that I was the perfect person for the position. However, now I had a big decision to make. I was informed that if I took this job I would have to discontinue my speaking for youth conferences at BYU because my employer would not allow me to take off that much time. I was also told that they had to have my decision by early the next morning.

As I drove home I kept thinking of all the pros and cons of going to work. At last I decided that this had to be a blessing from Heavenly Father and that I would take the job.

I dropped by my babysitter's home to pick up my two younger children and to inform my tender that she was about to have a new full-time tending job with my children. I'll never forget what she said when I told her of my good fortune. She said, "Vivian, I love your children and they love me, but they need their mother."

How could she have dropped such a bombshell on me? I knew she was right, but wasn't this opportunity supposed to be a blessing? Suddenly a stupor of thought set in.

When I arrived home I quickly took a casserole out of the fridge and put it in the oven for dinner. I told my husband that I had a speaking engagement at a Relief Society meeting that evening and that I would see him later.

As I walked out the door, Doug said, "What did you decide about the job?" I told him that I had decided to take it. Then he dropped another bombshell on me.

"Have you prayed about it?" he said.

Prayed about it? You've got to be kidding. When did I possibly have time to pray about it?

Finally the last bombshell dropped as Doug said, "I would never made a decision of that nature without consulting the Lord first."

I knew he was right. "Counsel with the Lord in all thy doings" is exactly what the scriptures say, and yet I had not.

How I got to my speaking engagement that night I'll never know. You see, I drove on automatic pilot the whole way. I literally grasped hold of the steering wheel and poured my heart out to Heavenly Father.

Just before arriving at the church I made a desperate plea to my Father in Heaven to please help me make the right decision. If this job was a blessing to my family, then I would take it, but if it wasn't and I was supposed to stay at home with my family I would do that. I just needed to know.

Then I did something a little selfish. I said that because the decision had to be made that evening I needed to know now. I didn't want any more stupor of thought; I needed a clear-cut answer and I had to have it *now!*

Because of my being so rushed all day, I felt that I hadn't done a very good job of speaking that evening. As I sat down after the talk I thought maybe this was the answer. Maybe Heavenly Father was trying to tell me that I was getting burned out on my speaking and that now was the time to move on to other things.

As these thoughts were going through my head the sweetest little old lady got up to give the closing prayer. You could tell from her gray hair and her weathered face that she was very seasoned.

She said all the normal things that one usually hears in a prayer, and then suddenly she stopped. There was a long pause. I looked up to see if she had had a heart attack or something. Then she continued with her prayer and said, "and bless sister Cline, Father in Heaven, that she will continue to teach. That she will know of the love that the sisters and youth of the Church have for her and of her need to share her talents with them."

Was that a clear-cut answer, or what?

I came up to her afterwards and told her that she was truly an answer to my prayers that evening. When I told her why, she smiled softly, and with all the wisdom that many years bring she said, "Sister Cline, there will be other opportunities like that one in the future. Now you are needed at home and in the Church."

Indeed, as I found out, sometimes the Lord answers our prayers through others.

Another way prayers are answered are with sudden thoughts in our mind. It seems like out of nowhere a thought will enter the mind and come up again over and over. (Remember, only good thoughts come from Heavenly Father. If it's a bad thought it comes from another source.)

This very thing happened to me. I was prompted for no reason at all to send money to a missionary in our ward. I had not heard of any financial problems with the family, so I pushed it out of my mind. Again and again I received the feeling that I should send some money to this particular Elder, but I didn't do anything about it.

The next fast Sunday the mother of this young Elder got up and said that she did not know who the person was that sent her son some money but that she was truly grateful. Apparently he had some expenses come up that he couldn't meet and the money was put to good use.

I felt so bad as I heard her testimony. I should have been the one to help out. I received the message but I didn't do anything about it. Because I did not heed the promptings, Father gave someone else the opportunity to share and that person received the special blessings for obeying.

You can bet from now on I will be more obedient to the promptings of the Spirit that come as thoughts in my head.

Scriptures are another way prayers are answered. Sometimes a scripture will pop into the mind as we are seeking an answer to a problem. This is an additional reason why we should read and become familiar with the scriptures.

Occasionally our Father in Heaven answers our prayers by the actual "hearing" of a voice. This happened to me once.

Summers are very hot in Utah, and because we don't have air conditioning in our home, my three sons often chose to sleep outside in their sleeping bags.

One summer morning I got up and prepared to go to BYU to speak to an EFY session. Because I am so busy I have learned to cut corners to save time anywhere I can. For instance, I have a routine in which I come out of our home, open the garage door, push the genie button, and hop into my car. While the garage door is going up I quickly back up, barely missing the garage door, then push the genie button inside the car to bring it back down.

This particular morning I went through my entire routine as I normally do until I began driving back in reverse. Suddenly I heard a voice literally *scream* (whether inside my head or audibly, I don't know), and say "Where are the boys?"

Immediately I slammed on the brakes and quickly looked over my left shoulder to see if the boys were sleeping in their designated area. To my shock, I saw only two sleeping bags—but I have three boys. Suddenly the reality of what happened hit me. We had told the boys never to sleep on the driveway, and yet as I threw the car door open, there behind my left rear wheel was a sleeping bag.

Terror such as I had never felt flushed through my entire body. I leaped as fast as I could from the car. There lay Walter, one of my twins, with the car's back tire rolled halfway up and onto his pillow. In another second I would have literally crushed my son's head.

Does the Lord hear and answer prayers? I bear you my solemn witness that he does.

May the Lord bless you with the desire to "pray always," that you may be guided and protected on your sojourn here on earth.

Vivian R. Cline is the owner of "The Finishing Touch" finishing school and is a former ladies health spa manager. She is an author and co-author and has also held the title of Mrs. Utah America. She has been a professional model, and is the director of the youth program "A Time for Youth." She is the wife of S. Douglas Cline and the mother of five children.

5

HOW IMPORTANT IS BEING POPULAR?

Paula Thomas

The woman was old and ragged and gray
And bent with the chill of the Winter's day.

The street was wet with a recent snow
And the woman's feet were aged and slow.

She stood at the crossing and waited long,
Alone, uncared for, amid the throng

Of human beings who passed her by
None heeded the glance of her anxious eye.

Down the street, with laughter and shout,
Glad in the freedom of "school let out,"

Came the boys like a flock of sheep,
Hailing the snow piled white and deep.

Past the woman so old and gray
Hastened the children on their way.

Nor offered a helping hand to her—
So meek, so timid, afraid to stir

Lest the carriage wheels or the horses' feet
Should crowd her down in the slippery street.

At last came one of the merry troop,
The nicest laddie of all the group;

He paused beside her and whispered low,
"I'll help you cross, if you wish to go."

Her aged hand on his strong young arm
She placed, and so, without hurt or harm,

He guided the trembling feet along,
Proud that his own were firm and strong.

Then back again to his friends he went,
His young heart happy and well content.

"She's somebody's mother, boys, you know,
For all she's aged and poor and slow,

"And I hope some fellow will lend a hand
To help my mother, you understand,

"If ever she's poor and old and gray,
When her own dear boy is far away."

And "somebody's mother" bowed low her head
In her home that night, and the prayer she said

Was, "God be kind to the noble boy,
Who is somebody's son, and pride and joy!"

                    —Mary Dow Brine

It really does take courage to be kind. Being thoughtful takes think-ing about others more than we think about ourselves. And we have to learn to like ourselves before we will ever lift or help others. Those are all facts. Finding courage, being thoughtful, and giving of ourselves to others will bring us more happiness and peace in our lives than we can even imagine. But we are the only ones who can decide what is right for us to do. Others cannot tell us how we should perform, cannot make the decision for us. It is up to each of us individually.

The question is, How important is it to be popular? The word *popular,* according to *Webster's New World Dictionary,* means: having many friends; being liked by many people. It says nothing about the kind of clothes we wear, or the homes we live in, or the cars we drive.

It doesn't refer to who the people are that we are liked by or hang out with. The word *popular* refers only to us: who we are, and how we treat others.

The reason we get confused about popularity is that there are two different kinds of popular. There is the world's way and then there is God's way. They are very different.

If we are doing popular in the world's way, three things happen that blind us to what being "well liked by many" really means.

Peers Become All-Important

Peers become all-important. We worry about what others might think of us and we think we can only be seen with certain people.

My son and a group of his friends, all in the eighth grade, came to our home after school. They were going through the fridge and pantry looking for food. My son had no idea that I was at home, because the car was in the repair shop; and I was in a back room studying and had not bothered to announce that I was only yards away from the commotion in the kitchen. Yes, the guys were acting a little different than they would have if they had known that I was within earshot of all that was being said.

First the jokes started. They weren't too bad at first, but they rapidly went downhill. Then the rough-housing began, and with that came some pushing and shoving, and one boy landed on the floor in the kitchen. In a moment of anger he blurted out the Lord's name.

I felt sick inside and wanted to make my way to the kitchen and give him a piece of my mind. But I was stunned as I heard laughter— and not uncomfortable laughter. It was as if nothing out of the ordinary had been said.

When they were through consuming large quantities of food, they made their way to their homes. My son was left alone in the kitchen to clean up the aftermath. He began walking down the hall toward the room I was in. I stepped into the hall. He instantly turned into "Porky Pig." He was earnestly trying to find the right words to ask the question, "Did you hear?" Before the stuttering subsided, I answered his question, "Yes I heard." I tried to express my concern about using the Lord's name in that manner, and how it seemed that not one person noticed or even felt the least bit uncomfortable. At this moment came the king of all copouts; the most popular excuse of this century left my sons' lips. "Mom, everybody does it!"

When we become locked into the importance of what people are thinking about us, we can make choices just because "everybody is doing it." These choices can bring us sorrow and even sadness. Just because we think that the whole world may be doing it does not make it right. In the history of God's dealing with his children on the earth you will never find an instance of his changing a wrong to a right just because everyone was doing it.

When we think that we can only associate with certain people who are "cool," we must first make the decision as to who is not so cool. Thus we set ourselves up as the judge of others. I don't think there are many of us that have earned that lofty a position. I watched as children in my elementary school abused other children. It certainly didn't stop with the first six grades. The abuse continued through junior high and high school. It always seemed to be the same people that were the abusers and the same people that were the victims. We destroy the lives of others with this practice.

It takes courage to be kind!

We Think Popularity Will Bring Us Happiness

As human beings it seems we are always looking outside ourselves to find happiness. Yet happiness comes from within. In looking for this great and wonderful gift we often let our perspective become distorted. If we really believe something, that automatically makes it true to us, because that is the truth we see. Thus if we believe we are dumb, we are. Not because we really are, but if we believe it we act it out. We *are* what we think!

When I was in the second grade (1952) my mom made me a beautiful white slip with a big red ruffle. The slip was so full that when I wore it under a skirt I looked like a square dancer. Have you got the picture? I thought this slip was the most beautiful thing I owned. When I had it on I really believed that I looked beautiful—beautiful like a princess. I thought how cool it would be to just wear my slip to school as a skirt. I would be the most beautiful person in my school.

I would go to my mom first thing in the morning and ask her if I could wear my slip to school as a skirt. I did this every morning for months. I would always ask the question as if I had never asked it before. My mom would always give me the same answer. "No, it's a slip. People will know it is a slip." When winter came, I stopped asking.

On the first spring day, I hit my mom up again with, "Please can I wear my slip to school as a skirt today?" Well, today was different. My mom said, "Yes, why don't you wear your slip to school as a skirt. Wear your red blouse to match the red ruffle, and your black patent leather shoes and white socks with the lace. You will look so cute!"

I followed my mother's instructions to the letter. I left a little late and had to run for the bus. When I was close enough that the other children could see how beautiful I looked, the boys were the first: "Paula, your slip is showing." "Hey, girl, you forgot your skirt." The girls were too embarrassed to speak. I wanted to just disappear. The moment the first boy yelled to me that my slip was showing, I was no longer in my princess uniform. I was standing in the middle of the road in my *slip!* I have never lived this story down. At my twenty-year class reunion, the conversation at the table was the time I wore my slip to school as a skirt.

Perspective is a killer. We have to make sure we are looking for the kind of happiness that lasts, not the kind that fades away with circumstances. I have discovered that the most meaningful happiness comes in our lives when we know for ourselves that God loves us individually; that he knows us and he knows our names. We can only find that out through diligent effort on our part.

Our self-worth is not a horizontal line the world would try to teach us; a line where we can see our performance. For example, you get an *A* in math, and that makes you feel good. You get asked to the Junior Prom, which makes you feel special. Maybe you play really well in an important basketball game. You couldn't feel better about yourself.

But what if you *don't* do so well in math, or get asked to the dance? What if it's your fault that the team lost—you missed the final shot? The only way on this earth that we can survive the things that we see as failure in our lives is if we discover for ourselves that we are linked to something far greater than our performance: even a Father in Heaven who loves us. Self-worth is a vertical line. This happens when we come to know God for ourselves.

We Leave God Out of the Plan

The final thing we do when we are doing popular the world's way is we leave God out of the plan. Instead of following in his footsteps, we don't even get on the path. We put ourselves in a position that we cannot hear (or won't hear) the promptings of the Holy Ghost. We become unteachable or hard-hearted.

In a New Testament class I was in, the teacher asked the class why in their opinion Jesus performed so many miracles. There were many different answers thrown around: "To attract attention." "To show he had power." "To gain a following." These were some answers given. The teacher commented that there was probably some truth in all of the responses, but he felt that Jesus healed because He could. He loved the people and He had the power to make their lives a little sweeter.

I hope that, just like the young man in the poem, when you have the opportunity to offer someone in need your arm or to "lift up the hands which hang down" (D&C 81:5) you will have the courage to act. That you, like the Savior, will serve because you can.

Paula Thomas has worked for Brigham Young University youth and family programs for twelve years. A mother and homemaker, she is completing a degree in family science at BYU. Sister Thomas has served as a ward Young Women president and with the Governor's Conference on Drug-Free Youth and Families. Her interests include reading, writing, and caring for her family and home. She and her husband, David, are the parents of six children.

6

KINDNESS: SOMETHING YOU AND I CAN DO

Randal A. Wright

When I was young I dreamed of being a star basketball player. I practiced every day with that thought in mind. There were a couple of problems with my life goal, though. One was that I was much smaller than others who were my age, making it harder to compete against the bigger boys. The other problem was that I wasn't any good at basketball. Since that time I have learned that there may be certain restrictions to some of our dreams. I can want to be a better basketball player than Shaquille Oneal, but the reality is that it will never happen, no matter how hard I try. Perhaps you have realized this same thing as you have chased your dreams. We are all different, with different abilities.

There is something, however, that you and I can do, and do well. We can all be kind to others. I know that may not sound like the macho thing to do, but it is the *right* thing to do. President Ezra Taft Benson said, "One who is kind is sympathetic and gentle with others. He is considerate of others' feelings and courteous in his behavior. He has a helpful nature. Kindness pardons others' weaknesses and faults. Kindness is extended to all—to the aged and the young, to animals, to those low of station as well as the high." ("Godly Characteristics of the Master," *Ensign,* November 1986, p. 47.)

"One who is kind is sympathetic and gentle with others. He is considerate of others' feelings and courteous in his behavior."

Being a basketball fan as a youth, I often watched the major college teams on TV. One season I was particularly excited that the University of Houston was ranked number 2 in the nation behind the traditional powerhouse, UCLA. During a twelve-year span, UCLA won ten national championships. Everywhere they played, tickets were in great demand and always sold out. During this particular season, UCLA was led by Lew Alcinder (Kareem Abdul Jabar), and the University of Houston had super-star All-American and future NBA star Elvin Hayes.

The game was being played in the Houston Astrodome, and my brother-in-law and I tried every way to buy tickets. After several unsuccessful attempts, I decided to call my friend Gary, who was attending the University of Houston, to see if he could get us some tickets. Again the message came back that the game was sold out. We were very disappointed.

Then one day two tickets came in the mail from my friend Gary. He wrote that he didn't really want to go to the game, so we could have his tickets. I knew that he was a big basketball fan, and this was by far the biggest game of the year, so I called him and told him we couldn't accept the tickets. He insisted, however, that we have them.

I couldn't believe he had done this for us. As we arrived at the Houston Astrodome, a part of the biggest crowd to ever view a college basketball game at that time, I thought we would be up in the "nosebleed" section. To my astonishment, we had seats on the front row, right behind the UCLA bench. That night the University of Houston upset undefeated UCLA in front of the screaming home crowd. I doubt seriously that Gary has thought much about his kindness since that time, but I have never forgotten what he did. He gave up personal enjoyment so that others could experience something they badly wanted.

"One who is kind . . . has a helpful nature."
While walking through the student center at Brigham Young University, I saw a friend from Texas. He was with his son Neal, who was about to enter the Missionary Training Center. Seeing them again, I couldn't help recall an incident from Neal's life.

When he was a senior in high school he called his seminary teacher right before Christmas and told her that he needed a job to earn some money for a special Christmas present. Being retired and living on a fixed income, his teacher did not have a lot of extra money. But knowing that Neal must really need the money or he would have never asked, she agreed that he could work for her to earn the money for his present. She warned him that he would be working very hard that day doing farm chores.

When the work was finished, Neal came in and informed his teacher that he was through with the chores she had given him. She was very pleased with the work he had done, noticing that he'd done more than she'd requested, and pulled out her checkbook to pay him for a job well done. Before she could write out the substantial amount she'd decided upon, however, he smiled at her and said: "Merry Christmas! The present was for you."

Can you imagine the feelings of joy that both student and teacher felt that night? Do you think a new CD or new pair of shoes provides as much joy as does being kind to others? The Prophet Joseph Smith said, "When persons manifest the least kindness and love to me, O what power it has over my mind" (*History of the Church* 5:24).

"Kindness pardons others' weaknesses and faults."

One summer I had the opportunity to speak several times at a university in a midwestern state. After one of the talks a young man came up to me and told me that he was a member of the Church. I didn't pay much attention to him, nor did I do anything to try to get to know him better or try to encourage him in any way. Why? Well, you see, I noticed that he had a shaved head, and I couldn't help thinking he was simply in need of some attention and this was a way to get it. I thought to myself, "You don't have to follow the world just to get people to notice you. Just be yourself." Later, I saw him after another talk. This time he was on crutches, and I asked if he had hurt himself. He replied, "No, I have cancer in my leg and my lungs." He was wearing shorts and I could tell that one of his knees was greatly enlarged.

I had the sickest feeling come over me. To think that I had judged this young man as one who was following worldly fashions, when in reality he had lost all his hair because of chemotherapy for cancer! When I realized what he was going through I felt tremendous compassion for him. I tried to encourage him in his time of great trial. As I spoke kind words, a feeling of peace came over me.

One of the great needs of the human heart is encouragement. And the interesting thing is that when we try to encourage someone who is down, our own spirits are lifted. Try it next time you need a lift.

After my experience with the young man on crutches, as I was driving back to the motel where I was staying, I made a new vow to quit looking for weaknesses in others. From that point on I would do better. When I drove in to the motel parking lot hundreds of young people were gathered there. They were different looking than the people I associated with daily. Many of the young men wore tattoos on their bodies, while others had nose, ear, and navel rings. They were dressed in old worn-out clothing and appeared in need of a good shower. Many of the girls also had nose rings and were dressed in immodest clothing.

I soon found out that there was a heavy metal concert that night and these people had come from many states to see this band. They were not actually staying at the motel, but were just camping out in the parking lot. Their sleeping bags were laid out right on the pavement. As I walked up to my room I stepped over several who were actually sleeping on the walkways. I began wondering why this group of young people, who had almost no money, had sacrificed to travel to see a band that made over $50 million last year. How could anyone be so foolish? As I walked in the door, I found myself irritated with the whole group.

Then I remembered the vow I had made only a few minutes earlier after badly misjudging the young man with cancer. I asked myself why I had so much compassion and kindness for the young man I had met earlier at the university. Because he has cancer, I thought. But why was there no feeling of compassion for the young concertgoers outside the door? I quickly excused myself by saying that they did not have cancer; they were only rebellious. Then I realized that they needed kindness too. Didn't Jesus say, "Verily I say unto you, Inasmuch as ye have done it unto one of the least of these my brethren, ye have done it unto me"? (Matthew 25:40.)

Again, I made a new vow to do better. The next morning I did something I may not have done had I not met the young man with cancer. I treated the concertgoers with kindness. It made me feel so much better. I learned some valuable lessons as I quit looking down on them because they did not have the same beliefs and values as I did.

An unidentified author penned this verse:

I have wept in the night
For the shortness of sight
That to somebody's need made me blind.

But I never have yet
Felt a twinge of regret
For being a little too kind.

"Kindness is extended to all—to the aged and the young. . . ."

A few years ago, I attended a youth conference in Birmingham, Alabama. A service scavenger hunt was planned as part of the conference. Each group was given a score sheet showing different acts of service that could be rendered at the homes of non-LDS families. Items included mowing yards, weeding flower beds, washing cars, cleaning windows, and so on. Each item had a certain number of points assigned. Points were also given for singing a Church hymn and giving away a copy of the Book of Mormon. The youth left with their score sheets in hand ready for the excitement of competition, each team hoping to tally the most points.

During testimony meeting that evening several young people told of their experiences. One young girl said that at the first house they told the man who opened the door that they were LDS youth and would like to do service at his home. He quickly agreed, and soon they were busy washing his car and cutting his lawn. A youth leader who was assigned to the group visited the man while the youth accomplished their tasks. The man said, "These kids don't look disabled to me!" The youth leader replied, "They aren't disabled. Why would you think that?" He said, "I thought LDS stood for learning disabled students."

At the next home they took a little more time explaining who they really were. Toward the end of the day, this group came up to a very humble home in obvious need of attention. They knocked on the door and an elderly lady opened it and invited them in. They looked into her kitchen and saw a broken kitchen sink and open cabinets with very little food. On a table was a well-worn Bible that had obviously been read many times over the years. The youth group quickly told her who they were and what they wanted to do. After their introduction, she started crying and said, "I knew the Lord would send the saints to help me." They all worked hard to complete their assignments and finally told the old widow good-bye after achieving the needed number of points.

As the youth climbed into the van, they discussed the elderly lady's situation. Soon everyone was pooling their money together. They stopped at a grocery store and bought her three bags of groceries.

Then they stopped by a hardware store and bought a part for her sink. Suddenly the competition part of the scavenger hunt didn't seem to matter anymore. They arrived back at her house and gave her the groceries and fixed her broken sink. Again, she cried. As they were leaving, they heard her say, "Thank God for sending the saints." Witnessing this act of kindness, I had a renewed desire to treat others with more love and respect. I realized that it usually doesn't cost anything to be kind to others, and the rewards are out of this world.

President David O. McKay said, "Life is made up not of great sacrifices or duties, but of little things in which smiles and kindness and small obligations given habitually are what win and preserve the heart and secure comfort" ("Spirituality, the Goal in Life," *Improvement Era,* December 1956, p. 914.) I've learned that it doesn't take great effort to be kind to others. We can lift others by a simple greeting, a smile, a word of encouragement, or just a short visit. These little things enrich the lives of both the giver and the receiver. Happiness increases when we are kind to others.

Our dreams of becoming a star basketball player may or may not come to pass, but kindness is something you and I can do. Let's begin today. We never know what tomorrow will bring. Someone has said:

If you would do a kindness, it is not wise to wait
You never know how quickly it's going to be too late.

Randal A. Wright *attended Ricks College and Brigham Young University, and recently completed a master's degree in family science at Lamar University. He is presently teaching Doctrine and Covenants at BYU while he works on a Ph.D. He has done much research on the modern world's impact on families, and has written articles for the* Ensign *and the* Church News *in addition to two books and a full-length drama. He has served in many Church positions, including stake Young Men president and high councilor. His hobbies include book collecting, family research, sports, and travel.*

7

FAITH, MUSTARD SEEDS, AND MOUNTAINS

Kim M. Peterson

Every grade-school morning at 8:45 A.M. I turned off the morning cartoons, picked up my lunch sack, and shouted good-bye to my mother as I started for school. Walking eight blocks 180 times a year for six years left plenty of time for kicking cans, sliding in the snow, running, and talking with friends. Once in a while the walk lent itself to deep and poignant thought.

Simultaneous with my grade-school experience was a weekly trip to Primary. Primary was held on Tuesday, Wednesday, or Thursday afternoon. Of the Primary lessons I can remember, one posed a significant problem. My CTR teacher taught us about faith. Her eight- and nine-year-old students were amazed by the implications of the scriptural idea that with faith as a grain of mustard seed we could move mountains. She showed us a tiny mustard seed and reassured us that we had faith at least as big as the seed.

The next morning I was impressed by the sunrise over Mount Olympus in Salt Lake City. My teacher's words still echoed in my heart, "If you have faith as a grain of mustard seed . . ." Concentrating my gaze and attention at Mount Olympus, I held my breath and tried my hardest to move the mountain. Nothing happened. Several mornings that year, and for the rest of my grade-school experience, I tried to "muster" the faith to move Mount Olympus. Nothing ever happened.

Did I have faith? Was the scripture true? Can mountains really be moved? Studying faith is a rewarding experience. Personal stories, faith-promoting experiences, and good questions can help us appreciate faith. The ability to apply faith to our everyday challenges, however, may be described most accurately by scripture. If you are interested in increasing and learning to apply your faith, I invite you to get your scriptures and study the chapters outlined in this chapter. By simply reading the stories and doctrine outlined in these scriptures you will demonstrate a portion of the faith you wish you had!

Our earthly experience is filled with insurmountable mountains. In Mark 9 we find the record of Christ's transfiguration. The Mount of Transfiguration may be Mt. Tabor, a mountain that rises almost 1900 ft. above sea level and stands "apart" (see v. 2). After the Savior's descent from the mountain, a father implores Him to cure his son of a devil. The disciples have tried unsuccessfully to cast the devil out. Christ teaches the father (and all of us) by saying, "If thou wilt believe all things I shall say unto you, this is possible to him that believeth." The father's humble reply helps us understand the role of humility and faith: "Lord, I believe; help thou mine unbelief." (JST Mark 9:20–21.) Christ rebukes the spirit and revives the boy.

The disciples, troubled by the fact that they had been unable to cast the devil out, ask the Savior why they were unsuccessful. Christ responds by saying: "Because of your unbelief: for verily I say unto you, If ye have faith as a grain of mustard seed, ye shall say unto this mountain, Remove hence to yonder place; and it shall remove; and nothing shall be impossible unto you" (Matthew 17:20).

The volume of a mustard seed is roughly .000016 cubic inches (that's 16 millionths.) The volume of Mount Tabor, by comparison, is roughly 92,000,000,000,000 cubic inches (that's 92 trillion.) It would take 5,763,000,000,000,000,000 (that's 5.763 quintillion) mustard seeds to equal the volume of Mount Tabor. If Mount Tabor is the mountain to which Christ is referring, the comparison suggests that with a faith ratio of 1 to 5,763,000,000,000,000,000 you can move mountains.

To some, standards such as staying morally clean, keeping the Word of Wisdom, or being worthy to attend the temple may resemble immovable mountains. In an attempt to move the immovable we may work harder, set more goals, or become more resolved. These works may be comparable to moving a mountain with a pick, a shovel, and a wheelbarrow. One shovelful of dirt is roughly .5 cubic feet. By my calculation, we would have to dig and move 3,840,000,000,000 (that's 3.84 trillion) shovelfuls of dirt. Sounds impossible, huh? If you are more sophisticated, you may opt to spend over $2,000,000 to purchase the largest front-end loader: a Caterpillar Catloader 994. The 994 has a bucket capacity of 23 cubic yards. Even with a Catloader 994 it would still take 556,000,000,000 (that's 556 billion) bucket loads to move Mount Tabor. Symbolically, we are left to choose among a shovel, a front-end loader, and a mustard seed.

Enoch lived at a time when Adam's children had "gone astray" (Moses 6:28). Enoch was traveling in the land when the Spirit of the Lord "abode on him" and told him to prophesy to this people and say to them, "Repent" (see Moses 6:26–27). Wouldn't this be like walking in the halls of your high school, trying not to look at the pictures people paste on their lockers, trying not to listen to what people say, and trying to avoid being offered drugs, tobacco, or alcohol? Imagine winding your way through this moral filth toward your school auditorium and having the Spirit whisper, "When the assembly starts, go up to the stage and tell everyone in your school to repent."

Like Enoch, maybe you would respond by saying, "Why me? I'm so young, and everyone would hate me" (see Moses 6:31.) Subsequently the Lord told Enoch what to say: "Say unto this people: Choose ye this day, to serve the Lord God who made you. Behold my Spirit is upon you, wherefore all thy words will I justify; and the mountains shall flee before you, and the rivers shall turn from their course; and thou shalt abide in me, and I in you; therefore walk with me." (Moses 6:33–34.)

You might expect that, because the Lord told Enoch what to say, his mission was easy. As would be the case with those in your high school, however, the people did not like to be told to repent, and "all men were offended because of him" (Moses 6:37). Despite the unpopular nature of his message and the hatred of the people, Enoch did what the Lord had commanded him to do. The prophecy of mountains fleeing before his presence was also fulfilled: "And so great was the faith of Enoch that he led the people of God, and their enemies came to battle against them; and he spake the word of the Lord, and the earth trembled, and the mountains fled, even according to his command . . . and all nations feared greatly, so powerful was the word of Enoch, and so great was the power of the language which God had given him" (Moses 7:13).

Mountains fled at his command! I've still never been able to move Mount Olympus. If Enoch's faith was as a grain of mustard seed, mine must have been pretty small.

As a sixth grader I climbed Mount Olympus for the first time. I remember counting a hundred steps and stopping for a breath. My father frequently asked if I was going to make it. Not wanting to disappoint him, I assured him I was all right, even though I wasn't sure. Just as the climb seemed impossible, we reached what to me looked like sheer cliffs. My dad asked if I wanted him to help me. I probably looked pretty haggard, and he offered me a rope tied to his belt. The steps I took, coupled with the help of my father, were enough to climb the hill I couldn't seem to negotiate alone.

Your Heavenly Father loves you enough to give you the task you cannot accomplish without his help: "And if men come unto me I will show unto them their weakness. I give unto men weakness that they may be humble; and my grace is sufficient for all men that humble themselves before me; for if they humble themselves before me, and have faith in me, then will I make weak things become strong unto them." (Ether 12:27.)

If we come unto him, if we choose to be humble, and if we have faith in him, he (not we) will make weak things become strong. One of the most dangerous conclusions we can come to is that if we simply tried harder, we could accomplish what Heavenly Father has designed for us. Four climbs and four years after that first effort I climbed Mount Olympus unassisted. Without the help of my dad on the first climb I would have remained discouraged, unsuccessful, and just short of reaching the top. Just so, the effort you make to be righteous, coupled with the help of your Father, is enough to be righteous in a world where you may not be able to remain righteous alone. In fact, attempting to be righteous without the help of your Father is a dangerous risk.

Once on top of Mount Olympus I could see my home to the west, ski resorts where I loved to ski to the south, a canyon where I loved to fish to the north, and I knew another city was to the east. If I had been successful at moving the mountain as a CTR, in which direction would it have moved? Can you imagine the headlines in the newspaper: "CTR Chooses the Wrong and Kills Hundreds." I would have been famous . . . and deadly. Mount Olympus didn't move because I didn't really have faith . . . no, not even the size of a mustard seed.

Alma teaches us that faith is a "hope for things which are not seen, which are true" (Alma 32:21). My dangerous desire to move a mountain was not faith, because it did not meet the requirements of truth. Faith cannot operate contrary to the will of God. Instead, faith is access to God's will. The brother of Jared (who also moved a mountain—see Ether 12:30) approached the Lord with the problem of lighting (faith) the vessels he had made (works.) Notice how he spoke to the Lord: "And I know, O Lord, that thou hast all power, and can do whatsoever thou wilt for the benefit of man; therefore touch these stones, O Lord, with thy finger, and prepare them that they may shine forth in darkness" (Ether 3:4).

The brother of Jared recognized that it was God's will to benefit man. Subsequently he saw God because of his faith. You can be assured that God also has your benefit in mind. Through faith you can access the will of God concerning your decisions and your destiny.

Faith not only moves mountains but it also parts the Red Sea, kills giants, causes rain to end a drought, saves a prophet from the lions' den, helps a fourteen-year-old pray, and designs ships. After Nephi had left Jerusalem, returned for the plates, returned for the daughters of Ishmael, saw his father's vision, made a new bow, and followed the Liahona, the Lord came to him saying, "Get thee into the mountain." Like Moses who went to the mountain for commandments, and Abraham who went to the mountain to sacrifice his son, Nephi did as the Lord commanded. God instructed Nephi to build a ship after the manner which he would be shown. (See 1 Nephi 17:4–13.) Wouldn't this be a little bit like the Lord showing you a spaceship and commanding you to build it? Even if you did build it, would you get in it? And what would your friends think?

Sometimes it may appear that the Lord requires us to do almost impossible things. We are commanded to stay morally pure and clean in a society where that God-given standard has to a large extent given way to sexual permissiveness. We are expected to defend the sanctity of life when most teachers and social organizations teach that abortion is the choice of the mother whose life would be inconvenienced by carrying the child. We are even taught to abstain from tobacco, alcohol, and drugs when many popular people base friendship and acceptance on participation in substance abuse. Maybe you'd rather try building the ship?

Nephi's brothers were particularly annoyed at his attempt to do what the Lord commanded. They "murmured," complained, and called

Nephi a fool (see 1 Nephi 17:17–18). Are you surprised? Consider the fact that Laman also went into the wilderness, returned for the plates, returned for the daughters of Ishmael, traveled in the wilderness, and would eventually help Nephi build the ship. We can't be sure whether Laman hunted for food or just ate what Nephi provided. And we know that instead of asking to see his father's vision he just asked Nephi to explain it. To that point Laman did almost everything Nephi did. What was the difference? Laman complained and obeyed—Nephi simply obeyed. Nephi's faith helped him avoid complaining and made him an example to his older brothers. Do you complain and go to church, or simply attend your church meetings? Do you complain and read the scriptures or simply study your scriptures? Do you complain and wait until you're sixteen to date or simply wait until you're sixteen? If we complain and keep most of the commandments, maybe we are more like Laman than we think.

Laman began to understand, and even helped build the ship after Nephi explained that his brothers knew that the children of Israel were in bondage, that Moses led them out of it, that Moses divided the Red Sea, and that Pharaoh's armies were drowned. Nephi continued by reminding them that the children of Israel were fed with manna in the wilderness, and that Moses smote a rock and there came forth water (see 1 Nephi 17:25–30). Having listed these incredible miracles, Nephi continued with an important question: "And now, if the Lord has such great power, and has wrought so many miracles among the children of men, how is it that he cannot instruct me, that I should build a ship?" Not only did Laman and Lemuel help Nephi finish the ship but also they boarded the ship and sailed to the promised land . . . and complained.

Using Nephi's reasoning, couldn't we also ask, if God delivered the children of Israel from Egypt and helped Nephi build a ship, how is it that he cannot instruct you to _____ ? You fill in the blank.

At times, we may be tempted to use faith as a Christmas wish list. When I was younger I even tried to have faith that I would get a new Masserati, pass a test for which I had not studied, or even get a date. Today, I realize that faith is meant to be used for everyday righteous desires and for some incredible eternal desires: "But because of the faith of men he has shown himself unto the world, and glorified the name of the Father, and prepared a way that thereby others might be partakers of the heavenly gift, that they might hope for those things which they have not seen" (Ether 12:8).

A quick review of the miracles in my life reveals a number of tests passed, several scared prayers answered, a dating career that resulted in a temple marriage, and two wonderful children. Still no Masserati—and Mount Olympus, to my knowledge, has not moved yet. I am so grateful that the Lord does not answer my prayers the way I think he should at the time. I realize now that he wants so much more for me than I want for myself.

About a year after my first attempt to move a mountain, my father bought a motorcycle. Our family was ecstatic! He drove into the driveway with the huge machine strapped to the bumpers of the station wagon. After several neighborhood drives, he determined to take the motorcycle onto the trails in the mountains. I was thrilled when he asked if I would like to come along. We lifted the bike onto the carriers, jumped in the station wagon, and headed for the mountains.

I can remember figuring out how to strap on the helmet, seeing my father kick start the motorcycle, and clinching his belt tightly as we climbed trails that would have taken hours to walk. We slipped frequently into the muddy ruts of four-wheel-drive vehicles, but never fell. After mounting the crest of the trail, we turned back. At first the riding was smooth and the gears hummed louder with each downshift. The warmth of the exhaust pipe took the bite off the chilling wind.

Toward the bottom of the trail, mud started sticking to the tires and soon caked the fenders. Gradually the motorcycle skidded to a stop when the wheels could no longer turn. I helped my father find a stick and tried to work the clay from the tires, fenders, and chain. After several minutes and another attempt at driving, the mud collected again and the tires would not turn. Even though I was with my father, I was scared. I wondered if we could find our way back in the dark, if the motorcycle was ruined, if we would be stranded, and if we would freeze to death.

Mustering all the courage a nine-year-old could possibly find, I asked my father if we should pray. I'll never forget his tender response as he thanked me and suggested that we kneel down by the bike. My tears flowed freely as I heard my childhood idol thank Heavenly Father for the blessing of the outdoors and the chance to be with his son. Then he simply asked that we would make it home safely, and that no harm or accident would befall us. The "safety" and "no harm or accident" was a favorite line in our family payers, but this time I meant it when I said "Amen." We straddled the bike, started down the trail, and didn't stop again until the bottom.

I look back and realize that this small mountain, the tiny Honda 90, and a simple dilemma were not a life-threatening combination. I am so grateful, however, for Heavenly Father's answer to my earthly father's prayer. I knew a miracle had happened. I still recognize that my faith, and the faith of my father, allowed Heavenly Father to help us.

Since we have no reason to move Mount Tabor, the symbolic message of the Savior must be more important. If we exercise only a particle of faith (even 1/5,763,000,000,000,000,000th of a particle) the seemingly insurmountable challenges in our lives can be moved. With a particle of faith we can know the "word of God is true" (see Alma 32:22–34). With a particle of faith we can remain morally clean (see Genesis 39:9). With a particle of faith we can keep the Word of Wisdom (see Daniel 1:8). With a particle of faith we can be happy in this life and live with Heavenly Father in the world to come.

Kim M. Peterson is a seminary coordinator and institute instructor in the Denver, Colorado, area. He loves to ski and has been employed as a ski instructor during the winter months. Kim also enjoys cooking a variety of Eastern dishes. He and his wife, Terri, have one son and one daughter.

8

SYMBOLS OF CHRIST

Stace Hucks Christianson

I have always been interested in the challenge of recognizing and understanding symbols. I remember someone telling me that the endless circle of a wedding ring is a symbol of the eternal life of a couple who weds. When I look at my wedding ring I remember the promises I made to my Heavenly Father and stay faithful to those promises so that I might live with my best friend forever.

The scriptures teach us that all things in heaven and earth are meant to be signs that there is a God (see Alma 30:44; Moses 2:11; Helaman 12:15). The Lord himself declares, "All things bear record of me" (Moses 6:63). I think it is important to search the scriptures looking for clues to what the Savior and many of our prophets are trying to teach us. The guidance of the Spirit coupled with sincere prayer can cause our eyes to be opened, our understanding enlightened, and our testimonies grounded in the "Spirit of truth" (D&C 93:9).

I would like to direct your attention to Old Testament times and the commandments that were given to some of our ancient prophets. When our first parents were cast out of the Garden of Eden they called upon the Lord for direction. In answer to their prayers the Lord told them that they "should offer the firstlings of their flocks, for an offering unto the Lord" (Moses 5:5). After (see Ether 12:6) Adam and Eve had proven obedient, the Lord sent down an angel to explain why he had given this significant commandment. "This thing," said the angel, "is a similitude of the sacrifice of the Only Begotten of the Father, which is full of grace and truth" (Moses 5:7). *Similitude* means a "type" or "likeness" of something else. In this case, sacrificing the firstlings of their flocks was to remind them of a greater sacrifice, "an infinite and eternal sacrifice" (Alma 34:10), the atoning sacrifice of the divine Son of God.

Because the Lord wanted the people to understand what the sacrifice symbolized, he required certain characteristics of the sacrificial animals. They had to be the firstborn, without blemish, and were often male (see Exodus 12:5). Notice the similarities to the Savior. *Firstlings* means firstborn; usually it was the male to remind us of Christ's divine birthright. *Without blemish* means without sickness, broken bones, or imperfections.

In the scriptures, people's lives may also come to symbolize the Savior. In Old Testament times the children of Israel were being held in bondage as slaves by the people of Egypt. According to prophecy, the Lord would raise a prophet in their midst to deliver them out of bondage. Eventually Moses rose up and led the children of Israel out of slavery and away from Egypt. When preparing Moses for his mission, Heavenly Father told him he was in the "similitude of mine Only Begotten" (Moses 1:6).

What do the lives of the Savior and Moses have in common? Both of their lives were prophesied about long before they were born. Both were born in a time when the political leaders of their day felt threatened by these prophecies and the rulers ordered all male infants put to death; and both survived (Exodus 1:16–17; Matthew 2:13, 16). Both were to lead God's covenant people out of physical or spiritual bondage; and both of them did. Both of them lived in a time when new commandments were to be given to the people. Both lived worthy to receive the new laws that their people might reap the blessings of obedience. The more you study the children of Israel the more you will find (there is a bunch!); I'll leave the rest of the discoveries up to you and the Spirit.

In the New Testament and the Book of Mormon, the scriptures use analogies which can be thought of as symbols. Prophets make references to things we see in nature, like vines, trees, fruit, seeds, animals, birth and death, water, and light. Good teachers will use analogies and symbols that are cross-cultural; all people, no matter what their culture, can relate to them. Christ spoke of himself as the "vine, ye are the branches: He that abideth in me, and I in him, the same bringeth forth much fruit: for without me ye can do nothing" (John 15:5). Let's consider why he uses a vine as a symbol. First, although vines may differ in kind, they are found in every land. Right from the start, the Savior knows that everyone will have a chance to understand his meaning.

Second, we must ask, what is he trying to teach us in this scripture? One idea is that a vine carries the nutrients to the rest of the plant so that it may grow and live. Another idea is that the branches cannot grow without the vine, but with the vine they can grow and encompass a hillside! How can understanding this verse remind us of the Savior? If we connect ourselves with our Savior he can give us life, and we can grow strong and eventually be able to take on challenges that we never thought possible.

Let's look at some of our most basic priesthood ordinances. First, baptism. Why do we as Latter-day Saints believe in baptism by immersion? In Roman's 6:4 we read, "We are buried with him by baptism into death: that like as Christ was raised up from the dead by the glory of the Father, even so we also should walk in newness of life." How can understanding this scripture strengthen our understanding of Christ?

We must understand that when we are baptized we make covenants to take upon us the name of Christ, to keep his commandments, and to always remember him. Baptism is a symbol of our agreement to enter into these covenants. When we are baptized we are completely immersed in the water, to symbolize the death and burial of our old self. This is why baptismal witnesses are so careful to make sure every part of you goes under. You wouldn't want to be buried with your big toe out of the ground. Your coming up out of the water symbolizes a new, resurrected self that is washed clean by the atoning blood of Christ. It is also a reminder that the Savior has given everyone the gift of resurrection and the opportunity for eternal life.

There is another priesthood ordinance that helps us to stay clean through sincere repentance. That ordinance is the sacrament. In John 4:7–14 the Savior meets the Samaritan woman at Jacob's well, where he teaches her about his gospel, using the water in the well as a symbol of eternal life. He cleverly uses the symbol of a spring, the source of water that will never dry up. The water from the spring supports life and can be shared with others for the same purpose.

Later (in John 6:47–54) he refers to himself as the Bread of Life. He promises that if we eat of this bread we shall never hunger. Notice that both bread and water are found in all cultures. Note also that he says, "Whoso eateth my flesh, and drinketh my blood, hath eternal life; and I will raise him up at the last day" (verse 54). Clearly an allusion to the sacrament. If we eat the bread in remembrance of the sacrifice of his body for the Atonement, and drink the water in remembrance of the blood that was shed in the Garden of Gethsemane, again for the Atonement, and use this gift of repentance every week, we will have eternal life. This is the Lord's promise.

Christ can be found everywhere, if only we are willing to make the effort to seek him. I like to kneel when I pray, to symbolize my humility before my Father. I like to close my eyes to remind me that I cannot look upon him with my natural eyes. I like to bow my head in reverence to his power. I like to attend church on Sunday because it reminds me that even the Lord rested. Sunday is the day the Lord arose from death, which reminds us of the gift of the resurrection that we will all someday experience. I like to look for him in all the commandments and the ordinances so that I might be reminded of why I live them.

In the Book of Mormon my heroes are the people of Ammon who first gave up their weapons of rebellion as a symbol of their repentance (Alma 23:13). They then moved to a land of strangers, Zarahemla (Alma 27). They left behind their homes, possessions, and loved ones who did not believe. Many of these brave people died because they would not take up their weapons even in self-defense (Alma 24:11–27; 27:2–3). All this to honor their new covenant; they were serious about remembering Christ. Mormon describes the people of Ammon like this: "They did keep the law of Moses [and] . . . did look forward to the coming of Christ, considering that the law of Moses was a type of his coming, and believing that they must keep those outward performances until the time that he should be revealed unto them. Now they did not suppose that salvation came by the law of Moses; but [that] law . . . did serve to strengthen their faith in Christ." (Alma 25:15–16.)

May we follow their example by keeping the law, the commandments, in order to better know our Savior and his love for us. I bear witness that he lives and that we will recognize his work in these latter days if we search for him in all that he has asked us to do.

Stace Hucks Christianson *is originally from Southern California. She served in the Arizona Phoenix Mission, and graduated from Brigham Young University. She currently is a part-time instructor at BYU. She loves the outdoors and enjoys almost all water sports. She enjoys teaching aerobics and working with teenagers. She is especially thankful for the beach, missions, and youth conferences. She is married to Frank Christianson.*

9

BATS, BITES, AND THE VACCINE

Victor Harris

The morning of Friday, May 13, 1994, was a typical morning around our home—I was already at the Logan seminary teaching, while Heidi was busily trying to get our children off to school. Little did we know that sometime during the morning of this particular "Friday the thirteenth" a bat had slipped through our eight-year-old son Mckay's partially opened downstairs window and crawled under the covers of his unmade bed.

We had been hit hard by the flooding in our area in February; in fact, our basement had flooded with six inches of septic tank back-up sewage. During that awful experience the pump hoses were frantically shoved out Mckay's window, ruining the screen in the process. We had been planning to replace his screen but hadn't yet managed to accomplish it; a circumstance that allowed our unwanted intruder easy access into the room.

Mckay fell asleep around nine o'clock that evening and unknowingly spent the next six and a half hours with his strange bedfellow until he awakened Heidi and me about 3:30 A.M. and exclaimed, "Mom! Dad! I just got bit by a bat!" His reaction wasn't one of fear but rather of, "Cool! I just got bit by a bat!" We thought we were dreaming at first, but then I replied, "You what?" To which Mckay again exclaimed, "I just got bit by a bat!" Heidi told him that it was probably just a big moth and asked me to go and deal with the situation.

Mckay and I walked downstairs to his room, only to discover a brown bat squeaking like a mouse and flopping around on his floor. We ran upstairs, told Heidi it was definitely a bat, grabbed a pitcher and some paper plates, and headed back down to Mckay's room. The bat had moved from its original spot. After we found it again I placed the pitcher over it, which caused it to squeak again. Gently, I tried to maneuver the paper plates underneath the bat, but I must have pinched one of its wings because it began to hiss very loudly. This sound really unnerved me. Mckay later told friends and reporters that this was when his dad really "freaked out!" In fact, this was all the newspaper said about me throughout the whole experience: Mckay's dad really "freaked out!"

Anyway, we removed the paper plates, left the pitcher over the bat, and ran upstairs to find something with a flatter surface to slide underneath the bat. I found a shoebox lid, tore down the edges at one end, and Mckay and I headed back downstairs. During this attempt the bat hissed again, but we were successful in capturing it and securing a lid on the pitcher.

It was then that Heidi and I asked Mckay what had happened. He told us that a number of times during the night he had moved his foot over to the edge of his bed only to hear a squeak and to feel a prick on his foot. He thought he had left one of his squeaky bug or creature toys in his bed and that it just had a sharp edge on it. This "bat and mouse" game continued until about 3:30 A.M., when the bat finally bit Mckay on his toe next to the big toe on his right foot, and this time held on!

Mckay said that he felt a pain in his foot—a hurt nothing worse than a bee sting—and woke up. He then reached down and felt a furry thing on his foot. He grabbed it, pulled it out from under his covers, looked at it, and then threw it on the floor. When it continued to squeak and to move around on the floor, he realized that his squeaky toy wasn't a squeaky toy at all—it was *alive!*

"It felt like a big hairball," Mckay later recalled. "It felt like a little mouse." He also felt the wings. "They were really thin, and there wasn't much skin on them," and one wing was torn, "It had a big ol' hole in it."

After listening to Mckay recount his story, we immediately called 911, from which we were relayed to the emergency room at our local hospital. There had been so few incidents of bat bitings in the area in the last ten years that they didn't immediately know what should be done, so they promised to find out and to return our call as quickly as possible. Within minutes, the county animal control agent called and told us he needed to pick up the bat in the morning so that he could take it to be tested for rabies. He also told us to keep the bat doubly secured so it had no way of escaping. I couldn't decide where to doubly secure the bat until I turned and saw the microwave. I knew if it escaped from the pitcher into the microwave all I would have to do would be to hit "time: 10 minutes; power: high," and then the "start" button . . . bzzzz . . . if you know what I mean. Anyway, we kept the pitcher containing the bat in the microwave for the rest of the night.

The hospital called a few minutes after the control agent and stated that the first rabies shots needed to be administered that day. Later in the day we received a call confirming that the bat indeed had rabies; and Mckay received six shots within the next twenty-eight days. Although the shots are now given in the arm and not in the stomach, they weren't any fun. However, Mckay was brave.

He still loves animals, reptiles, and bugs, and he even wanted the bat back as a souvenir. We haven't instilled in him a fear of bugs, spiders, or other creatures, and for this reason I think Mckay's bat experience turned out to be novel rather than terrifying. His friends have asked about the shots, the bite, the pain, and the overall experience, and Mckay has enjoyed their attention. His story also received the attention of the media, and the news of his experience travelled all over the country. He was even in *U.S.A. Today.* He has received letters and gifts, and he even asked me one day, "Dad, am I going to be a movie star now?" One well-known radio talk show host from Chicago called and interviewed Mckay live on his program. Among other things, the host asked Mckay if he liked being called Batman by his friends. Mckay said that it was all right, but that he had a friend who had been severely bitten by a cat and that their friends now all called him Catwoman, so he figured being called Batman wasn't too bad.

Are there lessons that can be learned from Mckay's experience? Showing courage, becoming educated, overcoming fears, supporting each other in times of need, and appreciating those who possess and perform different skills in order to benefit us and our society individually and collectively—these are just a few of the things we have learned from our bat experience. Heidi also tells people that we have definitely learned to always make our bed. However, I believe there is something far greater than any of these things to be learned from our bat ordeal, and it involves the rabies "vaccine" that was administered to Mckay.

I shudder to think about what would have happened to Mckay if he had lived a hundred years ago—without the rabies vaccine. Those two little fang marks on his toe would most likely have been fatal. We would probably have lost our little boy to this unseen and destructive disease.

Our world today is suffering from another kind of destructive disease; and there have been many, in fact all of mankind, who have been bitten by its ravages. We call it sin. Our only hope, as with Mckay, is to administer the "vaccine" regularly. I testify with all my heart that this vaccine is the atonement of Jesus Christ. Repenting of our sins and forgiving others unlocks the powers of this sacred vaccine and begins to rid our souls of the poisons found there. I have found that what might seem tiny, insignificant spiritual wounds can often lead to great unhappiness and even to eventual destruction if left unchecked by the vaccine which is mighty to heal.

It was Alma the Younger who so magnificently expressed this process of being healed by the administration of the vaccine, when he exclaimed:

> And it came to pass that as I was thus racked with torment, while I was harrowed up by the memory of my many sins, behold, I remembered also to have heard my father prophesy unto the people concerning the coming of one Jesus Christ, a Son of God, to atone for the sins of the world.
>
> Now, as my mind caught hold upon this thought, I cried within my heart: O Jesus, thou Son of God, have mercy on me, who am in the gall of bitterness, and am encircled about by the everlasting chains of death.
>
> And now, behold, when I had thought this, I could remember my pains no more; yea, I was harrowed up by the memory of my sins no more.
>
> And oh, what joy, and what marvelous light I did behold; yea, my soul was filled with joy as exceeding as was my pain! (Alma 36:17–20.)

The process of repenting and receiving the vaccine is never easy, but it is a daily necessity if we are to be healed and to be made whole again.

So how do we repent? Personally, as I approach our Heavenly Father in prayer, I first begin to specifically thank him for all the beautiful creations and blessings I enjoy, until I begin to experience what I call an "attitude of gratitude." As this sweet feeling moves throughout my mind and heart, I begin to plead for a forgiveness of my specific and collective sins. I continue in this manner—pleading, begging—until I begin to feel the warm and peaceful feeling engendered by the Holy Ghost. As this sanctifying feeling grows I become aware and know that the Holy Ghost cannot dwell in an unclean tabernacle and, therefore, I am beginning to be cleansed and forgiven.

It is then that I begin to ask for what I desire, but now I ask according to the Spirit and for what God would have me pray. This is, I believe, the message behind my favorite scripture, which states: "And if ye are purified and cleansed from all sin, ye shall ask whatsoever you will in the name of Jesus and it shall be done" (D&C 50:29).

Prayer and being healed through the Atonement—this is such a beautiful process. The living vaccine destroys the poison and disease injected into our spirits through sin and brings us again into the presence of God.

In the world there are those who say that this vaccine, the atonement of Jesus Christ, doesn't even exist; there are those who have haphazardly tried to repent and who, as a result, claim that the vaccine doesn't work; there are even those that utterly refuse to try the vaccine; there are also those who have been bitten and infected so deeply that they have given up hope that, even if administered, the vaccine could heal them; and there are those who are searching for the vaccine but don't know where to find it.

I testify from the depths of my soul that the vaccine—the atonement of Jesus Christ—can heal all of the world's spiritual maladies, as well as our own if we will just let it be administered through the processes of repentance and forgiving others. I know this of myself because I, like Alma, have often exclaimed, "Have mercy on me, who am in the gall of bitterness, and am encircled about by the everlasting chains of death." But I too have also rejoiced so many times and exclaimed, "And oh, what joy, and what marvelous light I did behold; yea, my soul was filled with joy as exceeding as was my pain!"

I express my love to each reader, and I want you to know and feel that the path to happiness now and eternal life in the future is open to all of us. May the Lord bless us all to be obedient to his commandments, which will keep us free from worldly addictions, and to remember that when we fall, although the path back is difficult, Jesus Christ through Gethsemane and Golgotha has provided a way for us to stand tall again and to be healed—healed because he who has walked the road of humanity, he who has suffered in our place, has offered himself as the vaccine.

Victor Harris teaches seminary at Logan High School. He earned his bachelor's degree in psychology at Brigham Young University and is working on a master's degree in marriage and family relations. Brother Harris enjoys all sports (particularly tennis, basketball, and wrestling) and is also a singer and an entertainer, having performed with The Young Ambassadors and U.S.O. groups. Victor and his wife, Heidi, have three children.

10

AND THEY ALL LIVED PEACEFULLY EVER AFTER

Lisa Heckmann Olsen

Happenings in life don't always turn out like fairy tales. Sometimes experiences don't end the way we expect them to.

Take, for example, my friend Ruth. We received our mission calls on the same day. I was thrilled to find I was called to Geneva, Switzerland. Ruth was just as excited to be called to Fresno, California. After a few weeks of preparation Ruth said she had some news for me. She had been dating Brian, a fantastic young man in our ward. The relationship had turned to talk of marriage, and after consulting the bishop she decided to wait six months. I was excited for her but disappointed that we wouldn't share the mission experience together.

A few months later I received a letter from Ruth explaining that she and Brian would not marry after all. They parted good friends with no hurt feelings. Ruth left on her mission, and at home Brian dated. He met a new girl, Marie Osmond. They fell in love and were married in the Jordan River Temple. They have a wonderful marriage! Ruth was pleased that they were so happy, and she didn't worry about herself.

However, *Star* magazine put Ruth on the cover of the magazine with the headline, "Marie Osmond took the man *I* planned to marry! Mormon missionary reveals that she was dumped by Marie's two-timing fiancé"! Of course, the article was full of lies. It said mean and terrible things about Ruth, Brian, and Marie. Ruth was hurt and thought no good could ever come of the situation.

But a copy of the magazine somehow was sent to a prison in Ireland. An inmate read the article and was so impressed by Ruth's desire to sacrifice a year and a half of her life to teach about God and Christ that he wanted to know more about the Church and wrote to Ruth. She then wrote her testimony in a copy of the Book of Mormon and sent it to him. Ruth had *never* expected a missionary experience out of the situation! At times the Lord has a remarkable way of turning events. "All things shall work together for good for them that walk uprightly" (D&C 100:15). Sometimes a situation we perceive as difficult can be the very situation that blesses our lives.

At times things happen in teenage lives that seem completely unfair. As I write this I see the faces of my young friends who struggle to find peace amid life's trials. I see Dustyn, who lost his mother to cancer; Kerry, who moved to Utah and left all her friends in California; Isaac, who bravely bears major physical limitations; Tami, who is learning to adjust to her parents' divorce; and Jeremy, who can't pull himself away from the wrong group of friends. They, like all of us, just want to feel peace and know that somehow, some way, "*all* things shall work together for good."

I know that Heavenly Father is infinitely aware of our trials, large and small. He can turn what we perceive as a difficult or negative situation into a blessing. Perhaps you also need to feel peace as you heroically struggle to understand life's experiences. Wouldn't it be nice to have these types of feelings constantly: "But the fruit of the Spirit is love, joy, peace, longsuffering, gentleness, goodness, faith, meekness, temperance" (Galatians 5:22–23). These very peaceful emotions are brought about by the Spirit. They come only when we are close to our Heavenly Father and our Savior, Jesus Christ. In connection with baptism we are given the *gift* of the Holy Ghost, which means that the Spirit will be our constant companion as long as we work to keep it with us. Here is what I have observed about those who maintain this calm assurance: peace will come as we repent of wrongdoing, exhibit faith in our Savior, Jesus Christ, and serve others.

Repent to Find Peace

"And it came to pass that I was three days and three nights in the most bitter pain and anguish of soul; and never, until I did cry out unto the Lord Jesus Christ for mercy, did I receive a remission of my sins. But behold, I did cry unto him and I did find peace to my soul." (Alma 38:8.) Alma the Younger's despair reminds me of Marcus. He transferred into my class after moving from Texas. I still remember his first day because the girls tried so hard not to stare at him. He had dark hair and striking good looks. He was wearing a beautiful black leather jacket and cowboy boots. The girls didn't stop looking for a long time. On top of his looks, his thick southern accent was terribly charming.

There were times during class when he would come to talk to me. I remember one conversatoin about three weeks into school: he sat at my desk and just cried. This handsome young man cried, because he was having a difficult time trying to fit in and make friends. Finally he did find a group where he felt comfortable. Unfortunately, it was a bad crowd. I watched a literal physical transformation in this student. His black hair grew very long and became unkempt. He began to listen to questionable music and to change his style of dress. He began to smoke, drink, and experiment with drugs. This young man fell into a hole so deep that no one could get him out. He lost all sense of peace in his life. It finally came to a point that his parents had to move the family to get him away from his friends at school.

Like Marcus, Alma the Younger found a crowd of friends who were a bad influence, and instead of encouraging Alma to become a better person they pulled each other down into great sin. (Does this sound the least bit familiar?) Alma the Younger was "a very wicked and an idolatrous man. And he was a man of many words, and did speak much flattery to the people." (Mosiah 27:8.) Not only was Alma the Younger involved in serious sin but he also was able to influence many people to follow his lifestyle. One day he was going out to "destroy the church of God, for he did go about secretly with the sons of Mosiah seeking to destroy the church, and to lead astray the people of the Lord" (Mosiah 27:10). They were about this business of destruction when an angel of the Lord appeared to them and demanded to know why they were persecuting the Church. The angel also told them that he had come because of the prayers of the people, and especially the prayers of Alma's father, the prophet.

In our day many such prayers are offered for the youth of the world—for you. Many people love you and want you to enjoy the blessings that come with full activity in the Church. Most likely an angel won't come and tell you to repent, but you will rather feel quiet promptings (those peaceful feelings described in Galatians) to stop the negative things you are doing. Don't deny the promptings!

Alma was so astonished by the angel that he became dumb. He couldn't open his mouth, move his hands, or even walk. He was so helpless that his friends had to carry him home. They told his father what had happened, and his father rejoiced because he knew the Lord had answered his prayers. Alma and the priests fasted for two days and two nights so his son could speak again. Among the younger Alma's first words were, "I have repented of my sins" (Mosiah 27:24). Imagine how he felt as he admitted his mistakes. "Yea, and I had murdered many of his children, or rather led them away unto destruction; yea, and in fine so great had been my iniquities, that the very thought of coming into the presence of my God did rack my soul with inexpressible horror" (Alma 36:14). Now listen to the repentant Alma the Younger, after the process of repentance. "Yea, methought I saw, even as our father Lehi saw, God sitting upon his throne, surrounded with numberless concourses of angels, in the attitude of singing and praising their God; yea, and my soul did long to be there" (Alma 36:22).

If at this very moment you were to come face to face with God, which of Alma the Younger's feelings would you experience? Alma the Younger became a powerful missionary who assisted in the conversion of many souls.

Exhibit Faith to Find Peace

In Mosiah 4:3 Mormon describes the people after they had listened to King Benjamin's sermon: "The Spirit of the Lord came upon them, and they were filled with joy, having received a remission of their sins, and having peace of conscience, because of the exceeding faith which they had in Jesus Christ who should come." These Nephites had peace because they had faith—or confidence—in Jesus Christ. One of my favorite titles for the Savior is "Prince of Peace" (2 Nephi 19:6). Faith in Christ will bring us peace. Strong faith is developed by obedience. True faith in Jesus Christ includes an actual knowledge that the course of life one is pursuing is acceptable to him, and feeling blessings in life from God.

High school was a difficult time for me. I didn't always feel peace, mostly because I didn't feel good about myself. I disliked the way I looked. I had a load of naturally curly hair that I couldn't control, I wore glasses, I had braces, and physically I didn't look like the "popular" girls at school. I had only two dates during the entire time of high school. However, I always hoped that things would get better. Just out of high school, I made a plan for my life. On a sheet of lined paper I listed ages eighteen through twenty-five (I guess I thought that life "ended" at twenty-five) near the left margin of the paper. Next to each age I listed what would be happening to me that year. The list looked like this:

18   Graduate from high school and start BYU
19   School at BYU
20   Still at BYU
21   Leave for mission
22   Still on mission
23   Come home from mission and get a job
24   Go to Israel Study Abroad and then get married
25   Have first baby

My plans went well for a few years. When I came home from my mission I couldn't find a job for almost a year, so I didn't have any money to go to Israel. At age twenty-four, when I was supposed to get married, I still had never had a boyfriend and hadn't experienced that "first kiss." At age twenty-five, no prospects for marriage, and I certainly had no baby. I was frustrated. Why had my life plans not been realized? But I came to learn that God had a much different plan for my life and that my life course was pleasing to him.

I wrote this journal entry when I was twenty-six. "Today in church I was talking with my roommate, Luz, about the Relief Society president in our ward, Darcy. Recently she got engaged to a super sharp multitalented guy in our ward. Anyway, Luz said, 'She deserves it!' That is a nice comment and all. Actually I hear it quite often when people talk about engagements. I've been bothered by the word *deserve*. I guess the thing I think about and wonder is, don't I *deserve* to get married? I've been home from my mission for four years now. Sometimes I wonder if God really does hear all of my cries."

Have you ever had that feeling of "deserving" a blessing? You have been obedient, so why have certain things happened or not happened in your life? As I reread my journal, the passage that stands out is, "I wonder if God really does hear all of my cries." Of course he does! My greatest comfort has come through prayer, constant prayer.

At that point in my life I worked to exhibit faith through sincere prayer, and I was filled with peace, a feeling that God was very aware of my desires, and that the blessings would eventually come. (I finally met and married my sweetheart, Brent, at the age of twenty-seven—two months shy of twenty-eight! He was definitely worth all of the waiting!)

I have a favorite student, Cable, who has felt peace through faith in God and Jesus Christ. He seemed like any other transfer student on the first day of school. He had moved from a large isolated ranch in Wyoming to Provo, Utah. Cable is tall, handsome with thick naturally curly hair, and somewhat shy. He works hard in class, and when it came time for parent-teacher conferences I was pleased to hand his mom a progress report showing an A, almost 100 percent. She was a very kind woman, and as she left she handed me a letter and said, "I just want Cable's teachers to know a little more about him."

Cable was the seventh of eight children. He was a diligent worker on the ranch and had particular talent for fixing machinery. Cable had a great life, but like any other teenager he experienced disappointments. In that small town in Wyoming, anyone who wanted to be on the school basketball team could play as long as he attended practices. During Cable's sophomore year, when he had been on school teams for about seven years, a new coach was hired. Cable didn't have the skills the coach wanted and was told that he would have no playing time in the season.

Cable said his "pride was pushed down," that he felt like a quitter, and that those seven years had been wasted. But he didn't quit. He just decided to find another niche in life. He chose art. He figures that in his years of playing basketball he had spent over seven hundred dollars on basketball shoes. He now decided to invest equally in his new interest and began buying art supplies. He was devoted to his new talent and found great rewards.

So what's so unique about Cable? It's the way he copes with the difficult and the unexpected. From his mother's letter: "February 22, 1993, when Cable was fifteen, I ran out to the corrals to tell his dad a new grandson had been born and found my husband crushed to death. We were snowed in that day, and the kids had just hiked in from the bus. I ran to the house and got the three kids, and Cable was the only one who had the presence of mind enough to get a handyman jack and jack up the huge chute off his father's body; then he helped roll him over, checked his vitals, and pronounced his father dead. At the funeral

Cable spoke, and through his tears expressed his faith in God and fervent desire to 'make the ranch all Dad wanted it to be.' He did just that. The summer after his Dad's death, Cable supervised the building of new corrals, new fences, ditch improvements, and literally took over the work and responsibility of a grown man. While I was proud of him, it also broke my heart to see him so weighed down with work and his youth apparently gone."

I cried as I read the story of sweet Cable's life. I have since come to know him better. I once asked him how he has accepted his father's death. Without hesitating a second, he said: "The plan of salvation. I know the plan of salvation." He also told me that the thing that brought him the greatest and most immediate peace was reading and rereading his father's favorite scripture: "And now I would that ye should be humble, and be submissive and gentle; easy to be entreated; full of patience and long-suffering; being temperate in all things; being diligent in keeping the commandments of God at all times; asking for whatsoever things ye stand in need, both spiritual and temporal; always returning thanks unto God for whatsoever things ye do receive" (Alma 7:23). Although Cable still struggles daily with the loss of his father, he finds peace through faith in the gospel of Jesus Christ.

Serve Others to Find Peace

As one of our baptismal covenants we promise to serve others. "As ye are desirous to come into the fold of God, and to be called his people, and are willing to bear one another's burdens, that they may be light; yea, and are willing to mourn with those that mourn; yea, and comfort those that stand in need of comfort" (Mosiah 18:8–9). Great peace comes as we learn to reach out to others and lift their burdens.

One of my heroes is Ardeth Kapp. She has said that, while growing up, she "envisioned living in a small white house with a picket fence. I thought I would just take care of the flowers, be active in the Church, friendly with my neighbors—and have lots of children." However, the blessing of children did not come for Sister Kapp. "I think often that it really might have been easier to remain depressed and despondent and full of self-pity," she has said, "thinking that the fact that we didn't have children wasn't our fault anyway, so why should we have to go out and serve." (Ardeth Kapp, quoted in *Follow Me* [Relief Society Personal Study Guide 4, 1992], pp. 146, 148.) As you know, Sister Kapp did not withdraw from serving others—far from it. She has spent much of her life serving the young women of the Church and has had a powerful impact on their lives.

I have learned a lot from watching teenagers serving other teenagers—particularly Jason, a young man in our school who needed a heart transplant. Though many students didn't know him, they immediately started raising money to help his family pay for this surgery. These students literally gave him a new heart. On the day of his graduation his classmates gave him a standing ovation as he stood there—healthy, with a new heart, and with tears in his eyes as he received his diploma.

Lisa was senior class president. I was her advisor. She came from a prominent family in town, was well liked by her peers, and enjoyed a very happy life. But there was a secret side to Lisa that I never knew about until Christmastime. One day she came to visit me after school; it was unusual for her to be there at that time of day, so I knew something was wrong. When I turned my back, she started going through my roll book and my seating charts. I was surprised and demanded to know what she was doing. She swore me to secrecy, then told me that when she was a freshman she and a few friends formed a secret Christmas hit club. For the first few months of the school year they would watch for someone in "need" and then bring to them the "twelve days of Christmas." Their first year they chose a girl whose family was rather poor. They purchased her clothes, fun things to play with, gift certificates, and even food for their family. The only catch— they *never* revealed their names. She was now in my classroom to find the name of a young man they had chosen as their next lucky "victim." I watched Lisa talk about their secret service, her eyes sparkling, and I knew she loved what she was doing. Great love, joy, and peace will come as we learn to reach out to others.

The Lord has promised that peace will come as we repent of our sins, exhibit faith, and serve other people. Even the Savior, Jesus Christ, had to trust God in order to find peace during the most difficult time of his mortal life. As the Savior suffered in the Garden of Gethsemane he prayed for help and comfort: "O my Father, if it be possible, let this cup pass from me: nevertheless not as I will, but as thou wilt" (Matthew 26:39). He offered a second prayer: "O my Father, if this cup may not pass away from me, except I drink it, thy will be done" (Matthew 26:42). And he prayed a third time, "saying the same words" (Matthew 26:44). His loving Father, our Heavenly Father who also hears and answers *our* prayers, responded to his Son's pleas, "and there appeared an angel unto him from heaven, strengthening him" (Luke 22:43).

I know that as we experience life our Father in Heaven wants to help us and bless us with peace. But we are obligated to take the first step and reach out in faith. He is infinitely aware of our lives, knows us by name, and loves all of his children. This is the sweet peace he has promised us. May you feel the power of peace in your life.

Lisa Heckmann Olsen is married to Brent Olsen, who is an accountant with a great sense of humor. Lisa has worked for several years with the EFY programs. She is currently teaching at Timpview High School and is the student government advisor. She loves to go to Lake Powell. She has a pet snake name Rachid and loves painting, shopping, and making stained glass.

11

THE MIRACLE OF REPENTANCE

R. Scott Simmons

One day in seminary I asked my students what they thought was the greatest miracle Christ performed. Someone said, "healing the blind." Another said, "cleansing the leper." Yet another said, "causing the lame to walk." After some discussion they finally agreed that raising the dead was probably the Savior's greatest miracle. After all, what could be greater than raising someone from the dead?

We then turned to the story of the conversion of Alma the Younger and the sons of Mosiah. The scriptures tell us they were the "vilest of sinners," and yet the Lord was able to cleanse them so that they were promised eternal life (Mosiah 28:4, 7). The class then agreed that to cleanse a soul from sin was the greatest miracle the Savior performed.

Through the Atonement the Savior makes it possible for us to be cleansed completely. Have you participated in this miracle? No matter who you are, the Savior can clean you completely (see Isaiah 1:18). All he asks is that we be willing to repent.

Typically, when I ask my students what they think repentance is, they tell me it's suffering. This thought keeps many from repenting. For many young people, repentance brings all kinds of images of private interrogation and then public humiliation. If you are having any of these feelings, they are not coming from your Father in Heaven. Those feelings are coming from Satan, "for he seeketh that all men might be miserable like unto himself" (2 Nephi 2:27). While true repentance does involve suffering, your Father in Heaven does not want you to suffer or fear. Rather, he wants to relieve your suffering and alleviate your fear. Repentance is the process through which comes relief from suffering and fear caused by sin.

The word *repent* means to turn or change. When your Father in Heaven asks you to repent he is asking you to turn or change from being worldly to being more like Christ. Every time you try to be more like the Savior you are repenting. As we attempt to be like Christ there may be times when we will turn back to the world; we will sin (see 1 John 1:8). We then need to turn back to God; we need to repent.

How then do we repent? In his book *The Miracle of Forgiveness* President Spencer W. Kimball told us there are four steps to repentance. They are: sorrow for the sin, abandonment of the sin, confession of the sin, and restitution for the sin. Following are the four steps and questions my students have asked me about concerning these steps. I have done my best to answer each question with either a scripture or a quote from the prophets.

Sorrow for the Sin

President Kimball tells us that the first step in repentance is to realize you need to repent. In order to begin to repent we must first realize we have sinned, that we have turned from God to the world. This realization brings the sorrow necessary to repent. The questions asked are as follows:

What if I really don't want to repent?

For behold, I, God, have suffered these things for all, that they might not suffer if they would repent;

But if they would not repent they must suffer even as I;

Which suffering caused myself, even God, the greatest of all, to tremble because of pain, and to bleed at every pore, and to suffer both body and spirit (D&C 19:18–19).

If we don't repent we must pay for our own sins. We must suffer as Christ did.

What if I did not know it was wrong?

Sometimes we hear a youth in the Church say with regard to sex sins, "I didn't know it was wrong." This is unthinkable. . . . Where were the whisperings of conscience? . . . Some at least of these influences and promptings must have lingered in his heart to tell him that the act was wrong! Even if he did not know *how* wrong it was he knew it was sin. Otherwise, why would he hide the act and keep secret the error? (Spencer W. Kimball, *The Miracle of Forgiveness* [Salt Lake City: Bookcraft, 1969], pp. 153–54.)

Can I wait until I get caught to repent?

Yea I would that ye would come forth and harden not your hearts any longer; for behold, now is the time and the day of your salvation; and therefore, if ye will repent and harden not your hearts, immediately shall the great plan of redemption be brought about unto you.

For behold, this life is the time for men to prepare to meet God. . . .

. . . I beseech of you that ye do not procrastinate the day of your repentance until the end, . . . if we do not improve our time while in this life, then cometh the night of darkness wherein there can be no labor performed.

. . . That same spirit which doth possess your bodies at the time ye go out of this life, that same spirit will have power to possess your body in that eternal world. (Alma 34:31–34.)

Is feeling guilty a part of repentance?

For mine iniquities are gone over mine head: as a heavy burden they are too heavy for me (Psalm 38:4).

You have an alarm system built into both body and spirit. In your body it is pain; in your spirit it is guilt—or spiritual pain. While neither pain nor guilt is pleasant, and an excess of either can be destructive, both are a protection, for they sound the alarm "Don't do that again!"

Be grateful for both. If the nerve endings in your hands were altered so that you couldn't feel pain, you might put them in fire or machinery and destroy them. In your teenage heart of hearts, you know right from wrong. (See 2 Nephi 2:25.) Learn to pay attention to that spiritual voice of warning within you. (Boyd K. Packer, *Ensign,* May 1989, pp. 54, 59.)

How sorry must I feel?

For I am ready to halt, and my sorrow is continually before me.

For I will declare mine iniquity; I will be sorry for my sin. (Psalm 38:17–18.)

Now I rejoice, not that ye were made sorry, but that ye sorrowed to repentance: for ye were made sorry after a godly manner, that ye might receive damage by us in nothing.

For godly sorrow worketh repentance to salvation not to be repented of: but the sorrow of the world worketh death. (2 Corinthians 7:9–10.)

How can I prove to the Lord I want to repent?

Not everyone that saith unto me, Lord, Lord, shall enter into the kingdom of heaven; but he that doeth the will of my Father which is in heaven (Matthew 7:21).

In repenting of sin we must realize that what we have done has offended our Father in Heaven. Too many of us worry about the worldly consequences of our sins. What will happen if I get caught? What will I tell my parents? or What will my bishop think of me—these are common thoughts of someone who has worldly sorrow. In order to truly repent we need godly sorrow. Our thoughts should be, How can I face my Father in Heaven? and I would do anything to be clean again. With these thoughts we are ready to repent.

Abandon the Sin

The second step is to abandon the sin. We must permanently stop the sin. We are taught, "By this ye may know if a man repenteth of his sins—behold, he will confess them and forsake them" (D&C 58:43). Some have confused this one step as repentance. Just because they are no longer doing the sin they think they have repented. But there is a difference between stopping sinning and repentance. To truly be repentant we must complete all the steps.

How long must I wait to be forgiven after I stop sinning?

To every forgiveness there is a condition. The plaster must be as wide as the sore. The fasting, the prayers, the humility must be equal to or greater than the sin. (Spencer W. Kimball, *The Miracle of Forgiveness,* p. 353.)

What happens if I stop the sin and then break down and start again?

And now, verily I say unto you, I the Lord, will not lay any sin to your charge; go your ways and sin no more; but unto that soul who sinneth shall the former sins return, saith the Lord your God (D&C 82:7).

Confess the Sin

The third step is to confess the sin. This can be one of the most difficult and yet one of the most important steps. Many people lack only this step to be fully forgiven.

Must I confess in order to be forgiven?

The confession of sin is an important element in repentance. Many offenders have seemed to feel that a few prayers to the Lord were sufficient. They have thus justified themselves in hiding their sins.

Especially grave errors such as sexual sins shall be confessed to the bishop as well as to the Lord. There are two remissions which one might wish to have. First, the forgiveness from the Lord, and second, the forgiveness of the Lord's church through its leaders. As soon as one has an inner conviction of his sins, he should go to the Lord in "mighty prayer," as did Enos, and never cease his supplications until he shall, like Enos, receive the assurance that his sins have been forgiven by the Lord. It is unthinkable that God absolves serious sins upon a few requests. He is likely to wait until there has been long, sustained repentance as evidenced by a willingness to comply with all his other requirements. . . .

The bishop claims no authority to absolve sins, but he does share the burden, waive penalties, relieve tension and strain; and he may assure a continuance of activity. He will keep the whole matter most confidential. (Spencer W. Kimball, *The Teachings of Spencer W. Kimball* [Salt Lake City: Bookcraft, 1982], p. 85.)

To whom must I confess?

Remember that all sin must be confessed. We must first confess to the Lord. Next, we must confess to anyone we may have offended as a result of our sin.

And if thy brother or sister offend thee, thou shalt take him or her between him or her and thee alone; and if he or she confess thou shalt be reconciled (D&C 42:88).

Confess your faults one to another, and pray one for another, that he may be healed. The effectual fervent prayer of a righteous man availeth much. (James 5:16.)

Some sins are of such a serious nature that we must confess them to our bishop. A bishop is like a spiritual doctor. Let me explain. If I cut my finger, I know how to fix it. I clean it, put on some antiseptic, cover it with a bandage, and in a few days it's better. However, if I need to have my appendix taken out I can't just cut myself open and remove it. I need to go to a professional. I need the help of a skilled surgeon. Similarly, some sins need professional help. That is where your bishop comes in; without his help you cannot overcome serious sins.

By this ye may know if a man repenteth of his sins—behold, he will confess them and forsake them (D&C 58:43).

What must I confess to the bishop?

These sins include adultery, fornication, other sexual transgressions, and other sins of comparable seriousness (Spencer W. Kimball, *The Miracle of Forgiveness,* p. 179).

If there is anything in your past that is bothering you, it would be appropriate to ask your bishop whether it is something that needs confession.

What if I do not confess?

And the rebellious shall be pierced with much sorrow; for their iniquities shall be spoken upon the housetops, and their secret acts revealed. . . .

And he that repents not, from him shall be taken even the light which he has received; for my Spirit shall not always strive with man. (D&C 1:3, 33.)

Restitution for the Sin

The fourth step is to make restitution for the sin. Restitution means to replace that which was lost to someone else as a result of your sin.

How do I make restitution?

In the process of repentance we must restore completely where possible, otherwise restore to the maximum degree attainable. And through it all we must remember that the pleading sinner, desiring to make restitution for his acts, must also forgive others of all offenses committed against him. (Spencer W. Kimball, *The Miracle of Forgiveness,* p. 200.)

What if restitution is impossible, as in the case of chastity?

Once given . . . it can never be regained. . . . To be forgiven one must repent . . . convict yourselves of the horror of the sin . . . confess it, abandon it, and restore to all who have been damaged to the total extent possible; then . . . live the commandments of the Lord so that he can eventually pardon you and cleanse you. (Spencer W. Kimball, *The Miracle of Forgiveness,* pp. 196–200.)

Once you have completed the steps of repentance the question still remains: How can I know whether I have been forgiven?

What must I do next?

Seek ye the Lord while he may be found, call ye upon him while he is near:

Let the wicked forsake his way, and the unrighteous man his thoughts: and let him return unto the Lord, and he will have mercy upon him; and to our God, for he will abundantly pardon (Isaiah 55:6–7).

Will the Lord actually forgive me?

Behold, he who has repented of his sins, the same is forgiven, and I, the Lord, remember them no more (D&C 58:42).

Will my sins be forgotten, so that I need not worry anymore?

Come now, and let us reason together, saith the Lord: though your sins be as scarlet, they shall be as white as snow; though they be red like crimson, they shall be as wool (Isaiah 1:18).

But if the wicked will turn from all his sins that he hath committed, and keep all my statutes, and do that which is lawful and right. . . .

All his transgressions that he hath committed, they shall not be mentioned unto him. (Ezekiel 18:21–22.)

How do I know when I've been forgiven?

And now, for three days and three nights was I racked, even with the pains of a damned soul.

And it came to pass that as I was thus racked with torment, while I was harrowed up by the memory of my many sins, behold, I remembered also to have heard my father prophesy unto the people concerning the coming of one Jesus Christ, a Son of God, to atone for the sins of the world.

Now, as my mind caught hold upon this thought, I cried within my heart: O Jesus, thou Son of God, have mercy on me, who am in the gall of bitterness, and am encircled about by the everlasting chains of death.

And now, behold, when I thought this, I could remember my pains no more; yea, I was harrowed up by the memory of my sins no more.

And oh, what joy, and what marvelous light I did behold; yea, my soul was filled with joy as exceeding as was my pain! (Alma 36:16–20.)

Just because you remember your sins does not mean you have not been forgiven. Notice Alma didn't say he couldn't remember his sins. He said he couldn't remember his pains. The guilt and suffering were gone.

If you have turned from the Lord, if you have sinned, I plead with you to repent. Take the steps necessary to turn your life back to God. I testify that he can clean you. You can be made whole again. Participate in his miracle of repentance.

R. Scott Simmons was born and raised in Salt Lake City, Utah. He spent his summers working on a dairy farm and is a real cowboy at heart. He served a mission in Cleveland, Ohio. Following his mission he attended BYU and worked at the Missionary Training Center. He currently teaches seminary at Timpview High School in Provo, Utah. Scott loves the outdoors and spends as much time as possible hunting, fishing, and camping. Scott and his wife, Nancy, live in Highland, Utah.

12

HORSESHOES, HAND GRENADES, AND KISSING

Matthew Richardson

As I was growing up, my friends and I would share stories about our greatest conquests in sports, schooling, games, and just about anything that we thought was interesting. We noticed that nearly all of our stories included an *"almost* or *so-close"* event. "I *almost* hit a home run . . . it was so *close.*"

After hearing story after story (and my telling a few stories of my own) my friends and I started quoting a phrase that became well used over the years: "Close only counts in horseshoes, hand grenades, and kissing." Being close counts in horseshoes because you receive points for getting as close to the stake as possible; hand grenades are only effective if they land close enough to the object that is to be destroyed; and kissing—well, I don't think I need to explain how close and kissing work! Since our stories weren't about horseshoes, hand grenades, or kissing, our *almost* or *so-close* stories simply didn't count. From that point on, whenever one of us related how he *almost* aced a test, scored a touchdown, or got a date, he would hear in resounding unison, "Close only counts in horseshoes, hand grenades, and kissing."

It seems that human beings love to claim a certain closeness to doing something, being someone, or having something. We might poke fun at this "wanna-be" desire and counter with my "close only counts . . ." cliché. But maybe we were wrong about what really counts when it comes to being close. I've come to realize that *close* really does count in areas other than horseshoes, hand grenades, and kissing. Perhaps the following experience will illustrate my point.

When I was a young man my family went on a family vacation to a western state park. Maybe your family has tried this "nature bonding" experience. It wasn't as good as going to Disneyland but it was better than staying home and working in the yard! This state park, however, was different from the other parks we visited on vacations. It was desolate, dry, and apparently there wasn't much to see. My father quickly pointed out the main point of interest—a mesa called "Dead Horse Point." We walked out on the mesa and peered over a cliff that dropped straight down for 2,000 feet! In the bottom of the gorge below was the Colorado River. It looked like a blue string winding every which way.

I was impressed by the magnitude of the drop. What fascinated me, however, was the way other visitors reacted to the edge of the cliff. Some people would run directly to the edge, slide to a screeching stop, and lean over to peer straight down. They would throw objects over the edge and excitedly start counting "One-one thousand . . . two-one thousand . . ." or they would just stand there with their toes hanging over the precipice taking in the view. Others would cautiously approach the edge, somewhat nervous and timid. They would briefly look over and proclaim, "I've seen enough!" then quickly retreat to safety. Finally there was a group that remained in their car, seat belt fastened, as they yelled to those urging them to join them on the bluff: "I can see it just fine from here! Really, I'm just fine!" When it comes to this type of close—the fascination some of us have with seeing just how close we can get to the edge—it counts. Actually this type of closeness worries me—or even more candidly, scares me.

Whether it be the cliff-walkers at Dead Horse Point or the cliffs of sin, humans have an unfortunate fascination with just how close they can get to the edge. Elder David B. Haight referred to the cliffs of sin as "spiritual crevasses." He said: "Spiritual crevasses symbolize the temptations and pitfalls that too many of our youth are tragically encountering: alcohol, with its wine coolers and keg parties, drug tampering and dependency, R- and X-rated films and videos, which often culminate in sexual immorality" ("Spiritual Crevasses," *Ensign,* November 1986, p. 36). I believe that most of us know where the edges are in our life. We know the difference between good situations and bad, between righteousness and sin.

Those cliff-walkers at Dead Horse point aren't all that different from those who insist on, as President Spencer W. Kimball would say, "flirting with sin." It appears that there are three distinct groups in both cases. Some people approach the edge with carefree abandon, others are cautious in their approach, and then there are those who remain as far away as possible. One thing is certain: when it comes to flirting with the edge, close definitely counts!

Consider the first group, our bold thrill-seekers. This is the group that runs, leaps, or marches confidently to the edge. Within this group we find those who feel the need to test the limits, to see if there are consequences to their actions. It is almost a deliberate defiance. They act as if they live their life in a "test-pilot" mode. These test-pilots think that warnings, danger signs, directions, rules, and restrictions are for other people, not for them. They have to test or try everything for themselves. These are the types of individuals that have to touch the paint when "Wet Paint" is posted. They feel that they can handle life head on, full speed, and on their own terms. Sad to say, we live in a world where these individuals are encouraged or even praised for their attitudes. The world applauds those with reckless abandon by calling them courageous, independent, adventurous and so forth. "Why shouldn't I just try it for myself?" becomes their motto.

Some of these defiant individuals actually think that falling off the cliff will do them good in the long run. Do them good? "Experience helps you in the long run," they say. "You'll be able to better understand others. After all, a little sin never really hurt anyone!" Elder Dallin H. Oaks said: "The idea that one is better off after one has sinned and repented is a devilish lie of the adversary." To those who defy the wisdom of others, the warning signs, and fences, Elder Oaks offered: "We don't have to have personal experience with the effects of serious transgressions to know that they are destructive." To illustrate his point, he said that he was once asked by his son why he shouldn't just try something (harmful) for himself. Elder Oaks told his son that "if he wanted to try something he ought to go out in the barnyard and eat a little manure." His son recoiled in horror. "Ooh, that's gross," he said. "I'm glad you think so," Elder Oaks replied, "but why don't you just try it out so you will know for yourself?" (See "Sin and Suffering," *BYU Speeches 1989–90,* pp. 151–52.)

We have wise men and women who can provide guidance that is applicable to our lives. Teachers, advisors, bishops, and parents are willing to point out the dangers of the cliffs of sin and help construct appropriate protection—personal fences. Even more important, we have prophets who offer inspired direction, warnings, and advice. The scriptures lead and guide us by demonstrating examples of those who constructed fences to keep them from the edge as well as those others who fell. Elder David B. Haight suggested: "To help each of us avoid the pitfalls and crevasses in life, the Lord has provided the lifeline of the precious truths in the scriptures, which, if held onto, will allow us to escape both physical and spiritual danger" ("Spiritual Crevasses," p. 38). Far too many people find tragedy when they try to "do it on their own"; they approach the edge a little too quickly and their momentum carries them over the brink, or they leap from the edge with confidence, only to discover that the law of gravity applies to them too.

The next group, far more numerous than the first, are those individuals that make their way to the edge at different rates of speed and for different reasons. "I just want a quick peek." "It's not like I'm going to do something *bad*!" "You don't think *I* would fall off, do you? . . . I can handle it!" "Everyone else has looked over the edge. I don't want to miss out on something!" Some approach timidly, others walk with sure confidence, and some might even carelessly skip, but one common element is the belief that they honestly feel (some even claim to *know*) that they won't fall over the edge.

I remember one day while I was teaching and one of my bolder students raised her hand and queried: "Brother Richardson, how *far* can I go *without* having to go see the bishop?" I thought this was an odd question. In reality, she was asking, "How close to the edge can I get without actually falling off?" Perhaps she was wondering, "Can I have my toes hanging over the edge?" or "Is is OK to hang by my fingertips? . . . fingernails?" What an interesting position to put yourself in. President Spencer W. Kimball said: "Carelessness about proximity to sin makes us vulnerable to Satan's wiles" (*The Miracle of Forgiveness* [Salt Lake City: Bookcraft, 1969], p. 218). According to the prophets, close *does count* when it comes to where you are in relationship to the edge of the cliff of sin.

An adaptation of an old Chinese proverb states: "A journey of a thousand miles is taken one step at a time." This powerful proverb provides the practical insight that we don't fall off the edge all at once. It is a gradual process. Therefore, I guess it really doesn't matter how *fast* you approach the edge. Some of the cliff-walkers take only seconds to stand at the brink of disaster, while others approach the edge over the span of many years. Despite how you get to the edge or how fast you get there, when you *approach* the edge you are taking a serious chance of falling off. President Kimball felt that this "means that the boy who dates the girl of questionable morals, even just for once, is taking chances. He is dealing with a powerful temptation. The girl who has even one date with a vicious fellow is in danger. The youth who takes one cigarette or one drink is 'playing with fire.' The young person who begins to yield to sexual intimacies is in a perilous position. One step calls for another, and to turn back is not easy." (*The Miracle of Forgiveness,* p. 217.) This subtle process happens to even the very best, the most valiant people. Probably the greatest example and warning of this is found in the scriptures.

King David was considered by many to be the greatest of all Israelites. Yet few realize that this king was the same person who killed Goliath as a young lad. Years had passed since that triumph, and David found himself king of a mighty nation. As a matter of fact, David was *almost* the greatest king in history. He was so *close* to having his life turn out just right. Unfortunately, David's chosen direction led him closer and closer to the edge rather than farther away. Here is a story of a man with the Lord's favor, and talents galore, who then loses everything. How? Perhaps we can learn from this man's mistakes. Wouldn't we be foolish to repeat David's tragedy?

David's rendezvous with the edge came about in a way that some may deem rather innocent. David, while still far from the edge, found himself walking on the roof one hot evening. One may ask, "Is there anything wrong with walking on the roof?" But the real question should be, "Where should he have been?" The scriptures tell us that David should have been where kings were supposed to be at that time—at battle (see 2 Samuel 11:1). How many times is our direction plotted simply because of our geography? We can find ourselves in the right place at the right time or in the wrong place at the wrong time. David shouldn't have been on the roof to begin with. He should have been at battle with his soldiers. Unfortunately, David's immediate (and eternal) future started with this bad decision.

David's next step towards the edge was also rather innocent . . . to begin with. While he was walking on the roof, he saw a woman bathing (2 Samuel 11:2). It wasn't David's fault she was bathing. How was he supposed to know where he shouldn't look? Once again, a better question to ask would be, "What should he do now?" Apparently David continued to walk his set course. He had already failed to answer the first question, and now, facing new choices, he must decide the direction of his travels. Unfortunately, he did not stop in his tracks, turn himself around, and walk away from the edge. He noticed that she was beautiful (2 Samuel 11:2). How did he know that? Perhaps David looked long enough to determine her beauty, or maybe he looked more than once. Another step closer to the edge.

There is still time for David to turn around; it's not too late. But he then inquires: "What is her name?" (2 Samuel 11:3.) Innocent enough? Not really; another step closer to the edge. David now picks up the pace towards the edge—he invites her to his home. "I'm the king of Israel, I can handle it." What a tragedy! David loses his morality and takes a headlong fall into a deep abyss.

If only David had properly answered two simple questions! 1) Where should I be? 2) What should I be doing? My heart sorrows for David. He was so strong in so many ways, yet he inched towards the edge; cautiously at first, then confidently, and foolhardy at last. Once Satan had him close enough to the edge it didn't take much to push him over. "Being curious, or bold, or foolhardy, we often come perilously close to the edge; so often that we see just how far we can get from the iron rod without really letting go of our grasp—perhaps just keeping a finger still upon the rod. Then, if one of Satan's darts strikes too near the target, we slip over the edge with hardly a murmur. It was thrilling, though, while it lasted, teetering there on the brink, knowing we were so close to peril, but confident, oh, so confident, that we had things in control." (S. Olani Durrant, "Cliff Walking," *BYU Speeches of the Year,* July 10, 1984, p. 160.) Elder Haight admonishes: "Don't trifle with evil. You will lose. We pray that you will not display the somewhat arrogant attitude of some, who say, 'I can handle it!' or 'Everyone else does it!'" ("Spiritual Crevasses," p. 37.)

Now, finally, the third group of cliff-walkers, those who stay safely buckled in their cars, those who feel comfortable in keeping the edge in the far distance. Once again our scriptures provide us with an example of a young man with his safety belt firmly fastened. Young Joseph of Egypt was a hero of heroes. He was faithful, diligent, "a goodly person" (Genesis 39:6), and his course was set. When his temptation of drawing closer to the edge came upon him, in effect he answered for himself those two important questions: "Where should I be?" and "What should

I be doing?" Where should Joseph be? Not with Potiphar's wife, that much was certain. So what did he do? He went about *his* business, and when necessary he simply "fled, and got him out" (Genesis 39:12). What should Joseph be doing? Obviously, nothing Potiphar's wife suggested. Remember Joseph's reply to her temptations? "How then can I do this great wickedness, and sin against God?" and "he hearkened not unto her . . . or to be with her" (Genesis 39:9–10).

Both David and Joseph stood on a similar mesa. But one walked towards the edge while the other walked away. That seems to be the ultimate difference between David and Joseph—the agony and the victor's crown. President Kimball reminded us that "the difference between the good man and the bad man is not that one had the temptations and the other was spared them. It is that one kept himself fortified, and resisted temptation, and the other placed himself in compromising places and conditions and rationalized the situations. Hence it is obvious that to remain clean and worthy, one must stay positively and conclusively away from the devil's territory, avoiding the least approach toward evil." (*The Miracle of Forgiveness,* pp. 231–32.)

If we ended this chapter here, we would be leaving one group out. I know that I said there are three primary groups in this story, but what about those who have already trodden the path, approached the edge (by whatever speed, means, or reason), and have fallen off? If you have fallen and find yourself in a state of free-fall, please grab a branch, a rope—anything that will stop your fall. And then start the arduous task of climbing back up the cliff. It isn't an easy climb. It can prove very discouraging at times, even look next to impossible. But it is the only way to stop the pain, agony, and emptiness. We call this repentance, and it is real, it works, and it is right. Some of you may have been falling for so long that you have picked up momentum and think you can't ever stop. Yes you can! But only if you are willing to reach out and grab that branch sticking out from the cliff.

President Kimball felt that the proper pattern is to "prevent sin rather than be faced with the much more difficult task of curing it" (*The Teachings of Spencer W. Kimball* [Salt Lake City: Bookcraft, 1982], p. 163). There is an oft-told story about a stagecoach company who was in need of a new driver. Three men applied for the job. The newly hired driver would be required to drive a team over high, dangerous, and precipitous mountain roads. As the company owner asked each of the drivers how well he could drive, the first man replied: "I am such a good driver that I can drive my stage within a wheel's width from the edge." The second applicant, not to be outdone, boasted, "Oh, I can do better than that. I can drive the stage so accurately that the tire of the wheel will lap just over the edge." The employer silently wondered how the third man could possibly outdo the other applicants. The third man, to the surprise and delight of the owner, humbly said: "I try to stay as far from the edge as possible." It goes without saying which of the men received the job.

It is my hope and prayer that we might develop an attitude like that of the third applicant. I hope we will be determined to stay as far away from the edges of life as possible. "The Lord has promised to the valiant, 'All that I have is thine.' To reach these lofty heights and limitless blessings, you must take no chances. Keep your lives sweet and clean and pure, so that there will never be any forfeiture. To do this, you will do well to avoid 'the very appearance of evil' and 'the very approach toward evil.'" (Spencer W. Kimball, *Faith Precedes the Miracle*, p. 168.)

I encourage you to look for the warning signs and then heed them. Pray, listen to the prophets, and read your scriptures, for these are the fences that keep us safe from a possible fall. I hope we can become like Joseph of Egypt: knowing where we should be and what we should be doing—and doing it in every place and circumstance.

Matthew Richardson was born and raised in Murray, Utah, and served a mission in Denmark. He graduated from BYU in communication, later received a master's degree in educational leadership, and is currently a doctoral candidate. He is a part-time instructor in the Department of Ancient Scripture at BYU. He loves sports, art, and movies, and he makes excellent Mickey Mouse pancakes. He and his wife, Lisa, are the parents of three children.

13

"I WANT TO BEAR MY TESTIMONY": *THE PREPARATION BEHIND THE DECLARATION*

Mark Ellison

One of my favorite things about visiting youth conferences and co-directing EFY sessions is hearing you young men and women bear your testimonies. Often, I'll take notes on the things I hear and learn from you. Always I'm uplifted and inspired by the Spirit's presence.

Testimony meetings are special activities in the Lord's church. "Rich outpourings of the Spirit are frequently manifest in such meetings, and as a result faith and devotion are increased in the hearts of the spiritually inclined who participate in them" (Bruce R. McConkie, *Mormon Doctrine* [Salt Lake City: Bookcraft, 1966], p. 787).

What Is a Testimony?

One time my wife's father, who isn't LDS, visited church with her on testimony Sunday. He listened intently during the meeting, and afterwards he turned to my wife and asked, "What's this thing called testimony?" After an hour of hearing quite a variety of things said from the pulpit, he was still unsure about just what a testimony was. Maybe that says something about how well we members of the Church understand what a testimony is, and how we should share one. "A testimony of the gospel is the sure knowledge, received by revelation

from the Holy Ghost, of the divinity of the great latter-day work. . . .
'The testimony of Jesus' must come by 'the spirit of prophecy.' This is
received when the Holy Spirit speaks to the spirit within men. . . .
Receipt of a testimony is accompanied by a feeling of calm, unwaver-
ing certainty." (Bruce R. McConkie, *Mormon Doctrine,* p. 785.)

One day when I was in early-morning seminary, one of my friends
raised her hand and said, "I don't think I have a testimony." We about
fell out of our chairs. (This often happened in early-morning seminary.) The girl explained: "I love the Church, I believe it's true, and I
follow its teachings. But I hear people say, 'I know the Church is true,'
and I can't say I *know* it's true, like I *know* that you're all here."

Now, she knew we were there because she could see, hear, or
touch us. Is a testimony knowledge received by sensory evidence?
Remember, Elder McConkie said it was "knowledge received *by revelation.*" Did my friend have a testimony? Of course she did! "I love the
Church, I believe it's true, and I follow its teachings"—that's a testimony. She knew *spiritually.*

Our teacher directed us to a great scripture, Alma 32:21: "Faith is
not to have a perfect knowledge of things; therefore if ye have faith ye
hope for things which are not seen, which are true." A testimony is a
declaration of one's faith in the gospel of Jesus Christ, a spiritual
knowledge. You do know it's true, but not because of tangible evidence; you know because your whole soul is convinced by the power
of the Holy Spirit, and your whole heart feels love for the truth.

But don't think that evidence won't come. Alma 32 goes on to
teach that we should "experiment" upon the word of God, obeying his
commandments and watching for the good results in our lives, which
is like planting a seed and watching it grow (see Alma 32:26–43).
Those good results are evidence that the seed is good, or that the
gospel is true.

How Do I Get a Testimony?

My former stake president explained: You don't walk onto a used
car lot, look at a car, and say, "I like that one—it has good gas mileage,
acceleration, brakes, transmission, and power steering." You don't
know those things about the car yet, not until you take it out on the
highway for a good test drive. You can't know the gospel is true until
you experience it, try it out, observe the effects of obedience in your

life. "If any man will do his will, he shall know of the doctrine, whether it be of God, or whether I speak of myself" (John 7:17).

In my studies I've noticed that three main things are emphasized over and over when gaining a testimony is discussed: praying accompanied by fasting, studying the scriptures and the words of the living prophets, and living the gospel over time so as to see its good effects. If this were an equation, it would read:

Prayer + Study + Righteous Living = Testimony

Consider some examples from the scriptures. Alma the Younger once saw an angel, but years later, as he was bearing his testimony and explaining how he got it, he didn't even mention that vision: "Behold, I testify unto you that I do know that these things whereof I have spoken are true. And how do ye suppose that I know of their surety? Behold, I say unto you they are made known unto me by the Holy Spirit of God. Behold, I have fasted and prayed many days that I might know these things of myself." (Alma 5:45–46.)

To get his testimony, Alma had to go through the same process we all do. Visions produce no faith in the faithless. Laman and Lemuel still had no more testimony after seeing the angel in the cave (see 1 Nephi 3:27–31). Notice also what the scriptures say about the sons of Mosiah after their mission to the Lamanites: "They had waxed strong in the knowledge of the truth; for they were men of a sound understanding and they had searched the scriptures diligently, that they might know the word of God. But this is not all; they had given themselves to much prayer, and fasting." (Alma 17:2–3.)

I know of nothing so critical to your life as gaining your own testimony. In 1867, Elder Heber C. Kimball made this prophecy:

Many of you will see the time when you will have all the trouble, trial, and persecution that you can stand, and plenty of opportunities to show that you are true to God and his work. This church has before it many close places through which it will have to pass before the work of God is crowned with victory. To meet the difficulties that are coming, it will be necessary for you to have a knowledge of the truth of this work for yourselves. The difficulties will be of such a character that the man or woman who does not possess this personal knowledge or witness will fall. If you have not got the testimony, live right and call upon the Lord and cease not till you obtain it. If you do not you will not stand. . . . The time will come when no man or woman will be able to endure on borrowed light. Each will have to be guided by the light within himself." (Orson F. Whitney, *Life of Heber C. Kimball* [Salt Lake City: Bookcraft, 1967], pp. 449–50.)

What If There Are Some Things I'm Not Quite Sure About?

If there are some questions that remain unanswered in your mind, can you still have a testimony? The answer is yes. Nephi said, "I know that [God] loveth his children; nevertheless, I do not know the meaning of all things" (1 Nephi 11:17). He bore testimony of what he knew, while still having questions about other things. This is an important part of developing faith. "Dispute not because ye see not, for ye receive no witness until after the trial of your faith" (Ether 12:6).

When I was a kid, our family assembled one of those multi-million-piece jigsaw puzzles on the dining room table over a period of several weeks. It was a picture of a harbor, with boats at a dock and several beach houses, and also—isn't this always the case?—about twelve square miles of clear, blue sky. "Real good puzzle," we all said. We started assembling the borders—they're easy. Next, the pieces with parts of the picture fell into place. But then we were left with several bazillion seemingly identical pieces of blue sky. What do you do in a situation like that? If a piece won't fit anywhere, you throw it in the trash, right? "That piece is a hoax!" you say. "In fact, this whole puzzle is a fraud!" Of course, you don't do that. If a piece won't fit anywhere you try it, you set it aside in the "Doesn't Fit Yet" pile. You come back to it later and try again. Voila! It fits, and you say, "Why didn't I see that before?"

Sometimes the gospel or life brings us something that we don't understand right away. We can't see how it fits in. We shouldn't say, "I don't understand this commandment, so it can't be true!" or, "The whole church is a hoax." We put doubt aside and go on in faith. We study, pray, and learn. In time, the Lord will show us exactly where things fit. Throughout it all, the Church is true, and God lives. President Spencer W. Kimball wrote, "If you cannot understand fully today, wait patiently and truth will unfold and light will come" (*President Kimball Speaks Out* [Salt Lake City: Deseret Book Co., 1981], p. 26).

Why Should I Vocally Bear My Testimony?

"With the receipt of a testimony comes the obligation to bear witness to the world of the divinity of the Lord's work" (Bruce R. McConkie, *Mormon Doctrine*, p. 787). Bearing your testimony will have a powerful effect not only on those who hear it but also on you. "The Lord pours out his Spirit upon a man when he testifies that which the Lord gives him to testify of" (Joseph Fielding McConkie, *Seeking the Spirit* [Salt Lake City: Deseret Book Co., 1978], pp. 4–5). Have you ever shared your testimony and felt this outpouring of the Spirit? You feel as though you sit down with a stronger testimony than you had when you stood up.

Elder Boyd K. Packer wrote a masterful article about the workings of the Spirit, entitled "The Candle of the Lord." If you want to learn more about testimony, reading it entirely would be a great place to start. Part of the article reads: "There may be more power in your testimony than even you realize. . . . Oh, if I could teach you this one principle. A testimony is to be *found* in the *bearing* of it! . . . Bear testimony of the things that you hope are true, as an act of faith. . . . The Spirit and testimony of Christ will come to you for the most part when, and remain with you only if, you share it. . . . Is not this a perfect demonstration of Christianity? You cannot find it, nor keep it, nor enlarge it unless and until you are willing to share it. . . . It is by giving it away freely that it becomes yours." (*Ensign*, January 1983, pp. 54–55.)

For some of you, the idea of standing to bear your testimony may be terrifying. I heard of a recent survey which found that people generally fear public speaking more than they fear death! It may help you to remember that you're among brothers and sisters who are on your side, and that the Lord will help you. President Kimball wrote: "Don't you sit there in your fast meeting and cheat yourself and say, 'I guess I won't bear my testimony today. I guess that wouldn't be fair to the other members, because I have had so many opportunities.' You bear your testimony. And one minute is long enough to bear it." (*President Kimball Speaks Out,* p. 24.)

What Should I Say?

Remember Nephi's words: "I was led by the Spirit, not knowing beforehand the things which I should do" (1 Nephi 4:6). Speaking as led by the Spirit will be a great, Nephi-like leap of faith for you.

The October 1993 *New Era* gives some helpful guidelines:

• Tell what you know about the gospel.
• Talk about the things you are striving to gain a testimony of.
• Pray for support and confirmation of your testimony before you bear it, even if it's just a small prayer in your heart.
• Take bearing your testimony seriously and sincerely. Peer pressure shouldn't influence you.
• Keep your testimony short and to the point.
• Don't tell long stories, whether they are about yourself or someone else. If you have a good story, it might be best to save it for the next time you are asked to give a talk.
• Don't describe the details of past sins and bad conduct.
• Don't take up too much time. Others may be waiting for their turn.
• Don't talk only about friends and family. Testimony meeting is a time to say what you know about the gospel.

Let me add a few words on that last one. If you've ever gone to a week of EFY, youth conference, or girls camp, you know these programs usually conclude with a special testimony meeting, and emotions are strong at such a time. Understand where your feelings of love for friends or appreciation for the week fit in. If the Spirit at a youth conference has helped you draw nearer to the Savior, can you see how it would be more powerful to *bear testimony of the Savior* rather than of the conference?

An Apostle has written that a valid testimony has its roots in three great truths: Christ is the Son of God and the Savior, Joseph Smith was a true prophet, and the Church today is Jesus' church and the only true church (see Bruce R. McConkie, *Mormon Doctrine,* p. 786). Your Spirit-sparked feelings in a testimony meeting will relate to one or more of those truths. Speak of those sacred truths. President Kimball said, "Don't you ever worry about triteness in testimony. . . . It never gets old, never gets old!" (*President Kimall Speaks Out,* p. 23.)

What If I Start to Cry?

When I was on the verge of standing to bear my testimony for the first time in my life, a friend sitting next to me noticed my nervousness. "What's wrong?" he whispered.

My heart was pounding, and I could hardly breathe. "I'm going to stand up," I gasped.

"Go for it," he said. "Just don't cry!"

I don't often cry when I bear my testimony, but on that occasion the Spirit affected my emotions in such a powerful way that I did cry.

The list of guidelines I quoted above goes on to reassure, "Don't be embarrassed if you get emotional" (*New Era,* October 1993). President Howard W. Hunter has this inspired guidance on the subject:

I get concerned when it appears that strong emotion or free-flowing tears are equated with the presence of the Spirit. Certainly the Spirit of the Lord can bring strong emotional feelings, including tears, but that outward manifestation ought not to be confused with the presence of the Spirit itself. . . . Let it come naturally and as it will, perhaps with the shedding of tears, but perhaps not. If what you say is the truth, and you say it purely and with honest conviction, [people] will feel the spirit of the truth being taught them and will recognize that inspiration and revelation has come into their hearts. That is how we build faith. ("Eternal Investments," address to CES religious educators, February 10, 1989.)

The Spirit will affect us in different ways at different times. Don't feel bad if you happen to cry while bearing your testimony, but don't think you're unspiritual if you don't.

How Should I Respond to the Testimonies of Others?

Perhaps this is the most important factor in whether the testimony meeting is a success to us. Our hearts need to be open to the Spirit and filled with kind feelings for our brothers and sisters. "Don't be critical of others' testimonies—we're all learning. Plus, you won't be able to feel the Spirit if you focus on the negative." (*New Era,* October 1993.)

What Effect Does Bearing My Testimony Have on Others?

There was a young man who investigated the Church for two years but was still unsure whether he should be baptized. Then one day he heard a shy, awkward Church member bear his testimony. I don't know the name of this member who, trembling and nervous, spoke of things he knew in his heart to be true. But the young man who heard him was Brigham Young. Here is how he described the effect of that testimony: "When I saw a man without eloquence, or talents for public speaking, who could only say, 'I know by the power of the Holy Ghost, that the Book of Mormon is true, that Joseph Smith is a Prophet of the Lord,' the Holy Ghost proceeding from that individual illuminated my understanding, and light, glory, and immortality were before me. I was encircled by them, filled with them, and I knew for myself that the testimony of the man was true." (*Journal of Discourses* 1:90.)

Brigham Young then decided to be baptized. Think of the far-reaching effect of that one testimony! "When a man speaketh by the power of the Holy Ghost the power of the Holy Ghost carrieth it unto the hearts of the children of men" (2 Nephi 33:1).

A young woman wrote me sharing the experience of bearing her testimony at a youth conference, and how it helped kindle a testimony in the heart of her friend:

> Remember me telling you about my friend? She's one of those kids who only comes to church because their parents make them. She's 16 and has never borne her testimony, because she's never had one. She even told me numerous times she didn't know if she believed and that she didn't care. . . . Anyway, at youth conference she just started laughing and clapping—she was enjoying a church activity! Of course I was just thrilled. At that overwhelming testimony meeting, she suddenly grabbed my hand. She had tears rolling all down her face. I then smiled, and looked forward, and made the decision, "I've got to bear my testimony, for her sake." [Which she did, and it was beautiful.] After the testimony meeting, we went back to the room to get my camera, and she hugged me and said, "I love you. Thank you for being my friend. I hope at the next youth conference I'll be able to do that."
>
> I said, "Do what?"
>
> She said, "You know, bear a testimony."
>
> I said, "Why didn't you today?"
>
> She said, "I wasn't sure about things, until you talked about that burning feeling right here" (patting her heart).
>
> I said, "Then why didn't you get up after me?"
>
> She said, "I guess I was nervous."
>
> I said, "So are you sure about things now?"

She said, "After that meeting how could I not be? Although there are some things I have trouble understanding."

I said, "Well, I guess that's why you've got me."

Yes, that's why we've got each other, "that when [we] are assembled together [we] shall instruct and edify each other" (D&C 43:8).

I want to bear my testimony to everyone who reads this: God lives and loves us. Jesus Christ is his Son and our Savior. He has restored his church in these last days through a mighty prophet, Joseph Smith. The Church today is, in reality, Jesus' church, and is directed by the Lord through living Apostles and prophets. These are the last days. I do know it's true, because my whole soul is convinced by the power of the Holy Spirit.

May you prepare by prayer, study, and obedience to be convinced by the Spirit of God, and may you feel the joy of owning that spiritual knowledge all the more as you freely give it away.

Mark Ellison was born in Germany, grew up in California, and now lives in Springville, Utah, with his wife, Lauren, daughter, Kasey, and new-born baby. He served a mission to the deaf in Oakland, California, and Phoenix, Arizona. He teaches seminary, enjoys composing and recording music for piano, synthesizer, and guitar, and regularly competes in triathlons (swim-bike-run endurance races).

14

SANTA CLAUS IS COMING TO TOWN: SOME MYTHS ABOUT FAITH

Art E. Berg

It was the night before Christmas, but all was not quiet in our house. If the mice had been making noises, we would never have heard them. A family of nine children can redefine even the noblest of Christmas traditions.

As a young man, within hours after the clock struck twelve on New Year's Day I dreamed of the coming Christmas morning. I loved everything about Christmas: the smells, candy, food, trees, decorations, giving, spirit, songs, and sights. But I especially loved the *getting* part of it. Throughout the year I would carefully compile my list of wishes. Every television commercial was an opportunity to discover an uncovered need. Toy stores were the breeding ground of creativity and quickly caused the list to grow by leaps and bounds.

As Christmas drew nearer, I would begin to prioritize my wants. All needs were immediately eliminated, as they were just expected to be provided as a part of the responsibilities of parents to their children. The list had to be confined to real wants; the kind of stuff you knew you couldn't get during the coming year. I knew that Santa had a budget, so I had to carefully choose those wants I had the best chance of getting, lest my parents would be forced to choose on their own and I would risk a disappointing Christmas.

On Christmas Eve my parents would gather all the children around the tree. We would read the Christmas story from the scriptures, have family prayer, and then we were allowed to open one gift each. It was kind of like a teaser. I am not sure why we always got so excited, though, because it was always the same present every year: new pajamas. After all, my mother wanted to make sure we looked good for Christmas morning pictures.

Sleep always came slowly on Christmas Eve because we were too excited by the anticipation of the coming morning. If we listened real carefully, we could hear Santa Claus bumping about downstairs wrapping the gifts and making sure everything was in its proper place. My mind would often race: "Will I get everything I asked for? Did I specify I needed that new bike in metallic blue? Did I leave enough obvious hints that Santa should know the priority of my list?"

It was a tradition that the next morning we had to go downstairs as a family. But there was a ritual which had to be observed first—I am sure, mostly as a form of torture to us children. Everybody had to be cleaned, scrubbed, showered, shaved, and neatly dressed in our new pajamas before we could begin the spirit of "getting." My mother would line all nine children up on the stairs for the ceremonious picture taking, which seemed to drag on for hours in the mind and body of a twelve-year-old.

Finally there came the moment we had been waiting 364 days for. My parents unanimously shouted, "Go!" Now the mad dash to the living room and the Christmas tree was on. Older children hurdled the younger ones in an effort to get there first. Seeing the room for the first time Christmas morning was always a treat. Santa had always wrapped about half of our presents and left the other half unwrapped and scattered around the room. When there are nine children, that makes for a lot of gifts everywhere.

Shrieks of joy filled the room. Paper flew through the air—we could not get the gifts unwrapped fast enough. The room strobed with the flashes of the camera and the relentless plea from my mother saying, "Look over here, now. Show me what you got. Now smile!" Flash!

Christmas was always the greatest day of the year for me as a boy, as it is for many children. Unfortunately, I brought some of those same childhood attitudes and perspectives into my relationship with God and my beliefs about the role of faith in my life. From those early Christmas memories and other experiences, I had created some misgivings and untruths about how faith worked. Fortunately, through successful missionary experiences, personal revelation, and a commitment to gospel study, I have discovered some common myths about faith that I would like to share with you.

Myth 1: God is some kind of a cosmic Santa Claus.

Somehow my childhood experiences of Christmas became a part of my relationship with God. Without meaning to, and without conscious knowledge, I was treating God as though he was some kind of a cosmic Santa Claus

In Primary and in my home I was taught the fundamentals of an appropriate prayer as follows: "1. Dear Heavenly Father . . . ; 2. We thank thee . . . ; 3. We ask thee . . . ; 4. In the name of Jesus Christ. Amen." While I understood and used that formula, I was always getting caught up on the "We ask thee" part. My prayers were becoming a "to do" list for God: "Please keep me safe. Watch over me. Help me score well on my test. Keep me out of trouble. Cause my parents to show mercy to me after they find out I wrecked their car. Help Jenny fall in love with me and say 'yes' to my invitation to the prom." And the list goes on and on.

Asking for help from the Lord is an important aspect of the prayer formula. However, for a long time, it was 98 percent of my prayers. I raced through the few, trite things I was grateful for in order to make sure I had plenty of time to get my full, prioritized list to the Lord so that he could get to work on it right away. Unfortunately, this approach to prayer and faith caused me a lot of discouragement, frustration, and misunderstanding. I had fallen victim to the myth that God's sole duty was to bring me pleasure and grant my wishes as I asked for them.

Now, if you had asked me if that was what I was doing or how I felt when I was doing it, I would have denied it vehemently. However, as I am honest with myself now and look back over the years of my behavior as it relates to faith and prayers, I would have to humbly confess my guilt. As I discovered the error of my ways, I began to search for a more appropriate means of communicating with my God.

The Lord has said, "And all things, whatsoever ye shall ask in prayer, believing, ye shall receive" (Matthew 21:22). I didn't have any trouble with the asking part. I had trouble with the believing. Faith is an action verb. Faith requires that we *do* something. To ask God to do something, we must first be willing to do our part. As I get older I have found myself much more cautious as to what I ask for. I first ask myself, "Am I willing to do all that is required of me?" Only after I can honestly answer that question affirmatively am I ready to petition the Lord for his help.

Another habit I have found worthy of sharing is spending more time expressing gratitude. While I was in the mission field my mission president taught me that, in effective leadership, before I expressed a constructive criticism I should always share at least two positive things about the individual I had a stewardship over. This practice always created a better foundation for communication and improved our relationship.

In prayer, I have tried to form the same habit of spending twice as much time thanking God for his rich blessings in specific detail as I do in creating my "to do" list for him. Aside from the fact that expressing gratitude to God is a commandment, it can also be an act of faith in and of itself. To exercise faith is to act "as if" our prayers have been answered. If I truly believed that God would hear and answer my righteous desire, I would spend more time thanking, rather than just asking.

When we stop treating God as though he is some kind of a cosmic Santa Claus, we will find that the nature of our prayers changes, our relationship with him improves, and our faith is strengthened. It is not God's purpose to meet our every demand, but rather to provide support, love, light, and strength. By seeing God as the great resource he is, we stop abusing our communication with him and start asking better questions. When we ask better questions, we will get better answers.

Myth 2: God will deliver us from the consequences of our bad choices.

While sitting in sacrament meeting many years ago, when I was ten years old, I was completely bored by the speakers' dissertations. Before long my mind was caught up in the fantasies and imaginations of a boy. I was envisioning the G.I. Joe which I had recently received for Christmas, the G.I. Joe figure which had a parachute strapped to his back. It came with a slingshot to shoot him high into the air; and I would then watch the small plastic figure float gently back to the earth with the parachute fully open.

It was then that I had my first major revelation. I thought, If G.I. Joe can do it, so can my younger brother. Excitedly arriving home after church, I dragged my little brother up to the top of our second-story roof. Bringing a sheet from the bed along with me, I instructed my brother to hold onto all four corners of the sheet and then jump off the roof. For some reason he was not as enthused as I was about this whole adventure. His refusal became more adamant as I pushed him closer to the edge.

Finally, tired of listening to his incessant complaints and fears, I took the sheet from him and declared that I would demonstrate how it all worked. Grabbing all four corners tightly, I jumped from the rooftop. About the time I was passing the balcony I had my second major revelation—I wasn't going to slow down. Suddenly, I became a fervent believer in prayer. My lips were moving so fast in my attempt to communicate with God that the wind was causing them to whistle! The fall seemed to last an eternity. I made more covenants with God during the descent than I could possibly have ever fulfilled. As you can guess, seconds later I crashed to the ground at full speed. The pain was excruciating. I thought I had broken both my legs.

While it is easy for me now to understand that my prayer and faith were somewhat misplaced, at the time I was disappointed that God had not saved me. Since that time I have had other experiences in which I made inappropriate requests to God in an effort to avoid the natural consequences of my own foolish behavior. But as much as God loves his children, it is misplaced faith that asks him to prevent all pain in this life; especially that pain which we create for ourselves. My mission president taught me that it was foolish to think I could sow my wild oats on Saturday and pray for crop failure on Sunday.

Unfortunately I have had many experiences with prayer which have been based on this myth. I have prayed that God would help me score well on a test which was critical to my educational future, yet I never studied for it. I have asked my Father in Heaven to bless me with good health while I was abusing my body with junk food and other poor eating habits. I have petitioned him for safety and then chosen to drive faster than the posted speed limit without a seat belt on. When we ask God to remove the natural consequences of our own behavior, we set ourselves up for disappointment and frustration.

Through Joseph Smith, the Lord declared, "If ye are prepared ye shall not fear" (D&C 38:30). Fear is the opposite of faith. If we want to exercise real faith and eliminate fear in our lives we must first be willing to do all we can do in preparation. I have heard of many experiences in which good-intentioned Saints have taken to heart the admonition of the Lord to "neither take ye thought beforehand what ye shall say." Unfortunately, this counsel is all too often used as an excuse to not prepare, in which case the person wonders why he experienced fear and why the results from his words were less than satisfying. What such good-intentioned Saints missed was the rest of the verse, where the Lord commands readers to "treasure up in your minds continually the words of life" (D&C 84:85). In short, prepare!

We cannot escape the natural consequences of our behavior by seeking to exercise faith and prayer, except as it relates to forgiveness from the Lord and his atonement for our sins. Asking or expecting the Lord to act in such a way is contrary to the purposes of faith and of this life, and it will only lead to frustration in our relationship with God.

Myth 3: If God does not answer our prayers, it is because we do not have enough faith.

In 1983, after breaking my neck in a serious automobile accident, I was left a quadriplegic; paralyzed from the chest down. It was the most painful experience of my life. Every day I prayed that God would heal me—change the physical condition of my life and restore me to the health I had enjoyed before the accident left me paralyzed.

After more than ten years in a wheelchair, I still persist in my prayers for that healing. However, over the years I have had to guard myself from feeling that because I have not yet been healed I do not yet have enough faith. While faith is a growing thing, and while I believe I can always find greater measures of faith in my life, I have also had to understand that some miracles just take time.

Oscar Wilde said, "If God really wanted to punish us, he would answer all of our prayers." If God answered all prayers, there would be no sick, no discomfort, no death, no hunger, no pain, no adversity, no poor, no challenges, no disappointments, and especially no freedom. If there were no pain, there would be no learning, no growth, and no change. Without these things . . . why are we here?

It is my testimony that God does love us. It is my belief that while we may cry out and wish that God would remove all the pain from our lives, sometimes he loves us more than that. He loves us enough to bless us with the miracle called time. By so doing, he provides you and me with the greatest opportunities for growth and change; essential ingredients on the road to immortality and eternal life.

*   *   *

No, God is not a cosmic Santa Claus. Faith is not intended to remove the natural consequences of our poor decisions. And just because God does not always answer our prayers in the way we desire, that does not mean we are absent of faith and are found wanting in the eyes of the Lord. These myths, among others, are often responsible for feelings of inadequacy and failure in the exercising of faith. Avoiding these myths, and exercising faith as God intended it to be used, builds our relationship with God and allows us to come before his throne boldly. Faith is more than just one of the basic principles of the gospel. It is the power which will bring us safely home again.

Art E. Berg is a businessman and president of Invictus Communications, Inc. A professional motivational speaker to business, church, and youth groups, he is the author of a book entitled Some Miracles Take Time. *He enjoys wheelchair racing, parasailing, boating, and traveling. Art loves working with youth and has served as a Sunday School teacher, Aaronic Priesthood adviser, and seminary instructor. He is married to Dallas Howard Berg, and they are the parents of one child.*

15

YOU TELL ON YOURSELF: WHAT YOU ARE INSIDE WILL SHOW UP OUTSIDE

Michael Weir Allred

I couldn't believe it. I had a square bald spot cut in my hair just above my ear.

I had told my wife that the way to make a tapered haircut was to hold the buzzers next to the skin and then, as the buzzers moved up, gradually move them away from the head. I didn't know if that was the right way, but it made sense to me. The only problem was that she forgot to move the buzzers gradually away as she moved them up. She laughed so hard she fell to the floor. We called my sister-in-law, who is a beautician, and asked for help. It was difficult for her to help, because she too was now on the floor laughing. Finally I had to settle for a similar cut on the other side of my head.

So there I was, two square bald spots, one on each side of my head, and I had to return to teach my seminary class on Monday. Have you ever been teased in school about something you are wearing, or the way your hair looked? Can you imagine my fear? Can you feel my pain?

Actually, the students were very compassionate. Not only were they kind in not making fun of me, but one of the boys even said it was the "baddest" haircut he had ever seen.

If I had purposely chosen that haircut you could probably tell a little bit about my personality. However, that is part of the problem—you can't always judge a book by its cover. But what is on the inside does seem to show up on the outside.

I want to make two points clear. First, I am not trying to present ideas on how to judge others. Second, people do judge us, so we need to be careful to stand as a witness for Christ in all things, and in all ways, and in all places. We will find out whether we are standing as witnesses by asking ourselves four questions:

Have I received his image in my countenance?
Does the light of Christ shine in my eyes?
Does the Father know his child?
Have I experienced a mighty change of heart?

Have You Received His Image in Your Countenance?

In 1984 I was going through training as a counter-intelligence agent for the National Guard. We were taught to watch our image critically. For example, during a surveillance it was vital that we blend into the surroundings. But as members of the Church it's different—we need to make sure that we stand up for what we believe in. There are times when the Savior needs us to be noticed.

In the general conference of October 1969, President David O. McKay recited this poem by an unidentified author (I've updated two lines to make them fit the 90s):

> You tell on yourself by the friends you seek,
> By the very manner in which you speak,
> By the way you employ your leisure time,
> By the use you make of dollar and dime.
> You tell what you are by the things you wear,
> And even by the way you wear your hair,
> By the way you laugh and the jokes you know,
> By the music you play on your stereo.
> You tell what you are by the way you walk,
> By the things of which you delight to talk,
> By the manner in which you bury deceit,
> By so simple a thing as how you eat.
> By the books you choose from the well-filled shelf.
> In these ways and more you tell on yourself.
> (*Improvement Era,* December 1969, p. 87.)

One's very countenance can be part of the judging process. Even in Old Testament times, those who participated in evil usually marked themselves. They would identify themselves with weird hairstyles, or by cutting or printing in their flesh (see Leviticus 19:27–28; 1 Kings 18:28). This doesn't sound like ancient times; it sounds like MTV. What was going on inside was showing up outside.

With all the stereotypical images in the world today, we should do some analysis as to which one helps the Lord. Even if the missionary is a cowboy from Montana—even if the missionary was the best skater in Seattle—the need is the same: When we are on the Lord's business we need to look the part in the eyes of those we are serving. We are actually taking on society's stereotypical appearance of a servant of the Lord. In the April general conference of 1973 President Harold B. Lee said: "Priesthood is the power by which Heavenly Father works through men, through deacons, through teachers, through priests. . . . They would always want to appear at their best when they are exercising their priesthood. Their hair would be properly groomed; their clothing and appearance would reflect the sanctity they should feel in the performance of their priesthood duties." ("Follow the Leadership of the Church," *Ensign,* July 1973, p. 98.)

I feel that this advice is equally important for the daughters of Zion. Both the young men and the young women who are trying to witness for the Lord need to ask themselves this serious question: Have I received his image in my countenance?

Does the Light of Christ Shine in Your Eyes?

The scriptures warn us of wolves in sheeps' clothing. Some of the most infamous killers of our day have looked like nice people. Jeffery Daumer and Ted Bundy were both successful in their evil partly because of their appearance. 1 Samuel 16:7 tells us that man looks on the outward appearance, but the Lord looks on the heart. Do our actions equal our appearance?

As missionaries in Japan, my companion and I were once asked why we were so light. We semi-sarcastically answered that it was because we were Caucasian. What the person was referring to, however, was more than an outward appearance. She had seen something in us that was a result of our actions.

Look at the daily routine of missionaries. They start with morning prayer and personal scripture study, and they avoid the things of the world. Here seems to lie the key to the light of Christ shining in our eyes. In 2 Nephi 32:3 we are told to feast upon the words of Christ, and that the words of Christ will show us all things that we should do. In this way the Spirit becomes our image consultant.

While growing up in the sixties and seventies, I had long hair. It was really cool, I thought. If a parent or leader asked me to cut it, I would use the familiar statement about the Savior having long hair. I had a testimony of the gospel; I believed the Church was true. I really didn't see the need for a shorter haircut.

Then one day my brother-in-law asked me if I had read the Book of Mormon. I said I knew it was true without reading it. He asked if I had a testimony of Joseph Smith. I said I did. He then invited me to read the Book of Mormon, because Joseph Smith said it was the keystone of our religion.

One of the reasons why I had not yet read the Book of Mormon was in the past. When I graduated from Primary I was presented with my own copy of the Book of Mormon. I took it home that night and read and read. I'm sure I read at least two chapters. I was feeling so spiritual that I even prayed as Moroni did in the famous painting. I knelt down and put my folded hands on top of my new Book of Mormon.

While I slept I had a really scary dream. I dreamt that I was in a large white house going up a staircase. At the top of the stairs was the traditional picture of the Savior. As I approached the picture it turned and snarled at me. I ran down the stairs and went to the local laundromat. Why the laundromat? I have no clue. I was so scared that I woke up. Out of fear I stopped reading the Book of Mormon. It's hard to believe I let Satan influence me like that.

While I was in ninth grade seminary the teacher was sharing the warm feeling that we get from reading the Book of Mormon. I raised my hand and disagreed. He then put his hand on my shoulder and said to me: "He succeeded, didn't he? Satan tried to scare you away from reading the Book of Mormon." I then determined that I would not let Satan beat me again. By this time I wasn't much into reading. So here I was with my brother-in-law, deciding to read the Book of Mormon from cover to cover.

My job at that time was in downtown Indianapolis, to which I took the bus to work every day. I would read on my way there and on my way home. I read to midway through Alma before the messages really started to stick. I was reading about a great man named Ammon. Ammon was like an Arnold Schwarzeneggar with a testimony.

By this time, instead of reading words I would start seeing the situations; I began visualizing what was happening. This visualization continued until I had completed the entire book. On the final day, when I was reading about the destruction of the Nephite people, I could hardly believe what had happened to them. So here I was, sitting on a crowded bus with tears in my eyes because of the destruction of a people I had never met but had grown to love. I was hoping that the people sitting around me would think I had hay fever.

When I returned home and found the house empty I knelt down and asked the Lord for another witness. I received my answer. I had already believed the Book of Mormon was true, but now I had read it. I learned to love the book during this time. My testimony was set on fire.

During this period I was sharing the gospel with my nonmember friend. Having had the experience in reading the Book of Mormon, I was now able to share some of my excitement with him. Soon my friend too felt the Spirit and wanted to be baptized. And he wanted me to do the honors.

It was just before his baptism that I approached my sister and asked her to cut my hair. Why was I choosing to cut my hair now? What about the statement about the Savior having long hair? Wasn't it okay to have hair like that and perform a baptism? While these thoughts went through my mind, I felt that the Spirit was telling me something. It is hard to use the excuse about the Savior having long hair when it is he who is telling you to cut it. The words of Christ were not only having an effect on my outward appearance but also were having a still greater effect on my heart. To find out how your heart is doing, answer this question: Does the light of Christ shine in your eyes?

Does the Father Know His Child?

Have you ever been told to ask yourself, "What would Jesus do?" I think this is great advice, but I would like to add one more part.

When I was ten to twelve years old my little nephew had been hurt and his mother thought he had a concussion. She called my mother and asked us to go get them and take them to the hospital. While we were at their house, my mother went inside with my sister and my nephew and left me alone in the car.

What would Jesus do? I loved this nephew very much and didn't want him to be hurt. So I knelt down on the floor and prayed to my Heavenly Father that he wouldn't have a concussion. He was too little: if someone should have to have a concussion, it should be me. Is that what Jesus would do?

When we arrived at the hospital, to our joy my nephew did not have a concussion. The Lord had answered my prayer. In fact, he answered it in every detail, because not long after that I fell in a shower and got a concussion. If I were to say that same prayer today, I would leave out that little part about *my* getting the concussion.

Not only should we ask what Jesus would do but we should also ask why. Why would the Savior go to church? Why would the Savior obey the Word of Wisdom? Why would the Savior study the scriptures every day? There are three main reasons why people do good: fear, pride, and love. The Savior's motivation is always love. When we begin to do *right,* we are going in the *right* direction. When we begin to do the *right* things for the *right* reasons, then we are *right*eous. In the general conference of October 1986 Elder Neal A. Maxwell said, "We cannot share in his power without sharing in his attributes. . . . We cannot reenter his house until our behavior would let us feel at home." ("God Will Yet Reveal," *Ensign,* November 1980, p. 54.) When it is time for us to come home, will the Father know his child?

To summarize this concept I quote a verse from the hymn "God Loved Us So He Sent His Son."

> In word and deed he doth require
> My will to his, like son to sire,
> Be made to bend, and I, as son,
> Learn conduct from the Holy One.
> (*Hymns,* no. 187.)

Have You Experienced a Mighty Change of Heart?

Have you ever had a dream that you didn't remember until someone said something that jarred your memory? I dreamed I was in a room and in front of me was a large door slightly ajar. Light was beaming from around the edges of the door. I knew the Savior was on the other side of it, so I walked over and pushed the door shut. I did not remember anything of the dream until later that day. I was riding in a car with a man who said he wished we had more spiritual experiences in our life. When he said this, I remembered the dream and said, "We could have more, but it is us who keep them out." In many instances we are the reason for the lack of contact with spiritual things.

John 7:17 says that we must do the Lord's will if we wish to know of the doctrine. We cannot live a life full of spiritual experiences while continuing to sin. We have to choose. From the beginning God has given us agency (see Moses 4:3; 7:32), and when he fulfilled the Atonement he took upon himself the sins of all who would receive him as their Savior. In doing so he felt all the effects of sin even though he was sinless. He felt pain as the soldiers nailed him to the cross. He felt loneliness as he was left by his disciples. He felt burden as he carried his own cross as far as he could. He felt humiliation as wicked men spat upon him. He felt the consequences of sin while still remaining perfect.

But there was one effect of sin he had not felt before, and that was the loss of the Spirit. While he was on the cross he said a phrase to his Father that is interpreted to mean "My God, My God, why hast thou forsaken me?" (Matthew 27:46.) Can you understand what it must feel like to be perfect and yet lose the Spirit? Can you imagine the joy that comes to a sinner who regains the Spirit? We can't afford to live without it. We must do everything we can to maintain or regain the Spirit. This was made possible through the Savior's atonement. I have tried to express my feelings about the Atonement in the following poem:

Live As He Lives

Oh consider in wonder how merciful he is
To condescend to our level that we could rise to his.
He came to this world though God from the start,
To take on infirmities, to succor man's heart.
His bowels filled with mercy, being tempted for all,
To loosen the bands of death from the Fall.
He must be a mortal, yet death as he willed,
He hath borne our griefs, with his stripes we are healed.
He made us free agents to act on our own,

All sins and their pains he bore all alone.
He paid the great price, our Savior, our King,
He requires from us this one vital thing.
This is the choice and consequence he gives:
Suffer as he suffered or live as he lives.

Doctrine and Covenants 19:16–18 says: "For behold, I, God, have suffered these things for all, that they might not suffer if they would repent; but if they would not repent they must suffer even as I; which suffering caused myself, even God, the greatest of all, to tremble because of pain, and to bleed at every pore, and to suffer both body and spirit."

Have you experienced a mighty change of heart and lost the desire for sin? Are you like your Father? Does the light of Christ shine in your eyes? Have you received his image in your countenance? Is there anything in your life that is interfering with spiritual guidance? If there is, change it.

Avoid the temptation to judge others, and always remember the Savior's need for us. May we always stand as a witness for him.

Michael Weir Allred *teaches seminary at Bonneville High School in Ogden, Utah, and is a graduate of Weber State University and the University of Phoenix. Before becoming a teacher, he served in the Army National Guard as a counterintelligence agent and Japanese interpreter. Brother Allred enjoys playing the drums and has taught drum lessons. He claims to love all sports "except synchronized swimming." He and his wife, Kathy, have four children, and he says he is currently developing skills to become a better home teacher.*

16

AM I TALKING TO MYSELF OR IS IT THE SPIRIT?

Todd Murdock

My parents taught me at a young age that if I died before I turned eight, automatically I would go to heaven. I loved that idea and quickly developed a desire to die before I was baptized a member of the Church and became accountable for my sins. I was very happy as a young boy but wanted to go to heaven, and death before eight seemed the easiest way.

I have a brother who is one year older than me, and before he had a chance to die he was baptized. In addition he also received a gift, the Holy Ghost, which meant nothing to me. I was happy that he was happy with this gift, but I still wanted to die.

One day we were playing a game of checkers in our living room. The phone rang in the kitchen. Mom answered it and then announced that the call was for my brother. Instantly my devious little seven-year-old mind went to work. I knew the game board could not be seen from the kitchen, so when my brother left to answer the call I could quickly rearrange the checkers and then win the game upon his return. I was ecstatic!

Standing up, my brother pointed a finger saying: "Don't move the checkers. I'll know if you move the checkers." I did my best I-would-never-think-of-it look. He warned me again, promising that he would know. I promised I wouldn't move the checkers and he left. When he was out of sight, I quickly moved the checkers. Victory was imminent!

Upon his return I acted innocent but hurried. "OK, let's go, my move," I said. I didn't want to look him in the eye for fear of giving away my next move.

Silence. Then finally he said, "You moved the checkers."

"Oh, I did not," I replied. "Come on, sit down, it's my move."

"Nope, you moved the checkers, and do you know how I know?" And then he said these words that I'll never forget. "I have the Holy Ghost."

My life was spared. I had my eighth birthday and was baptized and received the Holy Ghost. I expected that as soon as I received that gift a great change would take place in the way I felt and acted, but it never came. I felt the same as I always had. Soon after my baptism the novelty of having this "Holy Ghost" gift wore off, and I accepted that I had it only because my parents told me I did, and that was good enough for me.

Since that time I have wanted to figure what this gift really is. As years passed I heard stories of people who heard a voice and because they did they saved someone's life or their own or prevented an accident. The credit for this voice was always given to the Holy Ghost. Miracles seemed to happen because of this audible inspiration.

We are taught in scriptures that the Holy Ghost does speak to us. Look at some of the words used to describe the communicative ability of the Spirit. "Yea, behold, I will tell you in your mind and in your heart, by the Holy Ghost, which shall come upon you and which shall dwell in your heart" (D&C 8:2). "Howbeit, when he, the Spirit of truth, is come, he will guide you into all truth: for he shall not speak of himself; but whatsoever he shall hear, that shall he speak: and he will shew you things to come" (John 16:13).

Because I believed the stories and that the Holy Ghost could speak to mortals, I made the assumption that worthy persons would hear a voice that would direct them in their life; hence if I heard no voice and received no direction, I was unworthy. Therefore I really strained to hear an audible voice. I often questioned myself whether the voice I heard in my mind was the Holy Ghost or whether I was talking to myself. I began playing ridiculous games, giving myself instructions to walk a certain way, to open a door, or to do some other task that needed inspiration; each time questioning whether I was being so closely watched that all instructions were inspiration. Needless to say, this became very tedious and frustrating and boring. Eventually, I abandoned my desire to hear a voice.

In the summer before my high school senior year, I purchased a motorcycle. Red and shiny, it was the first vehicle I ever owned. Along with the bike came a helmet which I was instructed to always wear. I no longer had desires to die, so I was obedient. I loved to ride. I had a friend who loved to ride his bike with me, and together we covered many miles on our sleek machines.

Summer also meant football, and practices twice a day. One day after practice, I decided to ride over to my friend's house, and then together we'd go to a local church to shoot baskets, working out bruises encountered during the day. Because the distance to his house was short I decided not to wear my helmet.

My bike was parked in the driveway, screaming for me to come and ride. Again I was obedient. As I swung my leg over the seat and sat down, I heard in my mind, "Put your helmet on." The impression was so strong that I got off the bike. I thought for sure I was talking to myself.

I sat down again the second time. Again I heard, "Put your helmet on." "No way," I thought. "I'm talking to myself." I stood up again the third time, promising I wouldn't talk to myself.

I shook my hands, took a deep breath and then sat down. For the third time the voice came back. This time I heard my name. "Todd, put your helmet on."

I was amazed! "OK, I'm going to play along," I thought. "I'm going crazy, but I'll play along just in case this really is the Holy Ghost."

I then determined that in my effort of obedience I would ask my sister to run downstairs to my bedroom and retrieve my helmet for me. If she would do this, then I would wear the helmet; if not, I had done everything in my power to be obedient and the Lord would have to take care of me.

I walked back to the house, stuck my head in the front door, and asked my sister to get my helmet. I knew she wouldn't. We were at war with each other. At this time in our lives we had undertaken the tasks of making each other as miserable as possible. A simple favor from either one of us to the other was out of the question. In addition to this matter of our wars, she was now watching her favorite TV show, "Days of Our Lives," and I knew she would not part from it for me.

As soon as I asked, however, she jumped up, ran to the basement and into my room, came back with my helmet, handed it to me, then sat back down in front of the TV.

Inexpressible confusion filled my soul! "This isn't my sister," I thought, "this is the angel Moroni in disguise." Nevertheless I had my helmet, so I put it on and went on my way.

Second North in Kaysville, heading west, will take you under the overpass, over the railroad tracks, and then it's wide open road. An open road is an incredible stimulus for young teenagers to open the throttle on their bike and cruise. I did this, passing farmers' fields quite rapidly. I was alive, it felt great, it was me.

The road eventually intersects, and I slowed down to make a right-hand turn. Still no traffic, and I raced down the road again. However, the road did not continue in a straight line. It curved around an oak tree growing in the yard of a local farmer. Approaching the curve, I slowed down but wanted to take the turn as fast as I could. One of the joys of motorcycle riding is to lean the heavy bike and see how close you can come to the ground without wiping out. If you wipe out you've leaned too far.

I began my turn, and as I cornered at the top of the curve the farmer backed his truck out of his driveway and into my lane. I didn't see him until then because of the oak tree. I straightened the bike up to go around him in his lane, but he gunned his truck to get out of my lane.

It's a sickening feeling to know you're going to crash. I locked up my brakes and braced myself for the collision. It never happened. The blur of the truck flashed by in my peripheral vision as I headed for tall grass on the side of the road. It was slick but I felt I could keep things under control.

Suddenly the bike stopped and I went flying straight into the air. I could see the bike below me, and I thought, "Hmph, I'm flying straight in the air." Then, because my intelligence level is so high, I thought, "Hmph, I'm going to come down." Sure enough I did. I was heading for the ground head first, and a thought raced through my mind suggesting that I duck my head as if I were to hit someone in football practice. (Because of the circumstances I was unable to call a time-out to discuss other options.) I ducked my head and hit the ground. It was the best hit I'd ever had! The impact was absorbed in my head, neck, and shoulders, and I somersaulted gently onto my back.

The farmer stopped his truck, jumping out to see if I was OK. I assured him arrogantly that I was absolutely fine, almost acting as if I actually had fun flying through the air and landing on my head. I felt very weak. Eventually, I picked up my bike and headed for home.

As I walked in the front door my sister sensed something was wrong. I told her I'd been in an accident. Overly concerned, she told me to lie down and rest and wait for Mom to come home. I did this, then shared the experience with my mother as she listened sitting on the edge of my bed. I mentioned the "voice" that prompted me to put my helmet on. After I had finished, Mom pointed out that it was the Holy Ghost that had saved my life that day.

Reflecting on that experience I believe that I did talk to myself. I believe that I'm the one who said, "Put on your helmet." I also believe the Holy Ghost inspired me. Let me explain. As I sat on my motorcycle I felt impressed to do something. My mind searched to verbalize the impression. When I told myself to put my helmet on, that thought coincided with the impression and I knew what I was supposed to do. So what I really did was verbalize the impression in my mind. My mind and heart had the same answer, which is how the Holy Ghost works.

To verbalize our feelings is not so strange either. We do it all the time. For instance, when we're angry we verbalize with angry words. When we're in love and feeling those feelings strongly, we say something like, "I love you." At times we've felt strong feelings about something but find ourselves struggling to say what we feel. This happens often as we try to describe the Spirit.

I believe that in this life most of us will never hear an audible voice when prompted by the Spirit. I do believe it can happen, but more as an exception than the rule. All of us need to learn how to recognize the promptings of the Spirit; that is, we need to learn how it feels rather than how it sounds.

A great description of how the Spirit feels is found in 3 Nephi chapter 11. The surviving Nephites have witnessed terrible destruction of their lands, cities, and citizens by earthquakes, fires, and floods. They have experienced incredible darkness, and at the beginning of chapter 11 they are gathered in the temple area conversing about "this Jesus Christ, of whom the sign had been given concerning his death" (3 Nephi 11:2).

And it came to pass that while they were thus conversing one with another, they heard a voice as if it came out of heaven; and they cast their eyes round about, for they understood not the voice which they heard; and it was not a harsh voice, neither was it a loud voice; nevertheless, and notwithstanding it being a small voice it did pierce them that did hear to the center, insomuch that there was no part of their frame that it did not cause to quake; yea, it did pierce them to the very soul, and did cause their hearts to burn (3 Nephi 11:3).

It should be noted that in this account a voice is heard, but it is that of God introducing his Son, not the voice of the Holy Ghost. However, the feelings that attend this announcement are the feelings of the Holy Ghost. The function of the Holy Ghost is to testify of truth. As a member of the Godhead he testified truthfully that he who was introduced was Christ.

As the account continues, Christ does appear and introduces himself. Then he invites all those present to come forth and thrust their hands into his side and feel the prints of the nails in his feet. The multitude does this, "going forth one by one until they had all gone forth, and did see with their eyes and did feel with their hands, and did know of a surety and did bear record, that it was he, of whom it was written by the prophets, that should come" (3 Nephi 11:15).

We need to do the same. The invitation has been given to come to Christ. Symbolically, we must thrust our hands into the body of Christ and touch and feel for ourselves so that we can bear record of Christ. The invitation comes through the prompting of the Spirit to study the scriptures, to be obedient to our parents, to love our neighbors, to pray sincerely, to honor our priesthood, to honor ourselves with moral cleanliness, to keep the commandments and exercise our faith in Christ. These actions, and many more, will give us experience in recognizing the voice of the Spirit.

I express my gratitude for the voices that have influenced my life: prophets, parents, scriptures, prayer. Without them I would wander in darkness and not be familiar with the joy that attends living the gospel. I am grateful that during my life the Spirit has talked to me through feelings of love, joy, and peace and the knowledge that, if obedient, I will return home to the presence of God.

Todd Murdock *was born in Provo, Utah. He attended Ricks College and graduated from Weber State University in communications. Todd served his mission in Alabama. He loves sports such as hiking and skiing. He has participated in the Especially for Youth program the past three years and currently teaches seminary at Brighton High School in Salt Lake City.*

17

I'LL HAVE ONE CAPTIVITY AND
A LARGE ORDER OF DEATH
TO GO, PLEASE

Allen Litchfield

Harry Houdini was a magician of the early 1900s, the David Copperfield of his era. He performed many kinds of tricks, but his specialty was escaping. He could be wrapped in a straightjacket, chains, handcuffs, and ropes, then sealed in a trunk which was then weighted and dropped into a river. Then, apparently by magic, he would free himself and appear dramatically on shore.

When I was about eight years old I was a Cub Scout. We wore uniforms with loads of badges—if you could see any of the shirt at all, you didn't have enough badges. There was a badge for every activity, skill, or accomplishment in the world. One badge was called House Orderly—to get it you had to demonstrate that you could vacuum, do the dishes, and cook something edible. After several hours of my working on my House Orderly badge, my mother threatened that she wouldn't sign my badge completion form if I didn't stop immediately and go out and play so she could clean up the mess.

Other badges encouraged home destruction more directly, like Fire Starting, Power Tools, Chemical Warfare, Rocket Combustion, and Plague-Carrying-Rodent Pet Keeper. One of the more popular badges was Knot Tying. Remember that in the real world you never need to tie knots more demanding than those for your shoelace, unless you become a deckhand on a sailboat. After you get out of Scouts you just use granny knots for every situation. The Northern Hungarian Adjustable Sheetbend Rotary Knot for Icy Conditions is not something you will be called upon to do after you leave Scouts.

As Cub Scouts, however, we didn't know that, so we practiced lots of knots that we have never used since. One evening after our Cub meeting a few of us were practicing knots in my backyard. The knots themselves were boring, so we made the learning more interesting by taking turns tying each other to a tree. The kid being tied up could pretend he was Houdini, Batman, or the Shadow and had to escape in a certain amount of time. We had miles of rope and knew dozens of different knots, so getting free was quite a challenge. But if we couldn't escape and run to the front yard in the given amount of time, the others would come back and untie the unsuccessful little escape artist.

After we had done this for some time, the other boys tied me up really thoroughly, went to the front yard to wait, then got called home to supper and rushed away, forgetting about me. I was left tied to the tree. As the minutes went on I thought I might die there—perhaps my father would notice my body a week later when he came out to mow the grass. I wanted so badly to be free that I started to cry. When I finally worked my way out of the ropes I rejoiced in a way that I have only a few times since in my life. High school graduation seems like the closest comparison.

As I think back now, I wasn't really in serious bondage that day. I could have called out and someone would have helped me. In fact, I have never been in jail or a prison-like situation, except sometimes when I play the board game Monopoly, but I have seen a few prison movies and I visited Alcatraz once. I think I understand why people would want to get out of jail.

Papillion tells the story of two characters, played by Dustin Hoffman and Paul Newman, who try during the entire movie to obtain their freedom from various prisons. *Robin Hood, Prince of Thieves* begins the saga by showing that Robin and his Muslim companion risk everything to break out of a medieval jail. Matthew Broderick, early in the movie *Ladyhawke,* endures terrible challenges to escape from captivity. In the movie *The Great Escape,* military prisoners develop elaborate and persistent plans to get out of a German POW camp. Jean Valjean, in the book/play *Les Miserables,* demonstrates how much freedom means to him, adding many years to his harsh sentence by continually trying to obtain his liberty. Many Disney animated movies included a character who wants to be free: Aladdin, the Genie, Pinocchio, the ninety-nine Dalmatian puppies, Belle in the Beast's prison, the Tramp in the dogpound, and so on.

Without exception, characters in the stories are going to great lengths to choose liberty. Generally people crave freedom about as much as they do air and food. It seems that few people would choose captivity—even Houdini chose chains only because he knew he could escape. We wonder why anyone would choose to be in captivity, but the fact is that people choose bondage very often. In some ways choosing captivity might be the rule rather than the exception.

The Book of Mormon tells us that we are "free to choose liberty and eternal life, through the great Mediator of all men, or to choose captivity and death, according to the captivity and power of the devil" (2 Nephi 2:27). That seems like a very obvious choice, but it is not as easy as it looks. Men have always tried to keep other men in bondage, emotionally, politically, economically, so that they might have power over them for their own advantage (see Alma 43:8). For example, tobacco companies know that people who never smoke before they turn twenty will almost certainly never start. That is why they want young people to become "exposed to and committed to" their product while in their early teens (that phrase really means captured by an addiction). Men may want to make you captive, but God has always allowed his children the freedom to choose—and to receive the consequences of their choices.

President Howard W. Hunter said: "There has never been a time when man has been forced to do good or forced to obey the commandments of God. He has always been given his free choice—his moral agency." ("Motivations for Good," *Improvement Era,* June 1966, p. 514.) Elder Bruce R. McConkie explained further: "Unless we voluntarily choose good rather than evil, light in preference to darkness, Deity's way in preference to the devil's, it is philosophically impossible to be saved. Salvation is born of freedom of choice. Even if we were forced to believe the truth itself, in all its parts, and were compelled to worship in every proper way, it could not save us, for no agency would be involved." (*A New Witness for the Articles of Faith* [Salt Lake City: Deseret Book Co., 1985], p. 683.)

President Joseph Fielding Smith, like nearly all the prophets of the latter days, spoke on this theme as well:

[The Lord] knew that on no other terms, only through our free agency and the opportunities which would come to us in this life by knowing good from evil when we no longer walk by sight but by faith, would we be able to come back into his presence and be worthy of exaltation. Without free agency we would amount to very little, and the Lord granted unto us our agency, that we might act for ourselves—to choose the good, or to choose the evil if we desire—with the understanding that we would reap the reward of our labors in this life. (*Doctrines of Salvation,* Bruce R. McConkie, comp. [Salt Lake City: Deseret Book Co., 1955], p. 2.)

Now, this agency puts all of us in an insecure position, but one with the potential for exaltation. Some consider this precarious position and decide that "it is better that we should be in bondage" (Mosiah 20:22). Bondage sometimes looks better in the short term. Nephi taught that "it must needs be a good thing for [the children of Israel] that they should be brought out of bondage" (1 Nephi 17:25). I think most of us would agree that liberty for the children of Israel, getting safely out of Egyptian bondage under the direction of the Lord through Moses, was a good thing.

As a child, watching the movie *The Ten Commandments,* I saw the Israelites march past the pyramids heading for their promised land. They looked very happy. I don't remember thinking that they ought to stay in slavery in Egypt, that it would be too hard out in the Sinai desert and maybe freedom wouldn't be worth it. And yet numerous times after they left Egypt things were pretty hard (liberty often is), and the Israelites wanted to go back to the security of slavery in Egypt. They would say: "We weren't as hungry or as thirsty or as threatened back in captivity. Let us return into Egypt." (See Exodus 14:12; 16:3; 17:3; Numbers 14:2–4.) Basically, they were willing to trade their liberty for bread and water, and they didn't trust that God's way would allow them to meet their needs while maintaining their freedom.

Baltasar Gracian said that "freedom is more precious than any gifts for which you may be tempted to give it up" (in *Quotation Finder,* ed. E. M. Dirksen and H. Prochnow [New York: Harper and Row, 1971], p. 77). But people all over the world seem to forget that when things are difficult. The media tells us that there are people in the former USSR who want to go back to the "way things were." They would trade their increasing liberties for more bread and security; having the Berlin wall go down is apparently less important to them than having the groceries in the cupboard go down, even if the shortages are short term. Some former black slaves in the southern states of America weren't all that excited about emancipation and freedom initially; in some cases they chose to maintain a relationship similar to that with former owners rather than venture out into insecurity and the unknown.

These people discovered the advantages of bondage. In captivity there is often familiarity, perceived safety, basic comforts, short-term security, and diminished responsibility. O. Henry tells the story of a hobo (we would call him a "homeless person" today) who had spent much of his life behind bars. It was Christmastime, and the man was out in the cold with nothing to eat. He thought about how relatively pleasant it was in jail and decided to try to get arrested and sent there. He broke a number of laws, openly and blatantly, including stealing, vandalism, and even attacking a police officer with snowballs. Because it was Christmas, everyone kept forgiving him—he couldn't get arrested!

Dejected, he visited a church, and while thinking about his life and praying, he decided to make real changes. He concluded he would stop drinking, get cleaned up, find a job, reestablish relationships with family, and so on. Then ironically, he was arrested for vagrancy and sent to jail.

While few people deliberately try to get arrested, many people willingly enter a captive situation because of its perceived advantages. President Ezra Taft Benson explained one reason why this is so:

> One of the trials of life is that we do not usually receive immediately the full blessing for righteousness or the full cursing for wickedness. That it will come is certain, but ofttimes there is a waiting period that occurs, as was the case with Job and Joseph.
>
> In the meantime the wicked think they are getting away with something. The Book of Mormon teaches that the wicked "have joy in their works for a season, and by and by the end cometh, and they are hewn down and cast into the fire, from whence there is no return" (3 Nephi 27:11). ("The Great Commandment—Love the Lord," *Ensign,* May 1988, p. 6.)

President Benson suggests that many of us don't see the final end or result of the various choices we make. Perhaps we choose captivity because it doesn't look like bondage at the time of the choice. The devil leads us initially with a "flaxen cord" (2 Nephi 26:22) until we are held fast, then with more strong cords, and finally chains keep us in his control.

The most dangerous kinds of captivity are those that are so subtle and sneaky that the prisoner isn't aware of the bars. We have shown that when bars are apparent, prisoners will often devote all their energies to the goal of escape; but if they can't see the bars and are unaware of their captivity, they might live out their lives in blissful bondage.

People live in "all manner of bondage" (Mosiah 29:40) situations. Addictions are one kind of bondage. But people who are held captive by tobacco, liquor, harmful drugs, pornography, and other addictive habits sometimes think or pretend that they are the most free. Some youth brag about how free they are as they drag on their cigarettes outside of your school or partake of some illicit drug at a party. It seems to me they are the least free of all.

It is important that we see these addictions for what they really are in the long run. I remember sitting with a cancer victim who had had a blackened lung removed in surgery a few days before. Because smoking was not permitted in the hospital, we were outside in a bitter Canadian snowstorm. This poor man was huddled under blankets in his wheelchair smoking and sobbing. He kept saying over and over, "Tell all the young people you teach not to start smoking." What a terribly restrictive captivity! Of course, people can be held captive by forms of addictions that are more socially approved but which nevertheless control their behavior. Some people are addicted to eating, to gambling, to an unreasonable amount of exercise and dieting, to soap operas, to daily horoscopes, to shopping and debt, to negative angry music, to video games, and so on.

But addictions are not the only kind of bondage. We can allow ourselves to become in bondage emotionally to another person. Then that person can control us and get us to do things that are not in our best interests or even are contrary to the commandments of God. People who really love you will not try to keep you in bondage. As a bishop I once counseled with a young woman who wanted to repent and change some things in her life. She said it would be difficult to stop breaking the moral code, because if she didn't do what her boyfriend wanted he would stop going out with her. We prayed together that she would be strong enough to break free of this dominating, oppressive relationship and find the joy of liberty and eternal life. If her boyfriend had been holding her in a prison cell in his basement she would have tried to dig her way through the cement with a teaspoon. She would have made an explosive mixture from the year's supply stuff in his basement and blown her way out. She would have done whatever was necessary to escape her physical prison. But she had allowed him to hold her emotionally captive for many months without resisting.

Many peoples of the world are in political bondage. Sometimes, however, we get a distorted view of the world outside our own borders and assume that everyone that isn't exactly like us isn't free. Shortly after our family moved to Utah from Canada, a little girl came up to our youngest daughter Amber in her elementary class. The girl asked Amber how she was able to escape from Canada, and wasn't she delighted to be living now in the only free country on earth.

This little girl, while very patriotic, wasn't very well informed about political conditions in the world. But in some ways she was very much like better-educated older people—while we can see other people in the captivity of sin we might fail to see our own situation clearly. So we could read an article like this one and think, "My brother really needs to read this," or "Wendy is sure in bondage," or "I'm glad I'm not like that." Our own bars will usually be the most difficult to see. We ought to be aware that sin of any kind will make us subject to captivity and death. We surely ought to be concerned about the captivity of others, but our first responsibility is to obtain our own freedom from sin through Christ.

It may be especially difficult to appreciate our own captivity if we are dutifully going through ritualistic motions of living our religion. When Jesus came to the earth he met with a very religious group called Pharisees, who thought they were moving towards their God and heaven by obeying in a mechanical way hundreds of religious rules. They tended to pay tithing, attend meetings, pray, fast, read scriptures, visit the temple, avoid forbidden foods, dress according to their standards, remember the Sabbath, and so on. While Jesus agreed that these things were important, he tried to show them that they had "omitted the weightier matters of the law" (Matthew 23:23). Jesus wanted them to know the full truth of his gospel, for the truth would make them see they had been held captive in a pernicious mind-set, thinking that following a bunch of religious rules would save them, whereas what they needed was to embrace the Lord and his complete plan.

The movie *The Lion King* demonstrates an additional kind of less obvious captivity. Simba, the young lion cub, goes through a traumatic experience that leaves him on his own and feeling guilty. He is befriended by a fat warthog named Pumbaa and a skinny meerkat named Timon. Simba is then introduced to a seemingly wonderful life called in the movie "Hakuna Matata." This problem-free philosophy of life is "no cares, no worries, no responsibilities for the rest of our days." The three friends spend all their time just doing what they want, surviving and eating bugs, grubs, and whatever is easily available. But Simba is the son of a king with great potential and responsibility, and he has forgotten who he is. He is in the most difficult kind of prison, because he thinks he is free. The movie doesn't end there or it would be a tragic film, but many real lives are just this tragic, because young valuable lives are being spent by loafing around eating bugs.

The Book of Mormon tells us of a people who had to "study . . . to deliver themselves . . . from bondage" (Mosiah 21:36). Applied to us, this means that we have to think carefully about how we are in bondage and ways to obtain our freedom. Really God and his plan are the only way out of captivity. Mosiah reminds us that the people of King Noah were brought into bondage because of their iniquities, and why if it wasn't for the Lord they "must unavoidably remain in the bondage until now." But the good news is in the next verse: the Lord "did deliver them out of bondage; and thus doth the Lord work with his power in all cases among the children of men, extending the arm of mercy towards them that put their trust in him." (Mosiah 29:18–20.) I bear my testimony that I have felt the Lord's arm of mercy and that he can and will deliver us if we will reach out with faith to him.

Alma the Younger shares with his son Helaman his stirring testimony of this truth. He says their fathers "were in bondage, and none could deliver them except it was . . . God" (Alma 36:2). Alma then bears his powerful witness of his own conversion experience and the exquisite and sweet joy of liberty from sin through the Savior.

To go back to the story of the Lion King, Simba might just live out his life in this prison of his own making, the life of Hakuna Matata, but a prophet-teacher baboon named Rafiki wakes him up to his possibilities enough that he begins to see who he really is. Rafiki teaches Simba enough truth that he is able to receive a vision of who he is and what he must do. Simba is now prepared to hear the voice of his father and see his face in the night sky. His father, in vision, says to Simba, "You have forgotten who you are. Look inside yourself, Simba. You are more than what you have been. Remember who you are . . . you are my son . . . remember who you are . . . remember . . .". Simba now has the knowledge, courage, and commitment to escape from captivity and choose liberty and the plan of life (called the Circle of Life in the film).

I bear my witness that you are sons and daughters of God. He has prepared for you a wonderful plan of liberty and eternal life. The greatest joys you will experience in this life will come as you follow that heavenly plan. I urge you to avoid captivity and rejoice in the Lord's great plan.

Allen Litchfield is an instructor of religion at BYU. A former bank administrator, he has served as a seminary teacher and principal and as an institute instructor and director. Brother Litchfield enjoys reading and such sports as horseback riding and white water rafting and canoeing. He and his wife, Gladys, are the parents of six children, the oldest of whom is serving a mission in Japan.

18

OUR SPIRITUAL NEEDS— ACTION, NOT WORDS

Randall C. Bird

Several years ago I was reading a book called *Leadership* by Elder Sterling W. Sill. In his book he mentioned several principles that were essential in order for a person to develop spiritually. I would like to borrow the seven traits he listed as the focus for my message.

To Believe

While teaching seminary in Idaho, I received an assignment in the Church Educational System to move to Salt Lake City and work in the Church Office Building. That was a difficult decision to make, as many of you who have moved can understand. To adjust to a new area, leave our friends behind, find housing, send our children to a new school—these were just a few of the concerns that needed to be answered. In the midst of all of this I was asked to travel to Guatemala and Mexico and observe how seminary and institute classes were being taught in those countries. While there I was also to conduct some training meetings with the early-morning teachers of those countries.

I was excited to travel to those countries and meet with the good Saints who were teaching there. My excitement soon turned to fear as I was told it would be nice if I would deliver a message to these Saints in their native tongue (Spanish). I was in shock! The only Spanish I knew consisted of the word *si*. How could I ever deliver a message to these good people in their own language?

There's a great verse of scripture in the Book of Mormon in which Jesus says, "And whatsoever ye shall ask the Father in my name, which is right, believing that ye shall receive, behold it shall be given unto you" (3 Nephi 18:20). I decided that I would exercise faith and attempt to prepare the message. I only had a week before I was to leave for these countries, so if this was to happen, I knew the Lord was going to have to help.

My first step was to write my talk in English and give it to a friend to translate into Spanish. That took a couple of days. Next, I gave the talk to someone to record it in Spanish, on slow speed, so that I could learn to pronounce the words. I received the tape the day before I was to leave for Guatemala. I practiced giving my speech in Spanish only to hear laughter coming from the offices of my fellow workers who spoke fluent Spanish. Well, to get to the end of the story, I gave the talk—in Spanish—to those good Saints in Guatemala and Mexico. Though far from perfect, my Spanish was understood. Many of the Saints said thank you for my making such an effort to communicate with them. There was a good spirit present in the meetings, and I was grateful for the opportunity given to me. Certainly, one of the greatest needs we all have is to develop more faith in our lives. The ever-present need to believe is a trait critical to our spiritual development. It's interesting to note that the fourth article of faith tells us to not just have faith but to have faith in Jesus Christ.

To Belong

Shortly after moving to Utah, I noticed that my junior high school age daughter was having great fears as her first day of school approached. Many concerns occupied her mind. Who would be her friends? How would she do at a new school? And of course, the big question, Who would she sit by during school lunch? She had the great fear that no one would invite her to sit by them at lunch, thus leaving her all alone in some corner. Her prayers daily were for someone to ask her to eat lunch with them.

Well, the first day of school arrived and she left for the unexpected. How grateful I was when I heard that a group of girls invited her to join them for lunch! She came home from that first day of school so excited and relieved. This group of girls had helped her belong. She was now a part of that school and had some friends to associate with.

The sad thing is that not all have that good an experience in their lives. There are those who attend our schools with maybe thousands of youth walking by them daily, and yet they feel all alone. I'm reminded of a young man who, as he was growing up, developed differently than most other boys. His physique was abnormal. His sternum (chest) didn't sink in like most; instead it poked out, giving the appearance of a chicken breast. So since he looked that way, many called him by that name—chicken breast. He hurt each time someone referred to him as that.

On one occasion while he was eating his lunch at school, a bigger, stronger boy walked by him and called him that name. The young man stood and said, "Please don't call me that." The other boy replied, "Oh, and what are you going to do about it?" The two began to push each other back and forth until the bigger boy dropped the other to the floor with a blow to the head. Most of the onlookers failed to help the downed boy, but one Good Samaritan stayed behind to help him. He drove the boy to his home, where his family attended to his injuries. You see, in this case not only did the young man feel that he didn't belong, but others went to great lengths to ensure that he didn't.

The story ends on a sad note. This young man, who had been ridiculed during most of his life, finally made a decision to leave life early. He ended his life one day while the rest of his family was at church. One seriously wonders if the story could not have ended on a more positive note had others been willing to help him belong. Truly, the Savior said, "Inasmuch as ye have done it unto one of the least of these my brethren, ye have done it unto me" (Matthew 25:40). We need to feel that we belong.

To Behave

The third of our spiritual needs is to behave. In his remarkable address King Benjamin taught the need for all of us to "watch yourselves, and your thoughts, and your words, and your deeds, and observe the commandments of God" (Mosiah 4:30).

When first hired by the Department of Seminaries and Institutes to teach seminary, I was asked to teach in a small Idaho farming community. Upon our arrival in this area, my wife and I were asked to speak in a sacrament meeting. We were excited at this opportunity to address the youth and adults of the community in which we would be teaching. At this time in our lives we had been blessed with three children. Our first two girls were twins, and then we had another daughter about a year and a half after our twins were born. That meant we had three children under the age of two. It made life rather interesting around our home and occasionally at church.

The Sunday when we were to speak arrived, and we went through the usual chaos of getting everyone ready for church. With the three little ones Sundays could become quite hectic. Clothes, food, hair, bathrooms, and time all tended to be major players in the Sunday experience. Anyway, we survived all of this and made it to the church on time for our speaking experience.

We wanted to make a good impression in this first-time meeting with everyone. I had packed Cheerios, M&M's, and other items in the hopes of helping to keep the children quiet as my wife spoke (it should be noted that I have since learned there are much better ways of teaching reverence in church meetings than using food). My wife spoke first and did an excellent job. I used up all of the Cheerios and other items during my wife's talk and thus managed to keep the children fairly quiet. It now became my turn to speak.

After speaking for only a few minutes, I noticed my children beginning to make a disturbance toward the back of the chapel where they were seated. All the food items having been used up, my wife had nothing left with which to keep them quiet. She proceeded to move them out of the seats and into the aisle, where she hoped to "herd" them out of the chapel and into the foyer.

The chapel was of older origin and the back area sloped downward towards the front at quite an angle. My wife had moved the children into the aisle, but suddenly the twins got loose. Both of them now came at full speed down toward the pulpit at the front, where I stood delivering my message. With the third child in her arms, my wife was in quick pursuit. She reached the twins and was able to grab one and head out the side door of the chapel. That left one mischievous child near the light switches. Suddenly, lights in the chapel began to blink off then on in a continuous "strobe light" effect. I was humiliated. Should I leave the pulpit and snatch this child away, or should I hope that my wife would soon appear and rescue me? While I was musing upon these questions, the side door opened and in rushed the other twin with my wife in pursuit. I decided that now I would have to leave the pulpit and help my embarrassed wife. Just as I started to do so the first twin reached the piano, which was situated in front of the podium. Something less than beautiful music was soon filling the chapel. At that point, my wife, like a mother hen, was able to gather up both twins and take them out the side door. I returned to the pulpit, where I finished my talk.

On the way home from church that day my wife and I had a long visit evaluating the experience. We decided then and there that one of our main desires as parents would be for our children to behave in this life. We met as husband and wife and set up a strategy for teaching our children the importance of good behavior and reverence. I'm so grateful we did that. To this day I encourage all young people I can to see the need to behave. Truly, as King Benjamin taught, we need to watch ourselves, our thoughts, our actions.

One of the great thrills of my life was hearing a high school referee tell me, the football coach, how well behaved the young men on our team were during the football game. Can you appreciate how that made me feel? Many of these young men had learned that life was more than just a game, for which I was grateful.

To Love

The first great commandment is to "love the Lord thy God with all thy heart, and with all thy soul, and with all thy mind . . . and the second is like unto it, Thou shalt love thy neighbor as thyself." The Savior went on to teach that "on these two commandments hang all the law and the prophets." (Matthew 22:37–40.) All our human relationships hinge on our degree of love for God and his children.

I continue to marvel at the many acts of love that are being demonstrated daily by our Heavenly Father's children: The volunteer seminary and institute teachers who daily devote so much of their time and efforts to teaching; the many priesthood and auxiliary leaders who love the Lord and have answered the call to serve our Father's children; the thousands of youth who are faithfully showing their love of God by following him and his appointed leaders. Frequently I ask groups of youth that I speak to, to raise their hands if they are wearing a CTR ring. Large numbers of them raise their hands. Then I ask a second question, "How many have with you the Strength of Youth pamphlet?" Again, many hands go up. Though I know carrying a pamphlet or wearing a ring doesn't always translate into actual obedience to God's commandments, it does show an effort being made to be valiant in our testimonies of Christ. For Christ truly said, "If ye love me, keep my commandments" (John 14:15).

Another example of the need to love is found in the love of country. Several years ago the United States was involved in a war in the Persian Gulf. Patriotism was at a high in this country. Pledging allegiance to the flag took on a deeper meaning, as did the singing of "The Star-Spangled Banner." I remember attending a girls high school basketball game where the national anthem was sung prior to the tip-off. Due to the war in the gulf, and my love of this country, tears filled my eyes as the a cappella choir, in perfect harmony, sang the national anthem. The Savior's words came to mind: "Greater love hath no man than this, that a man lay down his life for his friends" (John 15:13).

To Be Loved

Not only should we give of our love to others, but it is nice on occasions to be a recipient of that love from others. Now, having worked with youth for quite a few years, I note that they sometimes have strange ways of saying they love someone.

Frequently, toilet paper seems to be involved in saying they care. I find it amazing that young people come together and say, "Who do we love? Let's go toilet paper their home." Now, isn't that strange? We love you—here, clean up this mess. Or there was the time that students brought every leftover Christmas tree from our community to my home and stuck them all in the snow around my yard. It looked like a forest. Birds came from miles around to lodge in my trees. All of this because my students loved me.

Now, remember, my last name is Bird, and as such I have had a lot of jokes directed my way over the years. One of the most original jokes occurred one evening when my doorbell rang and I opened the door to find a small bird hopping around on my doorstep with a note tied to its legs. I picked the bird up and unravelled the note, which read, "Hi! I'm a relative, can I spend the night?" You see, we all say we love people in many different ways. I would hope that a simple note, an act of service, or even the spoken word will find their way into a regular part of young people's lives.

To Serve

King Benjamin said, "When ye are in the service of your fellow beings ye are only in the service of your God" (Mosiah 2:17). One of our greatest spiritual needs is to serve. We truly come to love those we serve. On occasion when things may not be going well at home, I try to think of ways that we could serve one another in our family. If we can only do that, it seems life gets better. We become less selfish—we think more of others than of ourselves.

The Aaronic Priesthood and Young Women leaders are constantly thinking of ways that the youth could be of service in their homes, wards, and communities. Service projects, though striking fear into the hearts of some, are often the very thing that young people remember with fondness and talk about for years to come. Those combined activities, or even just single acts of service, seem to bring that inner peace that so many are seeking.

To Succeed

A great football coach, Vince Lombardi, once said, "Winning isn't everything—it's the only thing." I don't know that I exactly agree with the saying, but in the gospel of Jesus Christ everyone can be a winner. We all want, and can attain, eternal life. The spiritual need to succeed is exemplified in those two words. We want not only to live with the Father but also the type of life that he has. The scriptures teach that if we will continue to be faithful to our covenants and endure to the end we will have eternal life, which is the greatest of all God's gifts (D&C 14:7). May we all believe, belong, behave, love, be loved, serve, and succeed in the gospel of Jesus Christ.

Having taught seminary for over twenty years, **Randall C. Bird** *is now manager of seminary curriculum in the Church Educational System. A sports enthusiast, during his high school years he was named to the Idaho all-state teams in football and track, and he has been a high school coach in both sports. He also enjoys fishing, collecting sports memorabilia, reading, and being with his family. He and his wife, Carla, are the parents of six children.*

19

WHERE ARE YOUR FEET? IN THE GOSPEL OR IN THE WORLD?

Mitch Huhem

The following story has the potential to bring a great change to your life, one that will make you better, happier, and stronger than ever before. The reason is that if you follow through properly you will be completely grounded, rooted, settled, and established in the gospel of Jesus Christ.

It all began some years ago in a place far away from my birthplace; for I was born in Brooklyn, New York. My family was Jewish and very dedicated to that religion. Although both my parents were raised in New York, my father had the overwhelming feeling that he must not raise his family in New York but rather in sunny California. We sold everything we had and took off to the west in a blue Ford van. The trip was long, but I was young and did not mind it at all.

We made many stops during the trip, but it finally ended and we arrived in sunny San Diego. We got into our new home, and all was going normally until it happened! A knock came at the door. A lady on the doorstep said she was our neighbor and then handed us a loaf of bread. My mother quickly said no and assumed that the lady must be crazy, and that either the bread was poisoned or there was a knife inside. You see, in Brooklyn neighbors do not bring you bread unless they are trying to get rid of you. So although the lady tried to explain her good intentions, my mom did not accept the bread.

Persistence and endurance does pay off, however. That neighbor was a member of The Church of Jesus Christ of Latter-day Saints, and through her great efforts and the help of God we joined the Church. This experience was miraculous. It took months and many almost incredible happenings, but when we did finally receive baptism we were very strong and faithful.

I began to develop a firm testimony of the gospel, which from the beginning involved a dream of serving a mission. I wanted to be like the missionaries who had baptized us and taught us the gospel of Jesus Christ. All I wanted to be was a true disciple of Jesus Christ. At least, that was what I thought and said.

Years later I was awarded a full academic scholarship to Brigham Young University. This was going to be my first visit to Utah, and I was very excited about it. I needed to go for at least a semester and get straight As so I could put my scholarship on hold until I came back off the mission. While at BYU I had people tell me that I should stay the whole year and then go on my mission. I could not do that because my birthday is in March, and if I waited for the whole year I would not be done until April. I so badly wanted to be a disciple of Christ that I could not stand to wait any longer than I had to. My desire was so strong that I was planning to send in my papers at the earliest possible time so I could perhaps get into the Missionary Training Center before my nineteenth birthday in March.

While at BYU, I was paying all my expenses and also was planning to pay for my mission. But I was short on funds to do it all, and to help me my mother made a thousand Book of Mormon crossword puzzle books for me to sell and shipped them to me. I was now ready to go sell them all for five dollars apiece. I put on my churchgoing clothes and prayed to know where I should start. Why not the BYU bookstore? There were thousands of BYU students, and they all needed to know the Book of Mormon better.

At the bookstore I quickly found the buyer, then talked with her and explained how these Book of Mormon puzzle books would help all the students get a better and stronger testimony of the Book of Mormon. She listened as I poured forth my singleminded desire to serve God as a missionary and to leave BYU early and get into the MTC before my nineteenth birthday; and I told her again how this puzzle book would help everyone at BYU—and the store could have it for only five dollars a copy. She looked interested, told me to wait a minute, and left.

As I waited I prayed that she would buy. Sure enough, she came back with an order form. Inwardly I was so excited, but I calmly said, "So how many would you like?" I was thinking that with so many students she might order a thousand, or at least a couple of hundred. As I looked to her for her response to my question she softly said, "I think we will take ten."

I almost fainted. I turned blue, lost my breath, and could barely try to keep that smile—you know, the smile you display when inside you really are crying. I had nine hundred and ninety more books to sell. I walked out to the car devastated. Soon I was on my way again. The only thing was, I did not know where I was on my way to. Then I felt the prompting to go to the Missionary Training Center, which was close at hand. I had planned to first go there when I went through as a missionary, but the idea of two thousand missionaries all needing to know the Book of Mormon better made me so excited. This was it! I straightened my tie as I got out of the car, and I walked into the building with my hands filled with the Book of Mormon crossword puzzle books. The lobby was empty—in fact not a soul was in sight in any direction. I walked down the hall until I found an open door, but there was no one in the room. There was an open door, across the room, however, so I pushed it more open; and inside that next room was a man eating lunch. He looked up at me, and after a few moments he said, "Weren't you sitting halfway up, left-hand side of the Provo Tabernacle last week at the Missionary Preparation Class?" I told him yes, that was me, and again I began to tell my story—my desire to serve the Lord on a mission . . . leave BYU early . . . get in before my nineteenth birthday . . . how excited I was; and I was going to be obedient, dedicated, and enduring. Then I gave him the good sales pitch on the Book of Mormon crossword puzzle books. I let him know how the books could help all the missionaries get better testimonies of the Book of Mormon—and they cost only five dollars each.

He looked through the book and told me it was good. But it was not in his power to buy the books, he said, and I would have to go to Salt Lake City to make any sale to the MTC. A little discouraged, I said, "So who are you?" He replied, "I am President Pinegar, the president of the MTC."

I jumped up from my seat. "You are the president of the MTC? My name is Mitch Huhem. I can't wait to come into the MTC, and I am even leaving BYU early so I can get in before my nineteenth birthday."

President Pinegar moved his chair from behind the desk and rolled right up to my chair—so close that our knees where touching and he was looking right at me. Right then he said something and taught me a lesson that changed my life for the better and may change yours also.

At this point I need to quickly tell you something about myself, about my appearance. Having grown up in San Diego, I taught swimming lessons; I was a lifeguard for the city of San Diego; I worked in construction; and I surfed. I had a jeep and, yes, you can imagine—my hair was long, surfer style; I wore shorts and tank tops; and I looked like a pretty wild person. From my appearance you could not tell I had a strong gospel testimony and a desire to serve God. You see, I loved my hair. I thought I looked great with hair like that, and I had planned on not having it cut until the day I went into the MTC. I am serious; I had it all planned that five minutes before getting into the MTC I was going to have it cut, and no sooner.

Now, remember, my heart was good and dedicated, and it didn't matter that my hair was like that—or did it?

Come back with me to the office of President Pinegar, where we were knee to knee. He looked straight into my eyes and asked me this question: "Brother Huhem, do you want to be a missionary?" I immediately said "Yes," and then I explained again with much conviction that I was leaving BYU early to get in before my nineteenth birthday and all I wanted to be was a true disciple of Christ.

I did not understand when President Pinegar asked again, "Do you really want to be a missionary?" I didn't know what to say or what he meant by that. Then it happened. He said it. "Brother Huhem, if you want to be a missionary, *why don't you look like one?*"

I couldn't believe my ears. I didn't know what to say. Didn't he understand my heart and my inner intent? It didn't matter how I looked outside: it just mattered how I was on the inside. How could he not understand that? How could he say that to me?

As these thoughts raced through my head, President Pinegar stood up and walked over to the door. He opened it, faced the empty hallway, and pointed towards the hall. "What is that?" he asked.

I replied, "That's the hall."

"No," he said, "that represents the world."

He then pointed inside to his office and asked me what that was. I told him it was his office. He said, "No, this represents the gospel of Jesus Christ."

I watched as he put one foot outside and one foot inside the doorway. He then took a big step, and—*Boom!* The doorpost cracked him in his bald forehead and stopped him in his tracks. He turned his head to me and said, "When you have one foot in the world and one foot in the gospel of Jesus Christ you cannot progress." As he kept pushing against the doorpost with one foot in and one foot out I could clearly see that no progress was or could be made. I felt the power in his voice when he said, "You either have both feet in or both feet out."

My heart was pumping faster and more powerfully than ever before. I felt there were angels in the room. Still standing in the doorway, President Pinegar began to tell me about Jesus Christ. In the power of the Spirit he bore testimony of the Savior's life, his death, his resurrection.

I loved Jesus Christ so very much. You see, before we were converted to the Church my family and I had not believed in Christ, for the Jewish faith believes the Messiah has not yet come. But I knew that Jesus Christ lived and I felt so much love for him, which is why I had the intense desire to serve a mission. And now I felt the love of Jesus Christ filling the room. I was crying, the president was crying.

President Pinegar left the doorway and again sat next to me, knee to knee. As he looked in my eyes I felt it coming. He said, "Brother Huhem, if you want to be a missionary, why don't you look like one—*today?*"

And now the Spirit told me that, yes, although I had not thought of it in that way, I did have at least my toe on the side of the world. I was keeping it there for as long as I could. This was not right, for Jesus Christ did everything for me and made it possible for me to be happy. I must have both feet in the gospel *today.* I knew that meant getting my hair cut right now.

Wow! This was going to be tough! What was I going to do? What was I going to say to my friends? How was I going to look? I stood up and the president gave me a strong hug. We wiped our tears away and I immediately went down the hall to the pay phones, where I called a girl who cut my hair. "Mary can you please cut my hair today?"

She said, "What for? You just had me do it."

"I know," I told her. "But Mary, I must get my hair cut today, right now!"

As I drove to her I picked up some of my roommates, and they asked where we were going. I said we were going to Mary's and I was going to just get my hair cut. It sounds funny now as I look back, but everyone knew how much I liked my hair. It was important to me.

When we arrived at Mary's house my heart seemed to be going triple speed and my tongue was tied. I didn't know what to say or how to say it. How can I be doing this? I'm crazy. People are going to think I am crazy, ugly, and weird.

The door opened and Mary invited us in. My friends sat down in the living room as I was directed to the kitchen. I sat down on a cold kitchen chair, and Mary put her famous plastic cape around my neck to protect my clothing from the falling hair. As she did so my friends were talking and not paying attention until Mary asked me a question that I did not answer. She said, "Mitch, how do you want it?"

I sat in silence. No words were coming out. My chest was hurting and I was having trouble breathing. Then it came out. I blurted, "Give me a missionary cut!"

My friends immediately went ghost white, and Mary thought she had misunderstood me, so she asked again, "How do you want it?" I said again, this time with more confidence and surety, "Mary, give me a missionary cut!"

"You mean a real missionary cut, short and all?" she asked. I nodded my head, yes. I could see my friends all breathless. They knew about my going to get my hair cut just five minutes before going into the MTC as a missionary.

As Mary put her big scissors behind my neck and underneath my long hair and squeezed the blades together, I felt it. A big chunk hit the floor. Boom! I shut my eyes as she moved to another big chunk, then another, and then another. For a while I felt just the squeezing of scissors and the dropping of big chunks of my hair. Then Mary got into it with enthusiasm and began to really chop and chop and chop. I could tell she was having fun, but I dared not open my eyes for fear of seeing the result. With each chop I felt part of me falling. Luckily she soon finished and I was left sitting on the chair with my eyes tightly squeezed shut.

"Here's a mirror so you can see how it looks," Mary said. I kept my eyes shut but I lifted my hand so she could give me the mirror. I took it and began to open, just a little, one of my eyes, and I began to see. "Ouu Ouch! Ouu ouch!" Yes, she had given me a total missionary cut. I mean, it was all gone and then some. And I looked at myself I thought three things. First: Mitch, your head feels real light. Second: Mitch, you look pretty ugly. Last: I feel fantastic.

I felt so good that I wanted to jump up and down. I didn't care what anyone thought, for that day I did something that forever changed my life. I took my foot from the world and put both feet in the gospel of Jesus Christ. My heart was filled with gratitude and I felt a great happiness. More so than ever before. That day I dedicated myself 100 percent to God. I decided to be 100 percent obedient in all things and be a true disciple of Jesus Christ.

The joy I felt because of this cannot be explained by words but can definitely be explained vividly by your actually experiencing it for yourself. I mean, right now close your eyes and think sincerely and deeply of what you are doing, saying, wearing, thinking, or not doing that results in your keeping one foot in the world. With the Spirit, think of what it may be. What could you stop wearing, thinking, doing, or saying that would allow you to put both your feet firmly in the gospel of Jesus Christ and feel the incredible joy that I experienced.

You may think this is hard, and you may be saying, "Come on, Brother Huhem, I'm not ready," or "I really don't want to yet." But remember these words of Jesus: "No man can serve two masters; for either he will hate the one and love the other; or else he will hold to the one, and despise the other. Ye cannot serve God and mammon [worldliness]." It may seem tough because we might be concerned about what others may think of us. On this point Paul wrote: "For do I now persuade men, or God? or do I seek to please men? for if I yet pleased men, I should not be the servant of Christ." (Galatians 1:10.)

I know you are an incredible person. In the experience I have recounted I felt the Spirit and it caused me to do something I had not realized I ought to do—something I had thought was not necessary. As a result, I testify now that nothing can give you more happiness, joy, and peace than putting both your feet firmly in the gospel of Jesus Christ. Decide this day whom you will serve. Joshua said it best: "Choose you this day whom ye will serve; . . . but as for me and my house, we will serve the Lord" (Joshua 24:15). Have the courage to make right now the decision that will lead to the happiness, peace, and joy that comes from being 100 percent a disciple of Christ. You are fantastic, and I know you can do it!

Mitch Huhem *loves serving and helping others. He has given fireside talks at the Missionary Training Center and taught self-improvement seminars and workshops at BYU, and is currently the founder and president of E-Z Plan Corporation. He was a high school wrestler and one of the youngest Eagle Scouts in America. He has been married since May of 1993 to his wife, Patricia.*

20

FROM BOYHOOD TO MANHOOD?

Curtis L. Jacobs

I was in the seventh grade, my first year in junior high. Two of my friends and I decided we wanted to "sing" a song at the yearly North Davis High talent show. We had practiced several times. (We were young and stupid and didn't know how bad we sounded.) We were ready to shine.

The day came, and the show began. Finally our turn came to show the junior high what men we were. We hadn't realized that our high, squeaky, little-boy voices hadn't made the complete change to a deep, resonating, manly voice. There's no way around it—we sounded like Alvin and the Chipmunks. When we were done, through the snickers you could almost hear an applause. What made things worse was that after we were done a girl from the seventh grade sang a "solo," and her voice was lower than ours. I couldn't wait to get the talent show over with, hide the rest of the day, and then get home.

But then home only reminded me that I was still a "boy." I'd answer the phone, and the person on the other end would say, "Oh, little girl, is your mother home?" (I hated being called that!) I wanted to say, "I'm not a little girl; in fact I'm a young man, and if you can't tell the difference . . . well. . . . " But I never did. My voice would probably have cracked anyway.

I remember seeing boys in the ninth grade; some of them were already shaving. The girls would look at them and say something like,

"He's such a man." Me? I thought a lot about shaving, even picked up my dad's shaver a time or two, just to get into practice.

How many times had I heard (and have since even told my own boys), when I'd get hurt and start to cry a little, "You're not a baby anymore, so why are you crying?" There's even a song with the line, "Big boys don't cry, big boys don't cry."

For guys, and I'm certain for girls (I have a thirteen-year-old myself now), growing up can be wonderful and yet painful too. We see things all around us giving us images of what real men and women look like, how they act, even how they talk.

So, when does a boy become a man? When does a girl become a woman?

The world certainly seems to suggest certain things "men" can do. I remember a friend of mine who had always been a good example. One day (we were in about fourth or fifth grade) he decided he wanted to try to impress an older girl he kind of liked. He was a really tall but skinny guy. He wanted to show her what a man he was, so while riding on the bus one day, loud enough that she could hear he let out one "big" swear word. He was sure this would let her know he was "manly." She glared back at him, and without saying anything her face, her eyes, her whole expression told him she wasn't impressed in the least. It was almost like she was saying, "Why don't you grow up?" The very thing he thought would make him look older had backfired. You could tell that as she looked at him she was saddened by what he had said. She had thought he knew better.

I have a daughter in middle school. Several of the "boys" (and even many of the "girls") trying to act "mature" are still doing the same thing today. They think it's so "rockin' " to know every swear word in the book and then use them. But is real manhood or womanhood knowing how to use an incredibly impressive vocabulary made up primarily of *four*-letter words?

Other things seem to be "rites of passage." Remember when you approached (if you have had) your sixteenth birthday? I didn't turn sixteen until my junior year in high school. I wasn't even allowed to take driver's training until the beginning of that year. That meant I wouldn't even be able to get my driver's license until January of my junior year. It was the pits. Most of my friends were already driving around; they could go on dates. Me? Oh, sure, I could have gone up to somebody (after turning sixteen, but before I got my license) and said something like, "Would you like to go out with me? I could ride my bike (yes, a regular bicycle) over to your house and pick you up." I thought about it, but something told me I'd be better off not trying.

Finally I got my license. Now I was a man, right? I had more freedom, more space to cover. I was certain now that ladies would see my incredible five-feet five-inch frame (I'm now a huge five-feet-seven), watch me driving my mom's 1973 Duster with its 225 engine (it could go from 0 to 60 in about a minute and a half), and say, "What a man!"

One "boy" in a high school where I taught seminary used to come up to some of the young men who were members of the Church and basically tell them they weren't men until they'd had a beer or two or three. He really thought manliness was found in a beer can. Evidently one of the young men finally told him: "Boys trying to look like men have to drink. Real men don't have to drink; they're men without having to prove it by drinking."

I'll never forget running into a guy who had been on our high school basketball team; we both graduated the same year. I hadn't seen him in years. We weren't really friends back then, but the years between then and now seemed to make that unimportant. He finally asked, "Curtis, you didn't drink did you?"

"Well, no."

"Well, I did—a lot," he said. "Boy, was I stupid!"

The world has other rites of passage from boyhood into manhood. One time I bought a forty-five record. Now, for you of the CD age, records used to come in "album" size—a full cassette worth, or a forty-five with just one song on each side. (Your mom and dad perhaps have a few of these ancient items hanging around, or maybe even have them embossed on the wall.) I was listening to it one day at home. All of a sudden my mother said, "Curtis, do you know the words to that song?" I probably did, but it was one of those moments when I thought it was best to act like "I'm not sure what you're talking about." The song was about a young guy who happened to meet an older woman. They began talking, and finally they went down to the beach. The song then said something like, "I went to the beach a boy, but in the morning I returned a man." Oh, really?

Recently some "boys" (trying to be men) thought it would be "manly" to see how many young ladies they could get to be immoral with them. (I'm sure they didn't call it that.) They even kept "score" as to the number of "conquests." Is manhood based on "scoring" with some young lady? Much of what you see in the movies or on TV seems to say that a real part of "growing up" is to experience what the Lord has said must be reserved until marriage. This supposed "rite of passage" is one of Satan's greatest lies.

One day, while reading in the Book of Mormon, I was intrigued by how Nephi described himself. When you think of Nephi physically, what do you picture? I'm sure most of us see a huge, good-looking hunk, "large in stature," right? (thanks to all those Arnold Friberg pictures we've seen).

The scriptures do seem to bear out the fact Nephi wasn't a little boy. But would you notice something. Look at 1 Nephi 2:16, "I Nephi, being exceedingly young, nevertheless being large in stature, and also having great desires to know of the mysteries of God, wherefore, I did cry unto the Lord." Now, remember, the book of 1 Nephi comes from the small plates of Nephi, which weren't written until about thirty years after the Lehi group left Jerusalem (see 2 Nephi 5:28–31). In other words Nephi, in looking back on his own life, saw himself in 1 Nephi 2:16 as "exceedingly young, nevertheless being large in stature." Is he telling us he was really just a big kid? Maybe. But notice how he describes himself just a couple of chapters later in 1 Nephi 4:31: "And *now I, Nephi, being a man large in stature. . . .*" See the difference? Sure he's still big, but now he sees himself as a man. Why the change? I'm certain it didn't have anything to do with his voice!

If we look at what happens between chapter 2 and chapter 4 we might get some idea of what happened to change him from "boy" to "man." As far as Nephi's age between chapters 2 and 4 is concerned, there doesn't appear to be much time distinction. In chapter 2 Nephi is trying to find out for himself whether what his father Lehi has said is true. He prays, and later he records, "[the Lord] did soften my heart that I did believe all the words which had been spoken by my father; wherefore, I did not rebel against him like unto my brothers" (1 Nephi 2:16). Is part of becoming a man (or woman) trying to gain a testimony? Is it believing what the prophets have said to us? I'm certain Nephi would see it that way.

Now the brothers are told to go back and get the plates of brass from Laban. Laman and Lemuel, that "depressing duo," as Elder Neal A. Maxwell calls them ("Murmur Not," *Ensign*, November 1989, p. 82), do what they do best—they "murmur." Have you ever noticed that word? It seems it could go on and on—mur . . . mur . . . mur. . . . Why do they murmur? "because they knew not the dealings of that God who had created them" (1 Nephi 2:12).

They decide to draw lots, and Laman gets to go. (I'll bet he was excited about that.) Laban kicks him out of the house. Laman comes back and tells the others, "Sorry, guys, I tried." They try again, this time bringing their gold, silver, and precious things from home in an attempt to buy the plates. But Laban tries to have them killed, and they quickly conclude it's probably not best to stick around any longer.

Laman and Lemuel then get mad at Nephi and Sam, so they start beating them with sticks. (This is not an approved Church activity, by the way.) The Lord sends an angel, who convinces them to knock it off. The angel tells them they must go back again to Jerusalem, where the Lord will deliver Laban into their hands.

Now, you'd think real men might believe in an angel; it's kind of hard not to admit he showed up, right? But what do Laman and Lemuel do? Right . . . mur.

They go back to Jerusalem, but only Nephi goes inside the city wall. Now comes a big step to becoming a man. "I was led by the Spirit, not knowing beforehand the things which I should do (1 Nephi 4:6). Is part of manhood knowing something about the Spirit and when it's telling you something?

Nephi finds Laban drunk. The Spirit commands him to kill Laban, for "*the Lord* hath delivered him into thy hands." At first Nephi can't do it. Again the Spirit directs him: "the Lord slayeth the wicked to bring forth his righteous purposes. It is better that one man should perish than that a nation [like the Nephites without the brass plates] should dwindle and perish in unbelief." (1 Nephi 4:13.) Finally, Nephi obeys the voice of the Spirit. Can you imagine how certain Nephi must have been that it *was* the Spirit speaking? Can you imagine him saying, "Oh, hummm, I wonder if it's really the Spirit. Oh well, I'll take a chance and kill him anyway"?

One of the greatest steps in becoming a man, a real man, is in being willing to follow the Spirit, to follow what's right regardless of what might happen later. As the song says, "Do what is right; let the consequence follow." Had Nephi been caught after killing Laban, he could have been put to death himself. But, being a man, he finds the courage to follow the Spirit.

Nephi then is able, with the help of Zoram the servant of Laban (not to mention his constant following of the Spirit), to carry out the Lord's original command—he obtains the plates of brass.

I love the story of the young man who went to a video party with several of his friends. He'd made a promise not to see any inappropriate movies. Well, the video went in, and suddenly he realized that it was a movie his own family had heard was good, but when they started watching it at home they decided it wasn't appropriate and turned it off. Well, now, here's a interesting situation. Most of these guys were members of the Church. The movie wasn't even R-rated, so what's the big deal? He was just getting to know the guys in the neighborhood; he didn't want to look stupid. But he had to make a choice.

He got up and went over to the mother of that home and simply said: "I don't think I should be seeing this movie. Could I just go somewhere else until it's over?" The mother was so impressed that a day or so later she called his mother to apologize for having that movie shown at the party. She told this boy's mother how impressed she was that he would stand alone in doing right, as he had. I love that boy. You see, that boy was my son Joshua, and he was then only eight years old. Now, don't think that that decision suddenly made him a man, but it certainly was a step in the right direction.

Early in his life Nephi had become a man by doing the right things for the right reasons. He had learned to pray, to listen to the prophets and obey the voice of the Spirit. On the other hand it appears that neither Laman nor Lemuel ever really became a man. Not long before Lehi dies, he is trying to talk with Laman and Lemuel. He pleads with them: "And now that my soul might have joy in you, . . . arise from the dust, my sons, and be men, and be determined in one mind and in one heart, united in all things." (2 Nephi 1:21). While physically big (after all, they do whale on Nephi and Sam) they never "arrive" at true manhood.

In the October 1994 general conference President Gordon B. Hinckley told the story about a football player, during the Rose Bowl game, who picked up a fumble only to head in the wrong direction. Finally one of his own teammates had to tackle him or he would have made a touchdown for the other team. (How dumb would you feel? You would have simply shown how "bright" you are in front of potentially millions of people). "He had lost his sense of direction in a moment of stress. His mistake cost his team a victory." (See "Don't Drop the Ball," *Ensign*, November 1994, p. 46.)

Young people of the Church, make sure you're headed in the right direction; don't allow the world to get you "lost" in a moment of temptation.

One of my favorite scriptures is Helaman 3:29. In it you'll find the phrase "the man of Christ." To become men and women of Christ is to follow a different path than the one outlined by the world.

President Joseph F. Smith said: "To the young man or the young woman who is at a loss to know what to do, among all the various teachings that are extant in the world, I would say: Search the Scriptures, seek God in prayer, and then . . . you may defy the philosophies of the world. . . . The wisdom of men is not to be compared with them." (*Gospel Doctrine* [Salt Lake City: Deseret Book Co., 1977], p. 128.)

Each of you can follow that path and become men and women of Christ. You can do things every day that will help in this journey. Read those scriptures every day, for we are told, "and whoso would hearken unto the word of God, and would hold fast unto it, they would never perish; neither could the temptations and the fiery darts of the adversary overpower them unto blindness, to lead them away to destruction" (1 Nephi 15:24).

Don't forget to pray. Even when you make a mistake, don't forget to pray. As a bishop, I'm constantly having young people come to me who have stopped praying because they have done something wrong. Yet praying is one of the most important things they could do to get back on the path. Always remember Nephi's counsel: "If ye would hearken unto the Spirit which teacheth a man to pray ye would know that ye must pray; for the evil spirit teacheth not a man to pray, but teacheth him that he must not pray. But behold, I say unto you that ye must pray always." (2 Nephi 32:8–9.)

Some of my best moments occur when I take time to pray earnestly, to really let Heavenly Father know my feelings, my hopes, my fears. He will always hear; however, we must be willing to listen and obey. If we would pray sincerely every morning, asking our Father in Heaven to help us through the day, to help us resist temptations when they come, and then check in with him again each night, there would be less sin in our lives, less mistakes made by each of us.

In my many years of dealing with, talking to, and having fun with youth, I've noticed how important good friends are in keeping on the path. Choose your friends wisely. Elder Robert L. Backman tells of a young man, a football player, whose testimony was strengthened because of faithful friends. As they were about to graduate from high school, soon to be separated from each other, they decided to have one "last fling" together. Not the usual type of fling, either. These valiant future leaders in the Church met on the grounds of the Provo Temple. Late that evening these twelve young men bore their testimonies of the gospel and expressed their love for each other. (See "Youth's Opportunity to Serve," *Ensign*, July 1973, p. 84.) What friends! What men! (By the way, this *is* a Church-approved activity.)

A young man in my ward got up in sacrament meeting and told that during high school he decided he'd rather not go to church. Each Sunday one of his friends would call him about an hour before church and ask, "Are you coming?"

"No, not this week."

The caller and other friends would still get this guy involved on the weekends, doing good things together with them. Finally came the Sunday morning when the voice said, "Are you coming to church?" And before he could answer, the voice continued, "We'll be over in about thirty minutes to pick you up in whatever you're wearing." Click.

He decided he might want to be ready. They picked him up that morning and each week after that. Now, years later as a returned missionary, he said, "You know, if it hadn't been for those guys, I'd never have served the Lord on a mission." Then in front of everyone he called the one young man by name and said, "Thanks, thanks for being a true friend."

President Ezra Taft Benson, speaking at Ricks College, said: "Make no mistake about it—this is a marked generation. There has never been more expected of the faithful in such a short period of time than there is of us." ("In His Steps," *Ensign*, September 1988, p. 2.) In order to accomplish what is expected of you, you must become true men and women of Christ. Follow his example. Pray daily, read the scriptures and apply them in your life, choose your friends wisely. Above all, with faith in Christ, choose to follow the Spirit; it will help you make wise and righteous choices.

Oh yes, and as President Spencer W. Kimball would say, "Do it now."

A popular speaker, **Curtis L. Jacobs** *has worked for the Church Educational System programs since 1979. He has taught seminary and institute in Arizona, and has spent the last few years teaching at Utah State University. He and his wife, Jolene, are the parents of four very active children. Curtis is a racquetball fanatic and loves* Les Misérables.

21

HIGHWAY TO HEAVEN: THE SCRIPTURES WILL STEER YOU RIGHT

Vickey Pahnke

I am not mechanically inclined. You can ask anyone who knows me and they will tell you, "Vickey is not good at figuring out how machines work." Actually, they would probably say, "Vickey is pathetic when it comes to running machines," or something like that. Understanding mechanical things, directions, and all that, is a little beyond me.

Let me illustrate. A couple of years ago my family purchased a new answering machine. It was really cool and seemed simple to operate. I was excited to get it hooked up and record our message, so I decided to do the dirty work. Pulling the machine out of the box, I hooked up little things here and there, plugged it in, recorded the outgoing message, and waited for someone to call. (Around my house—with one husband, one wife, and four children—you don't have to wait long for the phone to ring.)

Maybe two minutes later came the familiar ring . . . two rings . . . three . . . four . . . the announcement didn't kick in! Several calls later I realized we had a malfunctioning machine. Stupid thing! It didn't even work! A little later the rest of the family got home. I shared my misery with them, lamenting over our dumb machine.

Then someone asked if I had read the instructions. Hmmm . . .

"You mean the ones that came with the answering machine?" I hadn't. So we pulled out the manual, read over the directions, and made a couple of little adjustments. Guess what? The machine worked after all!

I was a little embarrassed. This wasn't an intimidating device. To make it work, I just needed to be properly familiar with the manual. Sometimes I am "overly" anxious or "under"-focused, and don't take the time to *read the instructions*. I just need to *do it!* . . . dig in, read, study, and learn to understand whatever device is new to me.

Read the instructions. This is important in the way we run our lives, too. The holy scriptures are like a divine "owner's manual" from the one who knows and loves us best, and can be our instruction book—full of pertinent information, details, safeguards, and guidelines to help us function properly. Paul the Apostle wrote to Timothy: "From a child thou hast known the holy scriptures, which are able to make thee wise unto salvation through faith which is in Christ Jesus. All scripture is given by inspiration of God, and is profitable for doctrine, for reproof, for correction, for instruction in righteousness: that the man of God may be perfect, throughly furnished unto all good works." (2 Timothy 3:15–17.)

Unfortunately this most important of all books is often overlooked or underappreciated. We have a source of power and knowledge and understanding that can answer our questions, lift our spirits, "fix" whatever ails us, steer us through the difficulties—but we *have* to *read*. We have to familiarize ourselves with the instructions.

If any of you has a brother or sister on a mission, you can bet that when you send a letter your missionary savors it. He will read it, smile as he pictures you, and appreciate your help in supporting him. He or she would never put that letter, unopened, on a shelf and ignore it for days or weeks. Would you? Sad to say, though, we might set our scriptures, our "letters from home" (I remember Sister Ardeth Kapp calling them by that name), on a shelf, and neglect to read, to appreciate that which could help us the most.

What is your favorite movie? How many times have you seen it? I'm sure some of you have returned time and time again to view your favorite film. When I have asked this question at EFY or youth conferences, some say they have seen a particular movie as many as two dozen times! That's a lot of times. I have to admit that one of my favorite films is *Clue*. Sometimes I watch the movie all the way through following just one character, and I notice things I have missed before. I remember dialogue and setting and many details.

Now another question: How many times have you read the scriptures? At this point, if we were standing face to face, some of you would beam and look right into my eyes as you say, "I read and study the scriptures every day." Others of you might hang down your heads and admit you rarely take time to read these heaven-sent words. We all want to return home, to make it safely through our life's course, right? So let's turn to the source book, let's take time to read and reread these scriptures so that we have a better chance of staying on the road that will lead us home, remembering dialogue, settings, and details we may have missed.

"As [a person] thinketh in his heart, so is he" (Proverbs 23:7). If thoughts make us what we are, and if we are aiming at becoming like Christ, we need to be thinking Christlike thoughts. The more familiar we are with the Savior's word, the more we are able to think those thoughts, and the easier it is for us to move in a positive direction.

Let me illustrate the need for our reliance on our scriptures and touch on some ways that will help you in your study of these sacred words.

Do you know what it's like to be really hungry? At such a time it's hard to think about anything other than eating. Sometimes you might feel so "starved" that you will pass the hunger point and, though you are weak, you will not realize that you need food—even when it is within your reach.

Spiritual hunger can affect your spirit just as physical hunger does the mortal body. All of us have a need to nourish our spirits, to feed that hunger. But we might not realize how important it is to pick up the scriptures to fill that need. If you have ever felt "lost," or distressed over a problem, and then have resolved your difficulty by reading from the "owner's manual," you can relate to these lines from a wonderful poem written by S. Dilworth Young called "Know That I Am!"

> *Youth speaks:*
> I do not seek thee, Lord,
> In highest hill or
> Valley low.
> The cloudy sky
> Or stars which light the night

Are not thy face
I know.
Thou art the Son of God.
I thirst to touch thy garment hem,
To hear thy voice,
And to rejoice in thy
Calm presence, Lord.
A growing youth, I seek
To know thee and to
Hear thy word.

The Lord whom ye seek speaks:
My will is in my word:
Written in the rock
With iron pen,
Or graven in the
Gold of ancient plates.
My will is spoken
Unto men
Through prophets.
My voice speaks through
These chosen ones
Who write my words
On the page for all to see.
And reading them—
Given by my power
In the hour
Of their need—
They are my voice
To you,
Young friend,
And reading, you can say
That you have heard my voice
This very day.
(*Improvement Era*, April 1969, p. 49.)

Wow! As we read the scriptures, we hear the voice of the Lord and
he instructs us according to our need! No one else knows us so well.
The combination of personal prayer and understanding of the scriptures
allows us access to his advice.

Here are a few ideas to help you in your study:

1. Decide to *do it*. President Spencer W. Kimball had those two words on his desk. Maybe we should keep them in our hearts. If you say, "I'll try," it is easy to bail out for other activities. And Satan is really good at providing other activities to fill your time. Plan on thirty minutes a day, ten minutes, a chapter, whatever you can do to *begin* . . . just do it . . . every day.

2. Pray for help. I really mean this. Father wants to help you in your needs, but you have to be serious enough to ask. He will honor your righteous request and assist you in your plan.

3. Get your family involved. In some families scripture study is a given; in others it is foreign. Is it possible that you could lovingly (with the emphasis on "lovingly" here—not "naggingly" or "self-righteously") increase the desire for the rest of your family to study? It will be great to share the good experiences you are sure to have if the whole family becomes involved.

4. Get rid of distractions. You guys, the media is both a blessing and a curse. We don't even comprehend how negatively we can be affected by music, movies, or TV. And even if a show is wholesome and wonderful, if it takes your scripture study time it becomes a distraction. When you *are* reading, turn the TV or radio off and concentrate fully. Allow the Spirit to help you in this peaceful, quiet time.

5. Keep at it. If you miss a day, pick up tomorrow and add a little extra time. Soon your study will become a wonderful habit.

6. Imagine yourself in the scenes of the scriptures. What would *you* have done had you traveled with Lehi? Would you have recognized the Savior as he taught? How would you have managed at Winter Quarters?

7. Every day, talk about what you read. Whether to a family member, seminary teacher, or close friend, verbalize your feelings and thoughts. This will help you keep those spiritual whisperings in your conscious mind, and you will be apt to "travel" more carefully, keeping more Christlike thoughts.

If there is a "highway" to heaven, it isn't a super-wide one. The way is narrow and the gate is strait (see Matthew 7:14; 2 Nephi 31:18; D&C 132:22). Although it is well marked and properly defined, many fail to follow the road signs.

I love this quote from President Ezra Taft Benson: "The world would take people out of the slums. Christ takes the slums out of people and they take themselves out of the slums." ("Born of God," *Ensign*, November 1985, p. 6.) The responsibility is placed squarely on our shoulders.

As we allow the Savior to help us, we can rise above this murky, dimly lit world. Immersing yourself in the scriptures can transport you, at least momentarily, out of your difficulties, your hurts. You will feel the protective influence of the Holy Ghost to safeguard against unrighteous, dangerous influences or situations. You will be lifted to a higher place where you will feel more peaceful, more positively directed. Christ heals broken hearts, tends burdened souls. His love radiates from the words in the scriptures. Those words are for you.

I know of a ward that maybe is much like your own. It has a huge youth group. Jenni, a beautiful young woman, is a member of this ward. She loves the gospel, loves to get involved in activities with her friends, and is pretty much like you and me. Except that Jenni is blind. There are sometimes activities planned that she cannot participate in, and others that make her feel awkward or left out.

On one occasion the young women planned a special activity with their fathers. In preparation, an obstacle course was set up in the cultural hall, complete with tires, sawhorses, and so on. The object would be for the girls, beginning at one end of the hall, to make it to their fathers at the other end. One by one, each receiving instruction from her dad, they would move through this course. The equalizing factor was that each girl would be blindfolded. Jenni needn't feel left out, and it would be fun for all participating.

It must have been a hilarious night. Fathers were getting frustrated, daughters were getting agitated and falling all over the place. On the sidelines the others were shouting instructions and contradicting one another. Laughter filled the hall. Not one girl was getting through the course.

Jenni was last up. A quiet came over the hall as she stood ready for her turn. The other girls had whipped their blindfolds off. Jenni would not have the luxury of seeing this room when the games were over.

Her father quietly said: "Jenni, listen to me. Don't pay attention to what anyone else says, just listen to my voice. I will guide you through."

Jenni began her trip. Among those watching, eyes widened in amazement as she carefully maneuvered. Once or twice she stopped, got her bearings, had her dad repeat his instructions, before she moved forward. Jaws dropped as Jenni continued—never falling, never losing her composure. In time she made it to the other end and into the arms of her father, who swung her around as the others clapped and encircled the "winners."

"No way!" "Incredible!" The girls crowded around Jenni, amazed at how easily she had gotten through the course that they had failed to navigate. "How did you do it?"

"It was easy," Jenni said. "I just listened to my father's voice and did what he told me to do."

Jenni taught a powerful lesson that night.

My young friends, this life is a real obstacle course. There are unexpected turns and pitfalls everywhere. People on the sidelines often shout instructions, many times simultaneously giving different directions. It gets confusing. It is treacherous. And it is easy to fall.

Jenni gave us the advice we need. At the end of this life's course our Father in Heaven waits with outstretched arms. We must remember to listen to his voice and do what he tells us to do. Listening to the voices all around us cannot ensure our safety. But if we tune into his instructions we can make it back home. And primarily his voice speaks from the pages of the holy scriptures.

Open the scriptures. Nourish your spirit by reading and studying. Listen to his clear instructions as they teach you in the Bible, the Book of Mormon, the Pearl of Great Price, and the Doctrine and Covenants. Further strengthen your safety net by reading the words of our present-day prophet in the Church magazines.

We are members of Christ's church. He has made available to us an owner's manual. The more familiar we become with his teachings, the less we will experience malfunction. As we read, it's not that the obstacle course becomes easier; but *we* become better at listening for divine direction, learning to steer clear of detours that would throw us off course.

Just *do it*. The scriptures are for you. They are letters from home—given to help you return, and written with love.

Vickey Pahnke *is originally from Virginia. She studied musical theatre at BYU and works as a songwriter, producer, and vocalist. She is currently completing a master's degree in communication. She has been involved with many of the BYU youth programs—such as Especially for Youth, Best of Especially for Youth, and Outreach Youth Conferences—and has been a speaker for the Know Your Religion and BYU Education Week series. She is also on the board of directors for the Utah Special Olympics. She and her husband, Bob, are the parents of four children.*

22

AS FOR ME,
I WILL LIVE MY DREAMS

David L. Buckner

The day was cold but the skies were clear and I could see the canyon leading to Provo, Utah, in the distance. Heber City was just below me, and the snow-capped mountains of the high Uintahs were clearly visible in the distance. The mechanical sound of the Sultan ski lift was muffled by a gentle breeze. The anticipation felt by all in our group was put on hold for a moment as we paused on a snowy ledge at ten thousand feet to look at the world beneath us.

As I stared off into the distance my mind wandered back to the first time I ever flew in an airplane. I remembered the takeoff and could almost feel again the thrust of the engines push me back in my seat and the nervous butterflies in my stomach. I remembered looking out the window of the airplane and seeing the cars and houses quickly getting smaller and smaller. The world seemed so small, and the cities became a mass of lights and tiny miniature buildings. As the sun set, the clouds below looked like a thick snowy blanket. I remember wondering if all those people down there knew I was flying over their houses and schools. Could they hear the sound of the airplane overhead or sense the many eyes watching them from the windows of the plane? If they knew I was there, would they have come out to wave? Or would they have continued with their daily routine, consumed in their own lives?

It wasn't long before my daydream was interrupted by anxious skiers calling me from my perch atop the world. I took one last glance at the majestic valley below and the pristine mountains in the distance and left my private paradise to descend the rocky mountains below. But this time I left with a new vision of this place we call home and a greater understanding of what this "life" thing is all about. In a few precious moments above it all, I had once again been reminded of my Father, who loves me enough to give me time on this earth to prove myself worthy of all he has to share with me. And I had experienced an urgency to live life to its fullest like never before.

While speaking to a group of sixth graders, I asked them how many knew what they wanted to be when they grow up. Almost every hand went up. "I want to fight fires," exclaimed one young lady. "I want to be an actress," declared another. A voice from the back called out, "I want to be a forest ranger." And still another proclaimed, "I want to be a professional skier." That very same afternoon I stood before my graduating college seniors and posed the same question: "What do you want to be when you grow up?" The responses were very different. One commented, "I just want a job." After a moment of silence, another student spoke up. "I just want to make enough money to be happy." I couldn't believe what I was hearing. Could it be that sixth graders were better prepared to face the world than my graduating college students?

Time and time again I have asked this question, and every time the result is the same. The older and more experienced we get, the less we remember the view from the top of the mountain. We start at the top at a very young age with dreams and clear visions of our future. We see the majestic valleys below and the pristine mountains in the distance. We have visions of success and dreams of being great leaders and noble warriors. We promise ourselves we will always remember that gorgeous view from the top. Then we begin our trek down the mountain. Little by little we lose sight of the mountains in the distance. We forget the billowy clouds, the blue sky, and the miles and miles of rolling hills and valleys. And by the time we have gone down the hill of life's experiences, we have completely forgotten the view from the top and too often we have forgotten our purpose in life. Why is this so? How is it that in a few short years we forget our goals, abandon our dreams, lose sight of the vision of greatness, and give in to the temptation to just "make it through life"?

While reading the Book of Mormon one evening I began to understand why this happens. We forget that our timing and arrival on this
earth was all a part of "the great plan." The prophet Alma tells us that
we have been "called and prepared from the foundation of the world
according to the foreknowledge of God, on account of [our] exceeding
faith and good works . . . called with a holy calling" (Alma 13:3). We
are further told that we have been given "a land of promise; yea, even
a land which I have prepared for you; yea, a land which is choice
above all other lands" (1 Nephi 2:20).

Wow! We have been called to be here now! And with that calling
we have been given a land of promise, choice above all other lands!
Rarely had two passages prompted me to think so much about the
whole plan of life. As I continued to think about "the plan," I began to
wonder, Why do we find ourselves giving up, quitting, or settling for
less than our calling promises us? We are free to choose. We live in a
choice land. We have been called and prepared since before the foundation of the world. So why do we give in? Why do we find ourselves
saying, "I didn't have any choice," or "someone made me change my
mind"? How do we lose that mountain-top vision and forget our divine
nature and eternal destiny?

My young friends, it is called *adversity*. And simply speaking, adversity is the plan of the adversary. Satan would like nothing more than
to see each and every one of God's children overcome with adversity.
His desire is to defeat the plan of salvation by defeating us. He would
like to keep each of us from returning home to live again as a complete
family with our Father in Heaven. To accomplish his goal, Satan tries
to cover our eyes by telling lies. Often he will tell us foolish stories to
blind us and deceive us. He places obstacles in our way—such as sin,
immorality, jealousy, anger, and hatred—which make us forget the
beauty of life we saw from atop the mountains. But we must learn to
listen to the spirit of greatness, not to the beguiling discouragement of
the adversary. We must not let him take away our divine nature, our
royal heritage, and even our lives. For he will try. He will surely try.

The story is told of two young boys from a small western town.
They were great friends and would often spend their time playing by
the railroad tracks, hoping to see the trains forge their way through
town. From time to time the trains would stop for refueling, and the
boys would climb on board and pretend they were going to ride the
cargo cars to the big city many miles away. As the conductor would

sound the whistle they would jump from the train and watch until it rounded the bend in the distance.

One day, while waiting for the noon train, the boys noticed a small wooden shack nestled in the trees beside the tracks. As they quietly approached, the shack door opened and an old man called them. "Hey, boys, where ya goin'?" Slowly the boys turned to see the toothless old man, his skin blackened with dirt. "Come here and visit for a time," he said. The two boys looked at each other, shrugged their shoulders, and started toward the old man.

The three sat on the ground in front of the shack and the old man began to talk. "I seen you boys playin' here ever day. Ain't you afraid the train's gonna freeze ya to death?" The boys looked at each other with a puzzled look, then shook their heads. The old man continued. "It's been said people die when the train comes through town. Ya see, those cargo cars are refrigeration units. All it takes is five minutes in them and ya gonna be dead. I hear even the people in the big city die when the train comes through town. They try to unload it and they all freeze to death." The old man could see the fear on the faces of the boys as he began to laugh. As his laughter rang in their ears the boys jumped to their feet and ran all the way home, vowing never to go near the shack again.

Several months passed and the boys forgot the old man. Once again as the train's whistle was heard in the distance the boys would run to the tracks to see the big locomotive pass through town. As the train would stop, the boys would climb the ladders and again pretend they were going to ride the train to the big city many miles away. But one day the engineer didn't blow the whistle before the train started to pull out. The boys, on board, felt the train move and saw the ground start to rush by as the train picked up speed and the door slammed shut. It was too late to jump from the moving train now. They would have to wait until it stopped, then start the long trek home.

A few minutes passed then one of the boys remembered the old man's story. He turned to his friend and began to panic. "We're going to die," he said. "Remember the old man by the tracks—he said these refrigerator cars will freeze us in five minutes."

Both boys began frantically tugging at the door, but it was locked. They screamed for help and pounded on the door, but no one could hear them over the sound of the train and the blowing of the whistle. Finally, they both sat down and began to cry. "This is it," they said. "The old man was right. We are going to freeze to death."

What had been a warm July day now felt suddenly cold. Little by little the boys started to shiver and shake. They could feel the cold entering their bodies and slowing their breathing. "I can feel the cold already," said one boy. "I can't feel my toes or fingers," said the other boy. With each passing minute they continued to recount the old man's story time and time again. They remembered how he said some people would freeze in their tracks. Others had been frozen with ice so thick they took days to thaw. Again and again they commented on how cold it was getting and how tired they were feeling. Finally they turned to each other, closed their eyes, and fell into a deep slumber.

The train finally stopped and the engineer began to open the cargo doors. Little by little the cargo was unloaded from the train. A shout came from the livestock car: "Get a doctor quickly! I got two boys down here." When the doctor arrived he found two lifeless bodies huddled together. He quickly began to work his medical magic on the boys. One boy was still breathing, but the other could not be revived. It took the doctor three hours to awaken the breathing boy, but finally he opened his eyes and spoke. "What happened?" he inquired. Then he remembered the train and the cold and his friend. "Did I die?" he asked. "Because the old man said we would freeze to death in five minutes if we got on the train."

"Freeze to death?" the doctor asked. "How can you freeze to death in a cattle car? Son, that train was 45 degrees if not 50. You can't freeze in 50-degree weather."

The horrible laughter of the old man on the tracks filled the young boy's memory as tears filled his eyes. The cold, the shivers, the freezing toes—all these had been created in the minds of the two boys. They had believed the foolish story of an old man. They had listened to his haunting warnings of death and had believed his words. And now only one remained to see the foolishness of their mistake.

My young friends, the world is filled with people like the old man. People who spend their lives spinning stories of fear and failure. People who have not experienced the realization of their dreams. People who do not understand their divine nature or their own personal worth. They are frequent users of the four letter word *can't*. They are quick to judge and slow to learn. They possess an attitude of failure and compromise. They gave up trying to succeed long ago and want nothing more in the world than to sow seeds of failure for you. They are found among your friends, at your schools, even in your homes.

They do not see the world from the mountain tops but choose to live in the valleys below. Often they will tell you a dream is foolish, a goal is worthless, and a plan is hopeless.

This is not true! We are wonderful spirit children of a loving Father who has given us unlimited opportunities to grow and develop according to the righteous desires of our hearts. However, we are given one chance to be here on earth, one chance only. And during our stay here we are to do all we can to prepare to meet God. "For behold, this life is the time for men to prepare to meet God; yea, behold the day of this life is the day for men to perform their labors" (Alma 34:32). We are not here simply to pass time or to listen to the foolish stories of those who would like to see us fail. Because we can never relive a day on earth, we must learn to live each day as if it were our last.

In order to make it home to Father we must work every single day to overcome the discouraging influence of the adversary. To help you understand this mission may I share with you a new vision of life; one that I believe will help you through the challenges the world will place before you and assist you in fulfilling your greatest expectations for your earthly experience. For we have been promised that "he who doeth the works of righteousness shall receive his reward, even peace in this world, and eternal life in the world to come" (D&C 59:23).

Challenge No. 1: Dare to Dream

Earth life is made for dreamers. In my daily planner I have a section called "goals and dreams." I started many years ago writing down my dreams and goals. It began as a list of things I wanted to be when I grew up. Like every young man, I included the type of wife I wanted to marry as well as all the things I was going to do when I became a father. From time to time I would sit in a church meeting or in a class at school and get an idea to do something or be someone. Sometimes it was as small as "try out for the debate team" or as big as "be a U.S. Senator." As soon as the idea came to me I would open my planner and write it down.

One of the first dreams I had came at a very young age. I remember taking my first ski lesson at the age of six. The class was big, and many of the kids complained about the cold, the food, and anything else they could think of at the time. Our ski instructor was so patient and helpful that I decided that day I wanted someday to be a ski instructor. I went home that night and wrote it in my diary. The dream stayed in my diary for nineteen years until I went to college.

One day, while choosing my classes for the next semester, I came across a class offered for students wanting to become professional ski instructors. My heart raced as I remembered my nineteen-year-old dream. I might have forgotten the dream if I hadn't written it down. But there it was, a chance to chase a dream born long ago by a young kid who still had vision. I enrolled in the class, and after fifteen weeks I passed my professional ski instructor certification. For the last eight years my dream has become a part of me as I have been teaching skiing to young kids who are still dreaming, dreaming of their chance to make a difference in this world.

Some dreams are achieved on the heels of heartache. I met a young lady at a youth conference I attended who taught me the true meaning of chasing a dream even when all the adversity in the world was on her doorstep. As a young girl she had always been very popular with her friends. It wasn't easy as she would get up very early each morning to put hot curlers in her hair and prepare herself for the day. She had many dreams, but most of all she wanted to visit the beautiful Hawaiian islands at some time in her life.

The day I met this girl she looked quite pale and her hair was short and blonde. She sat next to me and told me of her life. A year previous she had been diagnosed as having cancer. The disease had overcome her body and had robbed her of her long, beautiful hair. Like the old railroad man, many had told her that she would never be able to fulfill any of her childhood dreams. She began to feel the cold of bitterness come into her life as the door shut on her dreams. Operations, radiation, and chemotherapy did not remove the disease. Her family and friends began to see her life slip away. She too saw nothing but a deteriorating body and miserable spirit. The dream was all but gone.

But something strange happened. As her physical life began to fade, her spirit began to receive nourishment from a heavenly source. Her bitterness was replaced with an incredible desire to serve others, to give back what she had received in her short life, and to live out her dreams. When her body was telling her to remain in the valley of bitterness and anger, her spirit was telling her to climb the highest peak and enjoy life to the fullest.

It was at this time she decided to fulfill her greatest dream to see the beautiful Hawaiian islands. Somehow, this young lady forgot what the world was telling her. She no longer listened to the voices inside telling her to quit, give up her dream, forget her goals. Amazingly, as she began to dream again her health got better. Her strength came back, and finally, with the financial help of a local charitable organization, she was able to take her lifetime dream trip to Hawaii. With her parents along as tour guides, she saw a part of the world she had always dreamed of but until recently never believed she would visit. She swam in the warm waters of the ocean and took a boat ride on the open seas, all the time living her dreams to the fullest.

Several months later the cancer ran its course and the body lost its fight with the disease. But not before this young lady had lived her dream. My dear friends, you must dare to dream! Dare to dream! Dare to dream!

Challenge No. 2: Aspire to Be You

Aspire to be what you want to be in righteousness, not what others think you should be. Too often we listen to the voices of the "old railroad man" before we listen to our own promptings. We have been promised, "If thou shalt ask, thou shalt receive revelation upon revelation, knowledge upon knowledge, that thou mayest know the mysteries and peaceable things—that which bringeth joy, that which bringeth life eternal" (D&C 42:61).

What an incredible promise that is, to be given personal revelation upon personal revelation! But how often do we use this "revelation" thing? And how do we know what revelation is? Before I went on my mission I told my bishop I wanted to come home from my mission with a knowledge of what having the Spirit felt like and an understanding of how I could get and use personal revelation in my life. It didn't take me long to learn how having the Spirit felt, but I really had a hard time understanding what revelation was and how to identify it in my life. Unlike so many returned missionaries I looked up to, I had never heard any voices or seen any visions on my mission. From time to time I began to wonder whether I would ever get a personal revelation, or whether I was not worthy of this promise. When I returned home from my mission, I talked again with my bishop.

I'll never forget our conversation. I walked into his office and sat down across the desk from him. Bishop Minnoch looked me in the eyes, and with a smile he said, "Welcome home, Elder Buckner. Sit back, relax and tell me about your mission." I didn't know what to say. I didn't know whether he wanted to hear about my mission, about the people, or about me and my own spiritual development. So I just blurted out: "Bishop, what does it mean to get personal revelation? On my mission I had two goals, one to learn what personal revelation was and how I could teach by its power. And the other goal, to learn what personal revelation was and how I could get it. I had a great mission, bishop, but I honestly don't know what revelation is or how to use it in my life."

I was sure Bishop Minnoch was going to send me back to Ecuador right then so I could learn what revelation was all about. Much to my surprise, a smile came across his face. He sat back in his big bishop's chair and paused before speaking.

He began, "Elder, do you have a list of goals?"

"Of course I do," I replied.

"Do you keep a daily journal?" he continued.

"Every day of my mission," I insisted emphatically.

Then the bishop looked directly into my heart and bore testimony of personal revelation. He said: "Elder Buckner, as you return home tonight I want you to get on your knees and speak with your Father in Heaven. Ask for guidance in understanding what personal revelation is all about. Then I want you to look at your goals and objectives as a young missionary. As you recall them to your mind, set them aside and begin reading your journal." He continued: "I bear testimony to you that you have indeed received personal revelation in your life. I bear witness that as you recount the experiences of your mission you will see the hand of the Lord revealed in all that you did and in many of the decisions you made." The bishop continued to counsel me as he taught me of the sweet influence personal revelation can have on our lives; that it does not have to come as a voice in the dark or a hand on the shoulder, but it often comes as a feeling of excitement or a motivation to do something which can have no other explanation.

As I did as counseled, I found that my life had been constantly guided by personal revelation. Time and time again I could not otherwise explain why certain events had occurred or why I had chosen certain paths in my life. My only explanation was the influence of personal revelation.

Many of us have received personal revelation but too often listen to the foolish advice of others. Such was the case with one of my dearest friends in his pursuit of his dream. Ever since I can remember, Blair wanted to be a pilot. When we were in first grade we would often play kickball in the school yard as the planes from the nearby air force base would fly overhead. The game would stop from time to time and Blair would give us a lesson in airplane types. "That's an F-16," he would declare. Then he would proceed to give us a short history of the plane and continue with an encyclopedic explanation of its construction and manufacture. All through our school years together Blair always talked of being a pilot and flying a Boeing 747, the world's largest passenger aircraft. He had a big picture of a 747 cockpit in his bedroom and he could identify every button and switch on the panel.

But as time wore on, so did the dream. Blair served a mission and returned to go to college, where many of his friends and roommates were not as impressed with aviation as Blair was. Often the roommates' discussions would turn to plans for the future, goals, careers, and how each would make his fortune. As Blair would talk of being a pilot, the conversation would turn away from his dream. Comments like, "Blair, why don't you go to law school or business school so you can make a real living?" or "why do you want to be a pilot? that's just a glorified bus driver," were often heard around the dinner table. Little by little those around Blair tried to suffocate the dream, and little by little Blair lost some of his childhood vision.

Upon graduation from college, Blair began the search for his lifetime pursuit. He studied for and took exams to enter law school and business school. After applying to a number of schools, he began to see that law school or business school was not where he wanted to be. Sure, many of his friends told him he could really make lots of money if he was a lawyer or the president of a company, but that was not part of his dream. For several years he had worked at various jobs, yet never really enjoying the path his friends had told him he should take. He had no passion, no real love for the path he had chosen. Sitting behind a desk was not a part of his vision of life.

With his car packed completely full, Blair left his home in Utah and drove to Las Vegas, Nevada, in search of a job with an airline. Having not had the experience necessary to pilot a commercial aircraft, he took a job at a ticket counter of a small airline. Each day he would watch the pilots come and go and would dream of the day when he would be doing what they were doing. With the money he made be bought time on an airplane, clocking hours as a pilot to get as much experience as he could so that someday he could fly the big jets. All his spare time and many of his holidays were dedicated to his dream, a dream that was almost killed by the "old railroad men" around him.

This last year I received a call from my friend in Las Vegas. He proudly reported that he had got the job! He was no longer selling tickets or trying to satisfy angry customers, and no longer watching the pilots come and go. He was now flying the plane. Twenty-four years after his dream began, he was now living it. Six years out of college he was now really doing what he had always wanted to do. He was a pilot!

Each one of you must always aspire to live your dream. Listen to the spirit of revelation given to each and every one of us, and remember the promise, "If thou shalt ask, thou shalt receive revelation upon revelation, knowledge upon knowledge, that thou mayest know the mysteries and peaceable things—that which bringeth joy, that which bringeth life eternal" (D&C 42:61).

Challenge No. 3: Never Say Can't

Never allow the world to tell you that you "can't" do it. Just like the old railroad man, there are many people out there who will tell you foolish stories of failure and gloom. They would make you believe that your dreams are foolish wishes and that you should settle for the simple life of an ordinary person. They are wrong. They do not see the world from the mountain tops but choose to saunter in the valleys below.

One day while walking through a park in London, England, I felt prompted to call my wife to see how she was doing and to let her know of my plans for the evening. As I entered a telephone booth to place the call, I noticed a small pamphlet wedged between the pages of the telephone directory. I pulled it from its hiding place and began to read it as I placed the call. The front page read, "The Society of West End Theaters Presents Its Annual Producers Workshop." I continued to read the announcement: "Twenty-five applicants from the theater industry will be chosen to attend this five-day conference focusing on how to produce Broadway theater. Conference mentors will include Cameron MacKintosh, producer of *Les Miserables, Cats,* and *Phantom of the Opera,* and Andrew Lloyd Webber, composer and producer of *Cats, Phantom of the Opera, Joseph and the Amazing Technicolor Dreamcoat.*" The list went on.

My heart started to race as I read the announcement. I thought back to the first time I had ever gone to the theater. As a child I had gone with my parents to see a local production of the musical filled with the song "To Dream the Impossible Dream." It was at that moment I had fallen in love with theater. I had always dreamed of becoming a producer of Broadway theater, where I could revive the old musicals and give life to new masterpieces.

As I finished reading the announcement I picked up the phone and called my wife. I was shaking a bit as I read the final words and asked, "So what do you think?" She paused for a minute then responded: "I think it's great! But it does say that only twenty-five will be selected and that each applicant should have some experience in the industry." It was then I started to think a bit more realistically. She was right. I really had no experience and they were only going to take twenty-five people. Maybe I shouldn't even bother to apply.

I hung up the phone and I said a little prayer. I sat in the park for a couple of hours and thought it all through. No voices came to me and I didn't feel any great impressions. But I began to think through all the options. At first all I could hear was that "old railroad man" spinning his stories of failure and loss. After all, I had no experience, and this was London, not some small town in Utah. I was just a dumb kid from Ogden, Utah. How could I ever meet the masters of Broadway theater and learn a business in which I had never been involved? It says only twenty-five will be selected. What makes me think I would ever have a chance? And it continued.

Then something strange happened. Like turning on a light I began to reverse all those questions and foolish feelings. I started to think, Why can't I apply? What have I got to lose? What if they say no, is that so bad? And what if . . . what if I actually do get into the conference? What then? Maybe I could become a producer of great musicals and wonderful stage plays. It was at that moment I began to feel great feelings of motivation and excitement. The exact feelings my bishop had told me about. Those feelings of personal revelation. All the feelings of "can't, can't, can't" left me. I was now more excited than ever. I was going to try something the rest of the world might think I had no chance of achieving. But as a part of my dream of life, I had nothing to lose.

I spent many hours writing the one-page essay required for the application. Finally satisfied with my effort, I mailed it off and awaited the reply. The announcement had said that successful applicants would be notified of their acceptance by April 5. I waited impatiently for the mail to come. But no letter arrived. April 2, 3, and 4, still no letter. April 5, and the postman, now familiar with my daily routine of waiting for the mail, arrived without the letter. That was it, I thought. I should have listened to my first instinct and not gotten my hopes up. I should have learned that I just "can't" do some things in life.

I guess it would be easy enough to say that the moral of this story is that there are certain things you should say "can't" to, so as to spare yourself the heartache. But this couldn't be farther from the truth. It was true I didn't get a letter on April 5, 6, 7, 8, 9, or 10. But on April 11, as I had given up all hope, I opened a letter which read: "Dear Mr. Buckner, The Society of West End Theaters is pleased to announce that you have been selected as a delegate to this year's annual producers workshop. You will be working with some of the finest producers in the business and will have an opportunity to get to know them personally." I continued to read; "You have been assigned Mr. Cameron Mackintosh, producer of *Les Misérables,* as your mentor for the five-day conference. We look forward to seeing you in London soon."

I couldn't believe what I read, so I read the paper over and over again. This was it—my chance to meet the masters of Broadway theater and learn of their wisdom! And to think I had almost convinced myself that I "couldn't" do it.

My young friends, never allow yourself to say "can't." Ella Wheeler Wilcox wrote: "There is no chance, no destiny, no fate that can circumvent or hinder or control the firm resolve of a determined soul." There is absolutely nothing you "can't" do if you put your mind to doing it. It doesn't mean that everything goes the way you dream it will, all the time. What it does mean is that as long as you continue to dream and work to live those dreams, you will be given many opportunities to fulfill your dreams. When you consult the Lord in all you do, he will provide many opportunities for you. You must dare to dream! Aspire to be you! Never say can't! We have been told that "the Lord is able to do all things according to his will, for the children of men, if it so be that they exercise faith in him. Wherefore, let us be faithful to him." (1 Nephi 7:12.)

Now is the time! Every choice you make today will impact your future. You must choose wisely, "for behold, this life is the time for men to prepare to meet God; yea, behold the day of this life is the day for men to perform their labors" (Alma 34:32). I challenge each one of you, at this young age, to begin each day by standing on top of the mountain. You can stand above it all by kneeling at the beginning of each day and asking for guidance in making your lifetime decisions. I challenge you to keep this earthly experience in perspective by remembering your view from the top as you make your daily decisions. Do not allow the "old railroad man" into your life. His foolish stories will only cause you to doubt your worth and may indeed convince you of your demise.

Finally, exercise faith, pray often, and obey the commandments of our Father. For "as it is written—Whatsoever ye shall ask in faith, being united in prayer according to my command, ye shall receive" (D&C 29:6).

I challenge you to live your dreams! As for me, I will live my dreams.

David L. Buckner is currently a part-time faculty member at BYU, where he graduated with a degree in international finance. He has a master's in international relations and is pursuing a law degree. He is an avid skier and has been a ski instructor at Deer Valley Ski Resort for seven years. David was born in Ogden, Utah, and grew up in Sacramento, California, where his dad was a mission president. David is married to Jennifer Jackson and loves traveling, scuba diving, tennis, and speaking to the youth of the Church.

23

ARE YOU MORMON?

Scott Anderson

It was just a typical day as I entered the plane and found my seat. Shortly before takeoff, as I was chatting with the people seated next to me, I found out they were college teachers from Texas, and were Christians. They asked where I lived, and as soon as they found out that I was from Utah, and even lived in the Salt Lake Valley, they asked, "Are you Mormon?"

I am not sure why the question hit me in the way it did. It could have been because I had been reading from Mormon's writings just the night before and, as is usual, had been filled with respect and admiration for this great man. Anyway, my response even surprised me. "Oh, no," I retorted, "if I were Mormon I would be large of stature, very impressive, and I might be wearing armor. I would be powerful, bright, and amazing! So, I guess it is obvious that I am not Mormon."

After waiting just long enough for the comment to sink in, I simply asked, "What do you think Mormon is?" They replied they thought it was a church.

"Oh, no, it is a man, a great example, and one of my personal heroes. Could I tell you more about him?" They were smiling now and said, "You probably will whether we say yes or no, right?" As they expressed interest I felt a little like Ammon must have felt when Lamoni said, "I will believe all thy words" (Alma 18:23). What an opportunity!

You probably know some ten-year-old boy, and I would guess that he is probably all energy without much direction. So it is amazing to us that when Mormon was only ten the prophet of God, Ammaron, came to him and put him in charge of all the sacred writings of his people. He explained that Mormon was to be very observant, and when he was about twenty-four he should go to the hill where the plates were deposited and write on the plates of his people the things he had observed. Imagine this young man being so impressive that a prophet could pick him when he was only ten!

The people where Mormon lived became so wicked that the prophets were taken from them, and this young boy explained that no one he knew received any gifts of the Spirit (see Mormon 1:14), which apparently means that no one even believed in Christ (see D&C 46:13). Can you imagine this young boy, so alone in his beliefs and surrounded by others who were becoming more worldly and wicked by the day? I try to imagine a thirteen- or fourteen-year-old boy without any support from others of his peers—so alone, but with a calling from a prophet to prepare himself.

When I was thirteen and fourteen my peers had such an influence in my life. The way they looked at me could make the difference between having a good day and a real loser. In fact, I remember my sisters coming to me when I was about this age and explaining that my curly hair was just not cool. For six weeks they talked me into sleeping with a nylon sock over my head to try to straighten my hair so that I could be "in." The weird thing is that I did it! Now that my hair is straighter, it is neat to have curly hair. Oh, well!

Even without support from others, especially friends, Mormon stayed so good that he quietly recorded in his journal, "And I, being fifteen years of age and being somewhat of a sober mind, therefore I was visited of the Lord, and tasted and knew of the goodness of Jesus" (Mormon 1:15). How can we begin to imagine ourselves in this incredible moment in this young man's life! Oh, the excitement and the joy! How much he must have wanted to tell others of this amazing moment in his life! But as he went to share this incredible experience, he was commanded not to tell others because they were not ready and had willfully rebelled. So rather than share it with them he shared his experiences with us in his writings.

Life became more complex for Mormon. Others could tell there was something extraordinary about this exceptional young man. He was big and strong, but the difference was so much more than that. They knew he was a natural leader, so much so that they were willing

to put their lives in his hands. Thus when he was only in his sixteenth
year the people of Nephi came to him and asked him to lead the nation's army into battle to defend their families, their homes, and their
very lives. I think of a day at the office when I saw one of my sixteen-
year-old students walking a block away from the school because he
was so worried that someone might see Mom picking him up in the
BMW (Big Mormon Wagon—the family station wagon) filled with all
the neighborhood kids and the dog. There are many youth today however, who are making life-altering decisions and who need someone
they can turn to as an example, someone who understands how to face
such a challenge successfully. No wonder Mormon stands as such a
powerful potential influence for good in this day of tough questions, a
time when our young people seem to need to grow up too soon.

Even though Mormon's army was almost always outnumbered in
the battles he fought, he almost always won. Wow! What a time for re-
joicing—the all-state, all-American general coming home with the trophy! How easy it would have been for him to brag or boast, but he
never did. He knew it was the Lord that had guided him in his suc-
cesses; but more, he saw the victories were not helping his people
come closer to their Heavenly Father. This was what he cared about
the most, and what he talked about. Even success can take us away
from our Heavenly Father. How he loved his people as he continually
risked his life for them!

He didn't love just them, he also loved us! When recording his
wartime experiences on the plates he refrained from including all the
terrible things he had seen, partly because he didn't want us, his readers, to be hurt (see Mormon 5:9). His son, however, when finishing his
father's record, quoted from Mormon's letter, which said that the
Lamanite armies were killing Nephite soldiers taken prisoner and feeding captive women and children the flesh of their husbands and fathers. Some of Mormon's men, he said, were just as evil in their behavior: having captured many Lamanite young women, they first took
from them their most priceless possession, their virtue, then cruelly
tortured them to death; then they consumed their flesh as "a token of
bravery." (See Moroni 9:7–10.) No wonder Mormon didn't record
such sad scenes on the plates. Perhaps Moroni added this note in view
of the R-rated society in which we would be living; that is, that in our
day constant scenes of carnage and immorality would be played before us.

The end had come. Mormon's people had been destroyed. What had happened to Mormon's wife and children? His son Moroni still lived. It was his last chance to write in his journal. Thousands of his people were heaped upon the earth in mounds of smoldering flesh. In his final entry he wrote a message of love and counsel to the descendants of those who had destroyed his people, killed his friends and his family. How could he be so strong? The words echo through the ages. He was one who took seriously the words of the Master to love one's enemies. How did he stay so good, so filled with love in the midst of all the anger and hatred surrounding him?

"So, you ask if I am Mormon." Struggling to hold back the tears, I replied: "I want to be, I wish I could be, I would love to emulate his life as one who could take the Savior's divine message and translate it into everyday acts of love and courage. But the wonderful thing is that he recorded his feelings and his insights about his own life experiences as well as editing most of the remainder of the story of his people and filling in with his insightful editorial comments. This is all recorded in a book called, of all things, the Book of Mormon. I just happen to have a copy of that book right here, and I would love to share it with you."

As I flipped through the pages and pointed out Mormon's writings I again was filled with love for this great prophet leader. And I said to those college teachers what I share with you now: I know for myself that this great man really lived. That he knew how to live and did live the Savior's teachings in his life. That he understood our day and the challenges that we would have, and that by following his example we can learn to overcome many of the challenges in our lives. That as you read his testimony throughout the book, it is obvious that his heroes were the great prophets like King Benjamin, Alma, Helaman, and Nephi. That it is obvious from 3 Nephi that his greatest hero is the Savior. That using the scriptures and following the prophets gave him courage not to follow the trend of his day but to stand strong and committed to principles that are eternal.

So I ask of myself and share with you a simple question: "Are you Mormon?"

Scott Anderson *was born in Salt Lake City, Utah. He and his wife, Angelle, live on a small farm in Bluffdale, Utah, where they raise goats, chickens, pigs, and children. They are the parents of seven children. He received a Ph.D. in marriage and family therapy at Brigham Young University and currently is an institute teacher at Utah Valley State College in Orem, Utah. He has taught in the Church Educational System since 1973 in programs such as Academy for Girls, Especially for Youth, Education Week, Education Days, Know Your Religion, and the Women's Enrichment Program. He serves as a high councilor in his stake.*

24

CONFRONTING THE COMPETITION WITH CONVICTION

Todd B. Parker

Much of the world around us is based on competition. It is a part of our daily thinking. We are interested in the outcome of different competitions. "Who is ranked number one this week?" "Who won the game Saturday?" "What score did you get on the exam?" "What grade did you get in chemistry?" "Did you ask her out? What did she say?" All of these questions indicate our interest in success, competition, and rising to the top.

In this chapter I discuss three aspects of competition and three questions involving competing in this world.

The three aspects of competition are:

1. Competition with disappointment.
2. Competition with forces vying for our time.
3. Competition between truth and untruth.

The three questions are:

1. How do I motivate myself to compete in a class at school for which I have no interest?
2. How can I increase my spiritual maturity as I compete with Satan's temptations?
3. Competition for power, money, property, and so on, seems to cause so much suffering in the world. Why does God allow it?

1. *Competition with disappointment.* At one time or another in our lives, each of us will have to deal with setbacks. These come in the form of disappointments, failures, unmet expectations, injuries, or even disabilities. These often cause us to lose hope. With loss of hope, often comes depression. We see no "light at the end of the tunnel." The writer of Proverbs stated, "Where there is no vision, the people perish" (Proverbs 29:18).

Depression and discouragement are states of mind. People choose the way they view their challenges. Following are two examples of people who chose to view their disappointments positively.

While attending BYU I saw a film entitled *One Day in the Life of Bonnie Consolo.* The first scene showed (I thought) a woman washing dishes at the sink with her hands. As the picture expanded to show the entire scene I was shocked to see that this woman (Bonnie Consolo) was washing dishes with her feet! She was born without any arms.

The movie depicted a typical day in her life. She cooked and served dinner, drove to the store and did shopping, wrote out a check, tied her son's shoes, cut his hair, put on her own makeup—all with her feet! As they interviewed her she said: "*Can't* just isn't in my vocabulary. I like to do difficult things like . . . what is something difficult? . . . I can't think of anything." She went on to say: "Most people try to be different. They spend their whole life trying to be different. I was lucky. I had it handed to me on a silver platter. I was born different." Many of us with such a disability could have given up and become dependent on others. Bonnie Consolo has become an inspiration to thousands because of her positive attitude toward her situation.

Another example is Tom Depsey. He was born without a right foot. As a child, he was fitted with an artificial wooden foot. It was with that foot encased in a football shoe that he kicked the longest field goal in history. Playing for the Detroit Lions in 1970 and behind by two points with two seconds left, he kicked a 63-yard field goal. The kick was from his own 37-yard line! As a boy he'd set the goal to be the first kicker in pro football to kick a 60-yard field goal.

Each of us has some area of deficiency. Weaknesses are given to help us become humble and strong (see Ether 12:27). By our setting goals, working hard, trusting in the Lord, and maintaining a positive attitude, the process of reaching goals can bring success, happiness, and fulfillment into our lives.

2. *Competition with forces vying for our time.* Each of us is a two-part being. We have a spirit body and a physical body. Every living thing in this world has a spiritual counterpart. We seem to be constantly faced with the challenge of where to spend our time. Prophets, Church leaders, scriptures, and our conscience tug at us to spend time in spiritual matters. Friends, school, and physical needs and desires tug at us to spend more time in pursuit of material things. What is a person to do? An illustration from Church history told by Elder James E. Faust and two statements by prophets may put this dilemma in better perspective.

In April conference of 1979, Elder Faust told the following story:

Some years ago President David O. McKay told from this pulpit of the experience of some of those in the Martin handcart company. Many of these early converts had emigrated from Europe and were too poor to buy oxen or horses and a wagon. They were forced by their poverty to pull handcarts containing all of their belongings across the plains by their own brute strength. President McKay relates an occurrence which took place some years after the heroic exodus: "A teacher, conducting a class, said it was unwise ever to attempt, even to permit them [the Martin handcart company] to come across the plains under such conditions.

"[According to a class member,] some sharp criticism of the Church and its leaders was being indulged in for permitting any company of converts to venture across the plains with no more supplies or protection than a handcart caravan afforded.

"An old man in the corner . . . sat silent and listened as long as he could stand it, then he arose and said things that no person who heard him will ever forget. His face was white with emotion, yet he spoke calmly, deliberately, but with great earnestness and sincerity.

"In substance [he] said, 'I ask you to stop this criticism. You are discussing a matter you know nothing about. Cold historic facts mean nothing here, for they give no proper interpretation of the questions involved. Mistake to send the Handcart Company out so late in the season? Yes. But I was in that company and my wife was in it and Sister Nellie Unthank whom you have cited was there, too. We suffered beyond anything you can imagine and many died of exposure and starvation, but did you ever hear a survivor of that company utter a word of criticism? *Not one of that company ever apostatized or left the Church, because every one of us came through with the absolute knowledge that God lives, for we became acquainted with him in our extremities.*

" 'I have pulled my handcart when I was so weak and weary from illness and lack of food that I could hardly put one foot ahead of the other. I have looked ahead and seen a patch of sand or a hill slope and I have said, I can go only that far and there I must give up, for I cannot pull the load through it.' " He continues: " 'I have gone on to that sand and when I reached it, the cart began pushing me. I have looked back many times to see who was pushing my cart, but my eyes saw no one. I knew then that the angels of God were there.

" 'Was I sorry that I chose to come by handcart? No. Neither then nor any minute of my life since. *The price we paid to become acquainted with God was a privilege to pay, and I am thankful that I was privileged to come in the Martin Handcart Company.'* " (*Relief Society Magazine,* Jan. 1948, p. 8.) (*Ensign,* May 1979, p. 53.)

I have often wondered why the pioneers seemed to have so many spiritual experiences. Why don't we have as many today? The answer may lie in the competition between the physical and the spiritual. The pioneers had practically nothing material (physical). They were consequently forced to rely on spiritual things. How could they be guilty of pride in material goods? "My handcart is more cool than yours." (I doubt it!) Today, however, we have so many material distractions that it's hard to focus on spiritual matters.

In 1878 Elder Daniel H. Wells made a prophecy about our day. He said, "There will come a time . . . in the history of the saints, when they will be tried with peace, prosperity, popularity, and riches" (*Journal of Discourses* 19:367). The pioneers' challenge was a physical one which resulted in their spiritual growth. Our challenge is a spiritual one. We must not let the materialism of this world occupy our time and interests to the point where we leave no room for spiritual things. Brigham Young said it this way: "The worst fear I have about this people is that they will get rich in this country, forget God and His people, wax fat, and kick themselves out of the Church and go to hell. This people will stand mobbing, robbing, poverty, and all manner of persecution, and be true. But my greater fear . . . is that they cannot stand wealth." (As quoted by Dean L. Larsen, "Beware Lest Thou Forget the Lord," *Ensign,* May 1991, p. 11.)

3. *Competition between truth and untruth.* Elder John A. Widtsoe said:

> Truth and untruth travel together side by side. Light and darkness both offer themselves to the seeker after truth, one to bless, the other to destroy mankind. Whenever a man sets out to seek truth, he will for a time be overtaken by evil. No seeker after truth is, therefore, ever free from temptation, from evil powers. No sooner had the Prophet reached the grove and found a place to kneel than evil sought to destroy him. . . . But he had come to find truth, and he fought against the evil power. He would not be overcome. He fought for truth; and as he fought, light appeared. Darkness was being driven away.
>
> That is an eternal law. If a seeker of truth has courage to fight off evil, denies his appetites, and works steadily in the pursuit of truth, he wins. ("The Significance of the First Vision," *Joseph Smith Memorial Sermon,* Logan, Utah Institute of Religion, December 8, 1946, p. 26.)

I have noted in my own life as well as in the lives of others that often, just before something spiritually significant or great is about to happen, there is a period of darkness or doubting. A knowledge of this principle illustrated by Elder Widtsoe can be a great key to hold onto when things seem bleak or dark. Just as Joseph had experienced darkness and despair immediately prior to the First Vision, so Joseph and Oliver apparently experienced hopelessness just prior to the restoration of the Melchizedek Priesthood. The following account comes from a letter of Addison Everett to Oliver B. Huntington dated 17 February 1881 recounting his recollection of what he heard Joseph Smith say in a conversation. Joseph and Oliver were running from a mob.

> They got into the woods in going a few rods from the house. It was night and they traveled through brush and water and mud, fell over logs, etc., until Oliver was exhausted. Then Joseph helped him along through the mud and water, almost carrying him.
>
> They traveled all night, and just at the break of day Oliver gave out entirely and exclaimed, "Oh, Lord! Brother Joseph, how long have we got to endure this thing?"

They sat down on a log to rest, and Joseph said that at that very time Peter, James and John came to them and ordained them to the apostleship.

They had sixteen or seventeen miles to go to get back to Mr. Hale's, his father-in-law's, but Oliver did not complain any more of fatigue. (Hyrum L. Andrus and Helen Mae Andrus, comp., *They Knew the Prophet* [Salt Lake City: Bookcraft, 1974], p. 15.)

So as you seek answers to prayers, a testimony of the gospel, or solutions to seemingly insurmountable problems, remember that, as Elder Widtsoe said, "truth and untruth travel side by side" and when the seeker of truth "fights off evil, denies his appetites, and works steadily . . . he wins." The scriptures encourage us similarly: "Thine adversity and thine afflictions shall be but a small moment; and then, if thou endure it well, God shall exalt thee on high" (D&C 121:7–8).

Let us now turn our attention to three questions concerning competition in the world around us.

1. *How do I motivate myself to compete in a class (to work toward a respectable grade) at school for which I have no interest?*

There's no magic formula here, but one suggestion and an example may be helpful. Once I sat in an English class for which I had little interest. We had to write a composition each week. I was not enjoying the class at all. We were given the assignment to write a composition on the "style of writing." It seemed like drudgery. I sat down and stared at the paper. "Well," I thought, "I'll do the usual. I'll quote things from authors we've studied, to impress the teacher. I'll say Shakespeare has this style, Whitman writes this way, Faulkner uses this style, etc." It was so dry you'd need to read it with a gallon of water. I wadded it up and threw it away. I thought, "I've got to do this thing anyway, so why not have a little fun with it." Paul says, "Whatsoever ye do, do it heartily" (Colossians 3:23). My attempt hadn't been made heartily. It would be a stretch to call it "half heartily."

I'd heard a man do a reading once using what he called an inflated language. I couldn't remember much about it, but I recalled the premise, which was that in the future words containing numbers, because of inflation, would have the numbers increase by one. So I entitled my essay, "The Style of the Future." I found myself searching the entire dictionary for words containing numbers which I could increase by one and use in my essay. For example, Cali*fo*rnia would become Cali*five*nia, *ten*nis would become *eleven*is, and so on.

Now what *had been* drudgery became exciting! I was frantically searching the dictionary for more words with numbers. As I found more and more I put them into my essay. I'd write a line and start giggling to myself. Soon I was laughing out loud. I got to the point that I couldn't wait to hand it in to see if I could crack a smile on the face of my English professor. Just for fun, I'll share part of the essay here:

Twice upon a time in sunny Cali*five*nia I had the mis*five*tune of meeting a young lieu*eleven*ant in the United States Air *Five*ces who just loved *three* play *eleven*nis. Two (one) day he barged in*three* the apartment where I was staying and said, "Any two five *eleven*nis?" (Anyone for tennis?) It was rather an asi*ten* question *three* ask of me since I was recuper*nine*ing from a pulled *eleven*don in my leg. Besides he was *two* of the top *eleven*nis players in the West. Any*two* who played him always came out feeling like a *ten*compoop because he was such a great player. When no*two* would make an *eleven*ative appointment *three* play with him, he became very angry and started throwing things. We almost had to call out rein*five*cements to retali*nine*. We were very *five*tunate, however, and did get him calmed down. It doesn't take a *five*tune teller or a woman's in*three*ition *three* know that no*two* wants *three* play *eleven*nis with some*two* so good that he humili*nines* you in front of every*two*.

Paul said "do things heartily." The Lord said "be anxiously engaged." (D&C 58:27). However you want to phrase it, the principle is this: If you've got a job to do, jump in with both feet and have some fun doing it. Use your creativity to make the completion of the task exciting. Your attitude will make all the difference.

2. *How can I increase my spiritual maturity as I compete with Satan's temptations?*

As a youth I used to read magazines at the corner drugstore. I used to look in the "Muscle Man" magazines at the advertisements. They'd often have a "before" and an "after" picture of a young man. In the "before" picture he was a skinny, ninety-eight-pound weakling. In the "after" pictures he had huge muscles, with girls in bikinis hanging on each arm. While reading the Book of Mormon I noticed a "before" and "after" description of Nephi. Note the wording of 1 Nephi 2:16: "I Nephi, being exceedingly young, nevertheless being large in stature." This is the "before" description. Now note 1 Nephi 4:31: "And now I,

Nephi, being a man large in stature." This is the "after" description. What caused Nephi to change from "exceedingly young, . . . large in stature" to "a man large in stature"? The answer lies in 1 Nephi 4:18: "I did obey the voice of the Spirit." A boy becomes a man, spiritually speaking, or a girl becomes a woman, when they learn to "obey the voice of the Spirit." We all enjoy watching the comparison of a young elder's missionary farewell with his homecoming. Often a "boy" leaves and a "man" returns. What causes the change? For two years he seeks diligently, like never before, to be led by the Spirit. This leads to the development of spiritual maturity.

While serving as institute instructor in Tucson, Arizona, I heard a full-time missionary tell this story. Prior to his mission he had been a roommate at Ricks College with a young man who had attended BYU-Hawaii. While there, he had a job as a lifeguard. One day, as he was packing up to leave work for the day, he had all his gear ready to go when the Spirit told him to check the shoreline one more time. Using binoculars he spotted a little girl who had been caught in the riptide. He radioed the coast guard for a helicopter, then swam out to rescue her. The helicopter airlifted her out, and he then swam back to shore. He didn't know her name or what happened to her.

Later he was called to serve a mission in Seattle, Washington. While he was there, the Spirit kept telling him to go back to a certain house. The father in that house just kept yelling at him to leave, but the Spirit persisted. Finally, as he went back and the father was again rejecting him, a little girl came running out and grabbed his leg, saying, "David!" It was the same little girl he had rescued two years before in Hawaii. Now the elders were invited in, and the family was taught and baptized. He had saved the girl temporally and then later had brought spiritual salvation to her. By learning to obey the voice of the Spirit we not only grow personally but we may also be an instrument in the hands of the Lord to save someone else's life.

One doesn't have to be a full-time missionary to learn to obey the Spirit. We can, in fact, do the things missionaries do that bring that result. This would include kneeling in prayer several times a day with others and by oneself. Missionaries spend most of their time focused on helping others rather than serving themselves. Missionaries also study, and memorize scriptures daily. Their conversations focus on the gospel rather than on the world. They avoid distractors such as television, inappropriate music, and circumstances that offend the Spirit of God.

3. *Competition for power, money, possessions, and so forth seems to cause so much suffering in the world. Why does God allow this to happen?* Hard questions such as this one are best answered by those who have been ordained prophets, seers, and revelators, for they give us the mind, the will, and the voice of the Lord (see D&C 68:4). President Spencer W. Kimball said:

> Is there not wisdom in his giving us trials that we might rise above them, responsibilities that we might achieve, work to harden our muscles, sorrows to try our souls? Are we not exposed to temptations to test our strength, sickness that we might learn patience, death that we might be immortalized and glorified?
>
> If all the sick for whom we pray were healed, if all the righteous were protected and the wicked destroyed, the whole program of the Father would be annulled and the basic principle of the gospel, free agency, would be ended. No man would have to live by faith. (*Faith Precedes the Miracle* [Salt Lake City: Deseret Book Co., 1972], p. 97.)

Elder Orson F. Whitney wisely observed:

> There is always a blessing in sorrow and humiliation. They who escape these things are not the fortunate ones. "Whom God loveth he chasteneth." (Heb. 12:6) When he desires to make a great man he takes a little street waif, or a boy in the back woods, such as Lincoln or Joseph Smith, and brings him up through hardship and privation to be the grand and successful leader of a people. Flowers shed most of their perfume when they are crushed. Men and women have to suffer just so much in order to bring out the best that is in them. ("A Lesson from the Book of Job," *Improvement Era,* November 1918, p. 7.)

Weight lifters gain muscle strength, in the weight training room, by adding more weight to the barbell to increase resistance and opposition to the muscle. So also do souls and spirits gain strength through trials. This world is for trials. We are not to escape them, but to grow stronger and become more like God as a result of the experience. If we always try to avoid adversity and trial and complain about it, this life will be disappointing indeed.

I've always enjoyed these lines by Jenkins Lloyd Jones that help keep things in perspective. Said he:

> Anyone who imagines that bliss is normal is going to waste a lot of time running around shouting that he has been robbed.
>
> Most putts don't drop. Most beef is tough. Most children grow up to be just people. Most successful marriages require a high degree of mutual toleration. Most jobs are more often dull than otherwise. . . .
>
> Life is like an old-time rail journey—delays, sidetracks, smoke, dust, cinders, and jolts, interspersed only occasionally by beautiful vistas and thrilling bursts of speed.
>
> The trick is to thank the Lord for letting you have the ride. ("Big Rock Candy Mountains," *Deseret News,* 12 June 1973, p. A-4.)

It is my hope and prayer that as we face the different aspects of this competitive world we will keep constantly before us these principles as taught by the scriptures and the Brethren to "guide us in these latter days."

Holding a bachelor's degree in English, an M.E.D. in counseling and guidance, and an Ed.D. in educational psychology, **Todd B. Parker** *is an associate professor of ancient scripture at Brigham Young University. Dr. Parker was a seminary teacher for fourteen years, and he has also been an institute instructor. An athlete himself, he remains interested in distance running, pole vaulting, gymnastics, and in coaching track. He is married to Debra Harbertson, and they have eight children.*

25

TOUGH TIMES TAKE THEIR TOLL: THEREFORE, TRIUMPH

Gary R. Nelson

It was only a practice football game. Besides, Beaver High was a 1-A ranked football team and we were a stronger 2-A opponent—or so we thought. My Dixie High School Flyer team had glided to a perfect seven straight wins coming into the game, and we were well on our way to state. We had had a taste of the state play-offs the year before, but then we could not get past the semifinals. We knew this was our year. We would not be denied.

My heart was also set on being named to the all-state football team in my senior year. It was a personal goal and dream I had envisioned throughout my high school days. Starting both as offensive right guard and defensive tackle seemed to enhance my chances of achieving this state recognition.

There is no doubt we looked past the Beavers, who later captured the state championship in their class. Down 21–0 at halftime, our sluggish team was dumbfounded and shocked in the locker room. We had underestimated this team. It was time for a wake-up call. We determined to regroup and get our scoring attack on track in the second half. I played only offense in the third and fourth quarters because of a sharp pain which persisted in my right side above my waist. Our highly explosive offense rattled off 44 points to Beaver's 27 in the second half, but it was still not enough. The only Flyer loss that year came at the hands of this overlooked, underrated, scrappy Beaver team which beat us, 48–44. It was a long bus ride home to St. George.

Even longer was that fateful Friday night. My much-needed sleep was interrupted many times by increased abdominal pain. The next morning I found myself in an emergency operating room with my family doctor. The removal of a ruptured appendix caused by a hit in the Beaver game sent my all-state football hopes to another lineman and kept me from a Sadie Hawkins dance that night. My date, a beautiful girl named Christine Putnam who, I might add, is now my precious wife), was kind enough to stay with me in my hospital room. (Through tribulation come the blessings!) There would be no dancing, no school, and no football for a few weeks.

After sitting out the next three games with my injury, I was finally able to play again in our quarterfinal, semifinal and state championship game at BYU Cougar Stadium. With my stomach wrapped tightly with Ace bandages over a padded incision, I started all three games at the right guard position. I just prayed that some opponent would not hit me in my tender, healing stomach. We won convincingly in all of these state play-off contests. What a thrill to pick up our winning coach, Walt Brooks, and march off Cougar field clutching the state championship trophy! The ecstasy of being escorted by family and fans into St. George and down St. George Boulevard, as the team rode on a local fire truck, is a memory I will ever treasure.

But to a young man who had his sights set on being one of the best linemen in the state it was one of the toughest trials I had ever faced. "Why did it have to be me?" "Why now?" "Was God punishing me for something I did or did not do?" These were some of the questions I asked myself during this time of trial and discouragement. I was not angry with God . . . just very disappointed with life in general. I did not understand.

Since my senior struggles, I have had other challenges. Adversity has tempered and continues to temper my life. It has given me much understanding about myself and God. I am still learning and growing through this "divine tutorial process."

Trials Come to All

Each of us will experience "tough times" in our lives. As sure as the morning follows the night, we will face adversity. A greater understanding of tribulations can assist us in coping and dealing with life's trials when they come. The old adage still applies, "When the going gets tough, the tough get going."

We should understand that a life filled with problems is no respecter of age or station in life. A life filled with trials is no respecter of position in the Church or social standing in the community. Challenges come to the young and to the aged—to the rich and to the poor—to the struggling student or the genius scientist— to the farmer, carpenter, lawyer, or doctor. Trials come to the strong and to the weak—to the sick and to the healthy. Yes, even to the simplest child as well as to a prophet of God. (H. Burke Peterson, "Adversity and Prayer," *Ensign,* January 1974, p. 18.)

Patience Is Learned Through the Struggle

The Lord counseled the Prophet Joseph Smith to "be patient in thine afflictions, for thou shalt have many; but endure them well, for, lo, I am with thee, even unto the end of thy days" (D&C 24:8).

Notice, the Lord did not say Joseph *would not have* afflictions, but rather that he would have *many* afflictions. The key is to be patient in the trial and suffering.

If we can bear our afflictions with . . . understanding, faith and courage . . . we shall be strengthened and comforted in many ways. We shall be spared the torment which accompanies the mistaken idea that all suffering comes as chastisement for transgression . . . I have seen the remorse and despair in the lives of men who, in the hour of trial, have cursed God and died spiritually. And I have seen people rise to great heights from what seemed to be unbearable burdens. (Marion G. Romney, *Improvement Era,* December 1969, pp. 68–69.)

Trials Can Make Us Stronger and
Better Latter-day Saints

Our attitude determines how well we make it through our trials. If we are in the mind-set of constantly blaming God and others for our condition, ours will be a dismal experience.

Elder Neal A. Maxwell categorizes suffering and adversity in three types:

— Type 1. Some things happen to us because of our own mistakes and our own sins.
— Type 2. Other trials and tribulations come to us merely as a part of living.
— Type 3. Another dimension of suffering comes to us "because an omniscient Lord deliberately chooses to school us." (*All These Things Shall Give Thee Experience* [Salt Lake City: Deseret Book Co., 1979], pp. 29–31.)

The hot piece of metal that is forged and fanned with the bellowing heat of opposition becomes more strong and tempered as it is struck with the heavy, consistent blow of the sledgehammer. Although we hate the constant pounding and rounding of our rough edges, we can be confident that God is crafting us "in the furnace of affliction" (1 Nephi 20:10) into useful, unique tools in his hands.

President Spencer W. Kimball has stated: "Is there not wisdom in his giving us trials that we might rise above them, responsibilities that we might achieve, work to harden our muscles, sorrow to try our souls? Are we not exposed to temptations to test our strength, sickness that we might learn patience, death that we might be immortalized and glorified?" (*Faith Precedes the Miracle* [Salt Lake City: Deseret Book Co., 1972], p. 97.)

The Prophet Joseph Smith knew firsthand the struggles with adversity. One cold Saturday night on March 24, 1832, in Hiram, Ohio, at the John Johnson farm, the Prophet Joseph lay in bed comforting eleven-month-old Joseph (one of the recently adopted "Murdock twins") as the baby struggled with a bad case of measles. A mob surrounded the house, busted open the door, and dragged the Prophet from his bed. They choked him into unconsciousness. When he came around he saw Sidney Rigdon's unconscious body on the cold ground, and he pleaded for his own life. The mob unsuccessfully attempted to shove the hot tar paddle into his mouth, then tried to force a vial of nitric acid into his mouth which broke against his teeth. They stripped his body of clothes and applied hot tar and feathers to his uncovered skin. They beat him and left him for dead.

After several attempts to rise, he finally made his way back to the house. His wife, Emma, fainted at his unsightly condition. Friends spent the night scraping off the "flesh-eating" tar from his body. Skin came off with the tar in many places.

I think this experience would be reason enough for me to stay home from church the next day—how about you? I think twice about going to church when I have a mere headache or a cold, but not so for the Prophet. He spoke to the Saints the next day in Sabbath worship services with several of the mob seated in the congregation before him. That afternoon he personally baptized three people. Joseph, the young Murdock twin, died the next Friday of exposure to the cold on that fateful night. (See *History of the Church* 1:261–65.)

This disgraceful incident of tarring and feathering, difficult as it was for the Prophet, strengthened him for future tribulations in his life. Imprisonment in the "temple prison" at Liberty and the martyrdom at Carthage serve as two examples. Like our beloved Prophet Joseph, we can become stronger and better Latter-day Saints through our trials.

Jesus Christ Can Bear Our Burdens and Comfort Us

One of our greatest friends, mentors, and allies is our Lord and Savior, Jesus Christ. He is "a man of sorrows, and acquainted with grief" (Isaiah 53:3). Through his infinite atonement, he can bear our pains and sorrows.

As Nephi taught the Nephites, "For behold, he suffereth the pains of all men, yea, the pains of every living creature, both men, women, and children, who belong to the family of Adam" (2 Nephi 9:21). Elder Neal A. Maxwell has explained: "Since not all human sorrow and pain is connected to sin, the full intensiveness of the Atonement involved bearing our pains, infirmities, and sicknesses, as well as our sins" (*"Not My Will, But Thine"* [Salt Lake City: Bookcraft, 1988], p. 51).

My beloved youth of Zion, did you catch this important insight? His atonement is infinite and eternal. It is complete. It covers not only sins but also every suffering, affliction, adversity, and hardship known to man! When Christ instructed us to "Come unto me, all ye that labour and are heavy laden, and I will give you rest. . . . For my yoke is easy, and my burden is light" (Matthew 11:28–30), he meant just that—to come unto him.

Let us lay our cares, troubles, and worries on him who can succor us, on him who can bind the wounds and give hope and peace to the heart. Christ is the Teacher, the Healer, and the Liberator (see Luke 4:18).

The Prophet Alma taught: "And he shall go forth, suffering pains and afflictions and temptations of every kind; and this that the word might be fulfilled which saith he will take upon him the pains and the sicknesses of his people" (Alma 7:11). Isaiah emphasized His complete suffering when he said, "Surely he hath borne our griefs, and carried our sorrows" (Isaiah 53:4).

A quadriplegic and former student at BYU, Stephen Jason Hall, has said, "I am reminded that Jesus Christ took on all our pains, also our sickness and our infirmities, that he might have mercy upon us" (*Feeling Great, Doing Right, Hanging Tough* [Salt Lake City: Bookcraft, 1991], p. 89).

We Can Choose to Be Happy in Tough Times

I have done a survey in dozens of classes and many fireside groups. I simply ask the class or audience to raise their hands *if they are not* dealing with a difficult struggle or problem right now in their lives. Every time I have asked this, not one hand has been raised. If everyone is experiencing difficult problems, then why are some people happy and positive while others are sad, negative, and prone to complain?

Happiness is a matter of choice. In a priesthood blessing I received during a difficult time in my own life, the Lord inspired a good stake president to say, "Choose to be happy!"

Such a statement is validated by the Lord in the Book of Mormon. The unbelievers had set aside a day in which to kill all the believers in Christ if the prophecy of the sign of a "day and a night and a day" of no darkness and a new star at the Savior's prophesied birth had not happened by that day. During this time of great stress and sorrow, the Lord's prophet, Nephi, "cried mightily to his God [all that day] in behalf of his people . . . who were about to be destroyed because of their faith."

The voice of the Lord came to Nephi saying, "Lift up your head and *be of good cheer,*" or in other words, "Choose to be happy!" He continued to say, "Be of good cheer; for behold, the time is at hand,

and on this night shall the sign be given, and on the morrow come I into the world." (3 Nephi 1:9–13.)

So here are the righteous believers of Christ ready to die for their beliefs, and the Lord tells them to be of good cheer. In the midst of "tough times," like those of the prophet Nephi and his people, one can still be happy. It is our choice. We have to decide. No other person can make us be happy.

Jacob counseled his people, "let us remember [God], and lay aside our sins, and not hang down our heads" (2 Nephi 10:20).

Some of your challenges might include: the death of a loved one, friend, or pet; the temporary or permanent loss of the use of a limb or other body part; physical, emotional, or verbal abuse from someone you love; being the victim of untruths at the hands of uncaring friends; feeling all alone; dealing with sin in your life; trying to understand your parents' separation or divorce; striving to keep the standards of the Church as one of its few members in your school; coping with not making the cast for the drama production, or the marching band, or the baseball team; not getting the job you had applied for; or simply failing a class. There are many things that can discourage and distress us.

A tape produced by the Church entitled "Bounce Back" provides us with ten ways to be happy and "not hang down our heads" in tough times:

1. Be your own best friend
2. Be realistic
3. Pick yourself up
4. Give of yourself
5. Give yourself a break
6. Get a move on
7. Talk to your family
8. Accentuate the positive
9. Learn from the hard times
10. Realize you're not alone

Dear youth of Zion, I stand in awe of all that you are and all that you are becoming. Yours is a generation that faces much trial and temptation. Know that the Lord loves and cares for you. Just as one football game caused me to readjust my sights and goals, so you can make it through your "tough times" through adjustment and acceptance.

Elder Marvin J. Ashton said: "Victories in life come through our ability to work around and over the obstacles that cross our path" ("Roadblocks to Progress," *Ensign,* May 1979, p. 67.) Let us be victorious. Never give up in our "tough times." One of my favorite sayings, embossed over the picture of the Savior praying in Gethsemane in one of his "toughest times," reads: "I never said it would be easy. I only said it would be worth it."

And the Lord triumphed. It was worth the struggle. It will be for you too. Tough times take their toll. Therefore, triumph!

Gary R. Nelson teaches seminary at Dixie High School in St. George, Utah. A popular youth and motivational speaker, he has been associated with EFY programs for many years. Gary is a former high school and collegiate football and tennis player and maintains an interest in all sports, especially BYU athletics. He has been a sportswriter for two local newspapers. In addition to writing and speaking, he enjoys making his "animal imitations," singing, playing the guitar and piano, hunting, fishing, camping, bodysurfing, and spending time with his family. Gary and his wife, Christine, are the parents of seven children.

26

WHEN LIFE HANDS YOU LEMONS, MAKE PINEAPPLE JUICE

Kim Novas Gunnell

My brother-in-law Brad Wilcox is the nursery leader in his ward. One Sunday his lesson was, "Heavenly Father Gave Us Food Because He Loves Us." All the children were seated on a blanket and listened as Brad asked, "What does a cherry tree make?"

"Cherries," said one little girl.

"What does an apple tree make?"

"Apples?" guessed a boy.

"Yes," Brad said. "And what does a lemon tree make?"

"Pineapples!" yelled another little boy. All the adults in the room began to smile. Brad said, "Buddy, if you can turn every lemon life gives you into a pineapple you're going to be just fine."

Brad told that little story at a family gathering just for fun, but I said, "I think that little nursery boy left church with a valuable lesson. According to the old saying, when life hands us lemons we are supposed to make lemonade, but I like the nursery boy's idea even better. Let's make a real difference. Let's turn those lemons into pineapple juice."

I remember a time in my life when I had to make pineapple juice from a lemon. I was in high school and, like a lot of young people, I worked for my father. He was a crop-duster, and while he sprayed the fields from his airplane I worked on the ground as his flagger. Every time he flew over I would run a few measured steps after waving my flag until he flew past me again.

Sometimes when he would stop to refuel there would be long periods of waiting time with nothing to do. This was especially true one winter when Dad was hired to do a job in Snowville, Utah. That week the place lived up to its name.

After the first full long day of work in Snowville I complained to my dad, "I'm cold! I'm wet! This is the worst! Anything would be better than this."

He said, "Kim, we've been hired to do a job, and we're going to do it; so make the best of it."

"Great!" I thought sarcastically. "How do I make the best of this? What could be worse than standing in this huge frozen field for twelve to fifteen hours every day with nothing to do but wave a flag?" I was used to working in the summer, when I could sit down on the soft dirt once in a while and get a suntan. Here I was now in the dead of winter, and the cold was like an endless torture.

The next morning my dad drove me out to my post in the field before going to his plane. The ride was pretty quiet because I was trying not to complain. I knew how hard Dad worked for our family and I didn't want to be ungrateful. Still, the thought of standing in this mini-Siberia for another day was hard to face. Dad broke the silence. "I think there's some reading material in the glove compartment if you want to take something with you."

I opened the compartment and shuffled through the contents. I said, "Dad, the only things I see are the Book of Mormon and some copies of the *Ensign*."

"Well, some people call that reading material."

I rolled my eyes and stuffed the book and magazines in my pocket. As I opened the door of the truck, I got hit by a blast of wind. I didn't think I could make it through another day of this. By late morning I was so cold and bored that I felt desperate. I needed something to take my mind off the situation. I thought of the *Ensign* magazines in my pocket. I was ready to try anything.

After Dad made his next pass in the plane I watched him fly off in the distance to refuel. I opened an *Ensign* and began reading. It wasn't as bad as I had thought. I read a short article first—I actually searched the whole magazine to find the shortest one. Then I read another, and another. The articles took my mind off my circumstance.

We had to sleep in the cab of the pickup because there was no hotel in Snowville. We each took turns stretching out on the bench seat while the other took the floorboard. We occasionally turned on the engine of the pickup through the night to take off the winter chill. I didn't notice the discomfort as much this night because Dad and I had such wonderful discussions about the things I'd read.

When my dad dropped me off the next day I actually didn't mind. It was still cold in the field, but I had enjoyed reading the magazines and I was surprised at how much I was able to read when there were no phones to interrupt me, no friends coming over—nothing but pure white snow in the middle of nowhere.

That day I read in the Book of Mormon. I'd get so involved I would sometimes forget to run and wave my flag. It was wonderful to be alone with my thoughts. I even had some wonderful talks with God. As the week wore on I couldn't wait for each evening when Dad would pick me up from the field and we could discuss some of the wonderful things I was reading.

Looking back, I realize that a lot of my earliest testimony was developed that week. What could have been a disastrous memory turned out to be a special week I will never forget. It also cemented a wonderful bond and friendship with my father. I had been able to turn a lemon into sweet pineapple juice.

That experience happened many years ago, but just recently a farmer in my ward hired me to do some truck and tractor driving on the Church farm. This time I was ready. Some of the newer tractors have wonderful stereo tape players. As I worked I listened to the Book of Mormon from start to finish, and then I listened to dramatized stories about great women of the Church such as Jessie Evans Smith and Eliza R. Snow. The whole experience could have just been a drudgery, but that John Deere tractor turned into a mean green learning machine. Now it is such a pleasure to work on the farm for a few weeks. I really look forward to that time of solitude and reflection.

Before I was married I had the wonderful opportunity to tour as the character Barbara in the musical *My Turn on Earth*. The music for the production was composed by Lex de Azevedo. I loved how he told of when he had to make lemons into some pineapple juice by mentally changing his environment:

I was signed to do the Sonny and Cher show. . . . It was 1970, 1971. That was an interesting experience. I found myself in a smoke-filled rehearsal hall eight hours a day, working with the interesting assortment of people that grind out a weekly television show. You had your choreographers, your dancers, your makeup people, your costume people, the directors, the musicians, not to mention the stars. Well, I found it to be one of the most hostile environments . . . to the Spirit of the Lord that I had ever worked in.

The standard conversation centered around the latest clothes styles, automobiles, the latest imported bottled water, movies, and continual sexual innuendos—not to mention the dress code of most of the people. . . .

I was becoming very depressed, I'd come home at night and I'd tell my wife how this environment was upsetting me. I found that it was hard to do my Church work. I was losing my motivation. . . . I was going to quit the show and I would have had it not been for my contract.

My wife said, "Why don't you try and create your own environment." I took my little cassette recorder, since so much of the time is spent waiting around; all the time I was waiting I would turn it on. I would listen to the General Authorities and other motivational talks. I took my *Ensign* magazine, and every minute when I wasn't playing the piano, I would create my own environment. The results were amazing. Immediately, instead of coming home drained, I would come home so excited, so stimulated, anxious to do Church work. . . .

We can create our own environment. (*Music and Morality,* audio tape, Embryo, 1983.)

Another of my brothers-in-law, Rocco, is from South Africa. He graduated from high school at age seventeen and, as was customary in that country, was drafted into the navy. He says, "Boys at that age are real conscious of having to appear tough, and I wanted to be the toughest guy there."

All 350 of the new draftees were taken to a navy base on the coast. Rocco remembers: "Everyone was nervous but no one wanted to show it. By the time our buses arrived it was already dark. We were divided into groups of thirty and herded into our barracks. We were all looking around seeing who we would be spending the next several months with."

Then the officer strutted in yelling about how all the new arrivals were a bunch of mama's boys and how he was going to make men out of them. The officer barked: "Now it's almost ten, and at three minutes to ten you will hear a bosun's whistle. That's the signal for any of you mama's boys who might be religious to count your beads or do whatever religious people do." Then the officer warned, "But you'd better be in bed when the next whistle blows at ten sharp."

Rocco says: "The officer really put the pressure on, because at three minutes to ten anyone who wanted to pray would have to do it in front of the whole group. I was afraid that if I knelt and prayed, as I had been taught to do, everyone—including the officer—would think I was a sissy."

Rocco thought that he might just say a prayer in his mind when the whistle blew, but then he thought of Peter denying the Savior, and Rocco didn't want to be in a similar position. Rocco knew exactly what he had to do. He can remember thinking, "All these guys are going to think I'm weird when they see me kneel down to say my prayers."

He was two years younger than most of the other guys there, and knowing how pecking orders develop, Rocco really worried about being labeled as the little preacher boy. But the promptings of the Spirit were clear: "You know what you have to do. You can't deny your faith."

When the whistle blew at three minutes to ten Rocco knelt down by his bed and began his silent prayer. He could hear the snickers up and down the entire barracks. At ten the officer yelled, "Lights out!"

The following day the men were busy getting uniforms, getting their heads shaved, and getting oriented to everything. Rocco didn't have time to worry about what the others had thought of his prayer. Then, that night, about half an hour before the whistle would sound, he began struggling with himself. "Last night I was obedient and I did what was right, but isn't once enough? If I do it again tonight they are all going to think I'm some sort of religious fanatic." His stomach could not be calmed. But sure enough, at three minutes to ten he knelt by his bed. Again he heard some snickers, but when he finished and got up he saw that three other guys were also kneeling down by their beds.

Rocco says: "The third night those three guys knelt down even before I could kneel, and by the next night there were seven other guys kneeling down. By the end of the week everyone in the barracks was kneeling down."

The following week one guy in the group approached Rocco. He was blonde, about six foot three, and liked to wear his sleeves up higher than anyone else to show off his muscles and his tattoo. Rocco says: "He looked like the kind of guy that would love to beat someone up for fun. I had chosen to stay clear of this guy."

Rocco was brushing his teeth when the guy came up to him and said, "What are you doing every night?"

Rocco thought he was accusing him of sneaking out or something. He said: "Oh, nothing, man. You heard what the officer said. If he caught any of us out at night we'd be dead."

"No, you idiot," the blonde guy said, "I'm not talking about that. What are you doing when you kneel down every night?"

Rocco said, "What do you mean, what are we doing? You're kneeling down too."

The guy said, "I'm just doing it because everyone else is, but what are you doing down there?"

Rocco said, "I'm praying."

The blonde guy said, "You idiot, I know you're praying, but what do you do when you pray?" Mr. Tattoo had never prayed in his life, and now he was coming to Rocco for a lesson. Rocco taught him the steps he had learned when he had first joined the Church.

Then the muscular guy came real close and said, "Look, if you ever tell anyone I asked you this you're dead."

Rocco said, "Your secret is safe. I won't tell anyone."

That night Rocco said a short prayer so he could open his eyes quickly and see, across the barracks, the big tough blonde kneel right along with everyone else and perhaps actually say his first prayer. Rocco had turned his lemon into pineapple juice for sure.

Whenever we find ourselves in situations that are far from perfect we need to remember that we can make a difference. We don't have to helplessly accept the negative situations we encounter; we can change them, make them better. If the trees in our lives are giving us lemons, let's remember what the child in Brad's nursery said and try to turn those lemons into pineapple juice.

Kim Novas Gunnell *is a homemaker, a violinist, and a former BYU Young Ambassador trainer. She was also Mrs. Utah 1993, has been a Relief Society teacher, and currently lives in American Fork, Utah.*

27

COMING HOME

Kathy Smith

Coming home! What images will jump out of your memory someday after you have left for college, for your mission, for the first real job?

My first real homesickness was overwhelming. While I was living for a semester in Grenoble, France, every site around me was foreign. I concentrated so hard to understand the language. I had constant headaches for the first few weeks. The humor was different, the writing on all the signs and stores was unreadable, hairdos and clothing and cars and scenery were totally unfamiliar. I felt that I had relocated on another planet.

The memories that I used to transport me to more familiar territory were similar to ones you have, I suspect. The fireplace with its warmth and spitting logs; long evenings on the phone with my friends; standing outside on the lawn with the hose and watching the sun spill red paint across the clouds as it disappeared. Will you remember autumn leaf fights after the piles of gold and brown and yellow leaves have been raked? How about cutting down Christmas trees in the snow? How about using the hot chocolate mug to thaw your ice sculpted fingers? And summer barbeques with corn on the cob and cousins to laugh with? We used to slip away from the crowd of family and go down to the stream and throw pebbles and wade and splash.

Home.

For some of you the memories of youth and family may bring back a different scene. Some of you have come to the gospel through very challenging doors. One summer, with others I visited two neighboring stakes made up of both inner city youth and of young people who lived in the more comfortable suburbs. As visitors, our first interest was to meet the youth and try to memorize their names. They were unbelievably patient with us as we barged up to them, interrupted their conversations, and introduce ourselves. As I was getting ready for my first attack, one of the stake youth leaders pointed out a husky black youth and told me his story. We'll call him Roderick.

This young man lives with his mother in one of the inner city high rise apartments. They have no car. No autumn leaves in a big yard to rake. Instead they live on poor streets with frustrated people who do not contribute to the ideal pumpkin carving, Christmas caroling, merit badge childhood.

Roderick and his mother found the gospel, but they live it in a very challenging environment. Even though their faithfulness does not insulate them from the realities of their lives, it does give them the courage and the tools to deal with the struggles they face. One day Roderick was waiting with his mother at the bus stop. Swaggering teens, clad in dirty jeans and matching bandannas, approached Roderick menacingly. He recognized the gang insignia and turned away. The gang leader shoved his shoulder. Roderick had no choice but to turn and face him.

"What gang do you belong to?" the cocky leader barked.

Roderick shook his head. "I don't belong to any gang."

The gang leader looked around at his friends and sneered. "Then you'd better join ours."

He shook his head again. Almost whispering, he said, "I don't want to belong to a gang." The other boy took a pistol out of his pocket and shot Roderick in the gut at point-blank range.

His mother screamed, and the ink-clad boys scattered like cockroaches vanishing into the woodwork. Her son was lying on the cement in his own blood.

There are many places where our earthly homes are not what they should be. In some homes there are harsh words which crack the surface of what could have been a place of trust and love. In some homes there is divorce. In others there is fear or poverty or sadness. One young woman asked a stake president what it was that she had done in the pre-earth life that was so horrible that her Heavenly Father had sent her to an abusive home, while other girls are sent to loving homes. The priesthood leader told her in a blessing that it was because of her valiancy; that she had volunteered to perform a Christlike service, to purify a lineage by absorbing the poison and not passing it on. (See Carlfred Broderick, "The Uses of Adversity," in *As Women of Faith: Talks Selected from the BYU Women's Conferences,* ed. Mary E. Stovall and Carol Cornwall Madsen [Salt Lake City: Deseret Book Co., 1989], pp. 177–78.) We cannot judge why we are given the particular set of life experiences that is ours. Our choice is to become stronger because of them.

One fact I urge you to realize is this: we all came from a perfect heavenly home. Our Father and Mother were loving and strong and kind. There was no anger there; no one was ignored or spoiled; no one was overworked or left out. We were all friends.

When the announcement was made that it was time to come to earth, there was excitement at the chance to come here and to prove ourselves. Maybe it felt a little like tryouts. Those of you who make the team or the performing choir or the orchestra or the cheerleading squad know the rush of that success. Then comes the effort, the practice, the sweat and concentration to succeed on the team. And earth life is like that. We have come here to make it possible to go home again— still as sons and daughters of God, to become like our Father and Mother in heaven.

My young black friend is a hero in my eyes. He may not drive a Jeep or wear whatever brand is popular this season, but his soul is dressed in incredible finery because of the honor he wears. Wouldn't it be easier if, once the gang leader had taken out the gun and really tried this boy's courage, the cameraman could have yelled "Cut!" and the "actor" playing the bad guy could have laughed and slapped Roderick on the back and said, "Hey, man, this was only a test! You passed! Gimme five"?

Instead his mother got Roderick to a hospital, where the surgeon feared he would have to remove his intestines. After the operation, a surprised doctor told the mother that somehow the bullet had bypassed all the organs and simply cut through the muscle. He had never seen anything like it. We understand, don't we? Heavenly Father did not leave his faithful son alone. We may not be able to see him with our physical eyes, but he can see us with his. And he watches over us like the tender parent that he is. I believe that part of the nature of our earthly tests requires that we choose him (and we choose home) on faith.

Even though we must experience the bitter and the sweet experiences in life, won't that day come? Won't Heavenly Father welcome us one day and say, "Well done! You passed the test." And there will be tears. I miss that home every bit as much as I missed America while I was a student living in another country. Coming home. I want to be there.

Many years ago I met a young man who lived in the same farming community where I was living temporarily. I would often see him after supper working on his father's fields as I took one of the horses out for a quiet ride. He drove an old red tractor which was as much rust as it was paint. It rattled along loyally as he plowed, hauled hay, and went through the daily ritual of feeding his father's beavers. Every evening he would fell what seemed like a whole forest! He grabbed his ax and after two or three strokes each tree would fall to the ground. He would pile the trunks effortlessly in the wagon behind his tractor.

I was intrigued, so I followed him home. His mother was a gentle, quiet lady who baked bread and taught me to can fruit. She shared secrets about this youngest son which only contributed to the heroic image I already saw. He played sports; he played the piano. He had perfect attendance at Sunday School and seminary, and he quietly lived the gospel he knew.

That summer I watched him and his brothers add onto their modest farmhouse. The old one had raised five sons in three rooms, and in one effort they now doubled the size. After all the construction was complete, the family realized that there was no money left to carpet the new wing. My young friend made a private trip to the bank and withdrew one thousand dollars from his savings account—money he had earned by hauling hay all the previous summer. Secretly he sneaked the money to his mother. She had her new carpet.

This boy grew up and all the qualities I saw just got better. He did the year of college before his mission and returned older and wiser from two years of service to the Lord. I had the script for the rest of his life all written out: Temple marriage. A youth leader. A little league coach for his own sons. A life of quiet faithful service to match the twenty-one years he had already lived.

Time did pass, but the script changed. I never knew what triggered it—he wouldn't tell me—but he made choices that took him on a detour. A friend died tragically in a boating accident. Did he doubt what he knew about eternal life? His father's hidden abusiveness surfaced again. Did he wonder how Heavenly Father could allow bad things to happen through people who should know better? Did the lure of temptation simply sound more tantalizing than the promises of the gospel? That seemed impossible, knowing what I knew of him. All I do know is that he chose a counterfeit. He closed the door on Heavenly Father and on all of us. This pearl of a youth—this hero that everyone loved—locked his heart away and was gone. I pounded on the wall he had built, but it was as if he was too far away to hear.

As the years passed, he never returned. Nothing I could say seemed to matter to him at all, but far from my letting go, he became all the more important to me. This was my friend, and if he didn't come back, home would be lonely.

He became a dairyman, married, and had two sons. Because he left the Church did he become hardened and bitter and sinful? No. He was still the gentle, smiling friend he had always been. There was a wall, and he kept us at a distance, but he stayed the man I had always admired, working as hard as ever. Only this time it was in the middle of the black morning hours milking a herd of cows. I don't understand anything about the economy, but I know that farmers depend on stable prices to make ends meet. I never could get the details into my head, but one year his farm failed, and he lost everything.

For a time he became a truck driver. He had a huge rig and drove it to all the corners of the United States; on the road for days and then only home for a weekend or so before leaving again. He began to hate what he was doing. Occasionally, when school was out, he would take one of his sons with him. Those boys loved the high seat, the huge wheels, and the bed in back. They constantly rummaged through the small fridge and ate whenever they wanted to. The boys felt as if they were on a giant moving playground. For my friend, it was not as much fun.

During this time he stopped at our home when his route took him our way, and we would sit over a meal and visit. One of these times he became very reflective, and he said to me with tears behind his eyes: "Kathy, I have come to realize how much family means to me. I don't ever want to do anything that would make it so I couldn't go home again." His boys didn't have their dad every day, and his wife had to be both the mom and the dad. He felt so hopeless being separated from them.

I stared at him. Don't you hear what you're saying? What about our heavenly home? What will it be like one day if you are not there and the loneliness I feel for you now becomes eternal?

We all have challenges in this life (even the people who live on the hill and seem to have it so easy and so comfortable). Heavenly Father has tailored each life's lesson in our own privately constructed classrooms. Trust your Heavenly Father. He knows what you are going through, and he is there. Just keep your focus on the fact that this life is a test. And every day, choose him. Choose home.

I recognize (from experience) that this sounds a lot easier than it is to do. As we get tumbled around in life's whirlpool, sometimes we grumble: "If I really had a Father in Heaven, he wouldn't let this happen to me." "Is this another fairytale like Santa Claus and the Easter bunny?" "Are Mom and Dad using this heaven and hell thing as a way to get me to do what they think is right?" When we buy into these lines, we open doors that take us out of the protection of the gospel net.

My cute son was thirteen the summer he discovered gasoline. He dipped used tennis balls into gasoline and then set them on fire and used a baseball bat to hit them. I was not home, of course, and it was great fun. By some miracle he did not kill himself or his friends, and I suppose you didn't either when you went through that phase.

One weekend when I was gone to a youth conference, he and a friend thought it would be fun to draw gasoline designs in the backyard grass and then set them on fire. He wondered what it would look like. So the boys ignited their design with a match, and the fire hissed through the yard, burning the lush thick green grass that my son's mother had spent tons of money and effort on. The design burned furiously, and my son saw that he would soon burn up the entire yard. He turned on the sprinklers in a panic and doused the flames. The next day his mom came home.

With sincere remorse in his eyes (and we moms can read eyes) I recognized that he meant what he told me. "Mom, I am really sorry. I honestly didn't realize it would *kill* the grass." He thought it would burn the gas but not the grass. I guess it didn't kill the cement when he had done something similar on the cement. "I won't ever do that again!" he promised. And I knew he meant, "Please don't kill me."

I think sometimes we do things because we really don't understand the consequences. We can hear it over and over, but curiosity still wins out, and we experiment. Then we have to choose again. "OK, I blew it. I can either admit that I made a mistake and ask for forgiveness, or I can stubbornly hold on to my mistake and convince myself that it is not a mistake. If there is no God, then there is no sin, therefore I cannot be wrong." Instead of stopping and turning around, we set the grass on fire over and over until there is no grass left. Along the way, we decide that God is a fairytale used by parents and leaders to scare us into complying with unreasonable rules. Which choice makes the most sense?

As I sensed his genuine remorse, my job was to forgive. I gulped back my first reaction (you can guess what that was) and hugged him and teased him. The grass grew back. Do you think your Heavenly Father is less loving and forgiving and understanding than your parents? He is the perfect example of the qualities we try to copy. He sent his Son to make up for the moments of weakness we fall into. He expected us to make mistakes, but he wants us to recognize that is what we are doing and change the negative patterns before they get set in concrete.

Once, many years ago, I was caught in the trap I have described. I felt that I just couldn't live the way celestial people lived (I had some image that other members of the Church were perfect—and then there was me). I decided I wasn't good enough, and since that was true I might as well "enjoy myself." That usually means we want to sin and are trying to figure out a way to justify it.

I had decided to leave the Church. I remember the morning after making this decision. I was combing my hair in the bathroom mirror. A face seemed to be looking back at me that wasn't my face. It was a kind, gentle, dark-haired man's face, and he had a soft short beard and incredibly sad eyes. He looked at me, and inside my mind I heard him ask, "Are you leaving me, Kathy?" I looked away because in my mind I knew that he knew, and I couldn't look at him. The face followed me. "Where are you going?" he asked again. I lowered my eyes and said aloud, "Nowhere." There is nowhere else. The path is set. I can walk on it, or I can leave it. I get to choose.

"Jesus saith unto him, I am the way, the truth and the life: no man cometh unto the Father, but by me" (John 14:6). I needed to retake my spiritual pulse. I had allowed dozens of little things to combine into a huge web that blinded me. Because of the atonement of the Savior, there are no sins common to man which cannot be fixed. It may take time; it may require a lot of humility and effort, but the grass will grow back.

A Lamanite king heard the gospel and wanted desperately to know if it was true. He asked, "What shall I do that I may have this eternal life of which thou hast spoken? Yea, what shall I do that I may be born of God, having this wicked spirit rooted out of my breast, and receive his Spirit, that I may be filled with joy, that I may not be cast off at the last day?" He too wanted to come home after earth life was over. "I will forsake my kingdom, that I may receive this great joy." (Alma 22:15.) Aaron explained how the king could obtain a testimony of the gospel. All he had to do was to ask in faith, and to repent of his sins. That is what we all have to do. "The king did bow down before the Lord, upon his knees . . . and cried mightily, saying: O God, Aaron hath told me that there is a God; and if there is a God, and if thou art God, wilt thou make thyself known unto me, and I will give away all my sins to know thee" (Alma 22:17–18).

The world holds out a smorgasbord of sins. They look delicious. They seem tantalizing. We are pulled like metal shavings to the magnet unless we decide to walk past the table. Trials can defeat us if we let them. Pain and hurt can defeat us if we let it wedge in between us and our faith in our Heavenly Father. Joseph Smith really did have a vision in a quiet grove of trees. It changed his life and it has changed ours. The Church is true. That is no longer the question. The question now is can we be true?

Coming home. Be there.

Kathy Smith was born in San Francisco, California, and joined the Church when she was fifteen years old. She teaches eighth-grade English and French in Provo, Utah. She has three daughters and one son. Sister Smith taught early-morning seminary for eight years and has taught at Especially for Youth and other programs since 1983. Kathy has traveled around the world and loves to cook Chinese food.